Anthropological Perspectives on Indian Tribes

Anthropological Perspectives on Indian Tribes

Subhadra Mitra Channa

Orient BlackSwan

ANTHROPOLOGICAL PERSPECTIVES ON INDIAN TRIBES

ORIENT BLACKSWAN PRIVATE LIMITED

Registered Office
3-6-752 Himayatnagar, Hyderabad 500 029, Telangana, India
e-mail: centraloffice@orientblackswan.com

Other Offices
Bengaluru, Bhopal, Chennai, Guwahati,
Hyderabad, Jaipur, Kolkata, Lucknow, Mumbai,
New Delhi, Noida, Patna, Visakhapatnam

First published by Orient Blackswan Private Limited 2020

ISBN 978-93-5287-999-1

032097

Typeset in
Amerigo BT 10.5/13
by Shine Graphics, Delhi

Printed in India at
Akash Press, Delhi

Published by
Orient Blackswan Private Limited
3-6-752 Himayatnagar, Hyderabad 500 029, Telangana, India
e-mail: info@orientblackswan.com

To my precious daughters

Megha

Navya

CONTENTS

ABBREVIATIONS

AFSPA	Armed Forces (Special Powers) Act
AZSU	All Zeliangrong Students' Union
BJP	Bharatiya Janata Party
CFM	Community Forest Management
CRPF	Central Reserve Police Force
CTA	Criminal Tribes Act
DPSP	Directive Principles of State Policy
FBD	Father's brother's daughter
HRLN	Human Rights Law Network
ICITIP	Indian Council of the Indigenous Tribal People
ILO	International Labour Organisation
IPT	Independent People's Tribunal
JFM	Joint Forest Management
MB	Mother's brother
MBD	Mother's brother's daughter
MBS	Mother's brother's son
MZ	Mother's sister
MZD	Mother's sister's daughter
MZS	Mother's sister's son
NEHU	North-eastern Hill University
NNC	Naga National Council
NSCN	National Socialist Council of Nagaland
NTPC	National Thermal Power Corporation
OBC	Other Backward Classes
PESA	Panchayats (Extension to Scheduled Areas) Act
PTG	Primitive tribal group
PVTG	Particularly vulnerable tribal group
R&R	Rehabilitation and resettlement
SC	Scheduled Castes
ST	Scheduled Tribes
UN	United Nations

WASP	White, Anglo-Saxon Protestant
WH	Wangham
WP	Wangpam
WS	Wangsa
WSu	Wangsu
ZNU	Zeliangrong Naga Union
ZPC	Zeliangrong People Convention
ZSUM	Zeliangrong Student Union of Manipur

PREFACE

An apology may be due for adding yet another book on tribes of India when so many excellent ones exist already. Much of the impressive scholarship on tribes, however, either focuses on specific issues or deals with specific regions. Hence, one can argue that a textbook was much needed to introduce undergraduate and even postgraduate students to the concept of tribe. This is the rationale behind this book.

The book does not claim to have the depth and incisive insights of more detailed anthologies and ethnographies, which deal more or less exclusively with one or another aspect of tribal life, although an effort has been made to include as many as possible of these works in the suggested readings and references. What this book sets out to achieve is introduce the young reader to a view of tribes that goes beyond many of the received concepts and prejudices that are set deep in the popular imagery of 'tribe'. Through extensive ethnographic examples and engagement with theoretical works, the student is taken through a broad-based and critical understanding of the category 'tribe'.

At the same time, effort has been made to keep to the framework of a fairly conventional anthropology syllabus for the benefit of students. Thus, the chapters follow the standard themes of family and kinship, modes of subsistence, religion and cosmology, and law and state power. But the book also attempts to raise the awareness of students to the issues and challenges of contemporary times. Each chapter engages with the theoretical understanding of the concepts used at a more general level and then moves on to a more specific account in the context of Indian tribes. This is to help familiarise students with the basic concepts even as we venture into more critical and evaluative discussions of those very concepts.

Theory is shown to be firmly rooted in the history and the socio-political context from which it emerges. The student is thus led into the discussion of the emergence of the concepts rather than being told to memorise the 'definitions'. In fact, in this book, the idea of definitions has been replaced by stimulating the student towards a critical understanding of what 'concepts' mean and, more importantly, how they emerge.

The understanding of tribe is thus within the framework of the political, economic and social contextualisation of the term—its construction and its use within particular political regimes. The student is encouraged to not take definitions as 'givens' and to develop a critical and analytical attitude towards the discipline. At many points, for example, the student is led into alternative discourses, with the foregrounding of different opinions and different explanations for the same phenomenon or process.

A common thread maintained throughout is the focus on dynamics, flexibility and change as an intrinsic aspect of all social phenomena. Society is a complex entity and nothing about it can be explained in monolithic, essentialist terms. The concept of tribe is itself the best example of how attempts to impose order on something that is inherently not amenable to order can create more chaos than order. This is why all studies of social phenomena need to be grounded in empirical data for it is the reality on the ground that can lead us towards a proper theoretical understanding.

As mentioned earlier, the book has attempted to consolidate most of the knowledge and theories about 'tribes' into broad categories: kinship, religion, subsistence, and law and politics. These have been chosen as the most basic principles of social organisation, which are fundamental for an understanding of social phenomenon. There are, however, important aspects that may have been left out, like the considerable literature on tribal health and medicine, indigenous knowledge, gender and tribal history. Some of these aspects have been incorporated wherever possible, while care has been taken to keep the gendered perspective wherever it is central to the topic concerned. But these aspects have not been detailed in separate chapters.

Concepts and processes are best understood through field experience and data, which are central to the discipline of anthropology. Hence, this book draws extensively on material from my own field research. This might appear as a subjective choice, but this subjectivity is inherent to all anthropological works. But the book also uses a wide range of works available so that students are introduced to the rich legacy of the discipline as well as some of the key debates and perspectives within the discipline.

There has been a conscious effort to include most of the classical works in anthropology in general and of the founders of tribal studies in India in particular. Since this book is meant to be conceptual in nature, it focuses on concepts that have originated from empirical work pertaining to India, while keeping references to statistical data to a minimum.

I am grateful to Moutushi Mukherjee, the commissioning editor of Orient BlackSwan, without whose proactive interest, I would not have thought of writing this book. It is essential to acknowledge the contribution of the copy-editor, Samprati Pani, who elevated the text to impressive standards. Years of experience in teaching students have gone into the writing of this book, and I am thankful to all my students who kept alive my interest in teaching. I also acknowledge the contribution of the anonymous peer reviewers, whose insights are always welcome.

1

TRIBE

Who, What and Why?

HIGHLIGHTS

- Tribe, ethnicity and the indigenous
- The concept of 'tribe': evolutionary, functionalist and postcolonial/post-structuralist perspectives
- Belongingness and looking ahead

INTRODUCTION

In this chapter, students will learn that the category, label or concept of 'tribe' is not connected to any objective reality but is a mere construct embedded within historical and political conditions. Different but related terms such as 'ethnic group' and 'indigenous people' also have their own theoretical and historical contexts. The anthropological approach to the concept of tribe is informed by different schools, each with its own theoretical framework. These theories are not simply products of the mind, but are intertwined with the social and political conditions of the times in which they were formulated. Students will thus learn the relationship between theory and context. More importantly, they will learn about the relationship between labels as conferred from the outside (often from 'above') and the self-identification of people. Many tribes do not identify themselves by the terms by which they are known to outsiders. There is often a disjunction between how one identifies one's self and how one is identified by others. Most tribes consider themselves to be the original work of the creator and as possibly the centre of the universe. Roy (1912: 358) has written that the Mundas call themselves Iloro-Ko (men) and their race Iloro (man); in other words, they are just 'human', not any subdivision or group within a larger entity but that entity itself. To outsiders, they are 'marginal', 'backward' and 'primitive', among other derogatory terms used for them. Padel (2011: 12) writes that the Konds asked him if there were Konds in his country as well. This simple question indicates, as Padel puts it, 'How differently Konds see themselves from the way the ethnographic tradition defines them—precisely as it defines other tribes, by locating them in a particular area and giving an exact figure for their population. Konds see themselves, quite simply, as one of the main races or divisions of mankind.' Being set aside as a tribe or *janjati* is a construct imposed on these people from the outside and is never an aspect of their self-recognition.

Many tribes do not identify themselves by the terms by which they are known to outsiders. Most consider themselves to be the original work of the creator and as possibly the centre of the universe.

Thus, this chapter will discuss identity and the politics of identity, as well as the explanations for why certain terms like 'tribe', 'indigenous people', 'ethnic group' and 'nation' are used for similarly situated people. The differences in the use of these terms are contextualised within the specific history and political ideology of the region of their use.

SOME KEY TERMS

What Is Tribe?

The term 'tribe' as we understand it today is the outcome of a specific historical situation, namely, colonisation by Europe of much of the non-Western world between the seventeenth and nineteenth centuries. In the English language, in general use, the term was often used in the context of 'likeness' or of people related by kin and blood ties. The *Compact Oxford Dictionary* (2001) defines a tribe as a 'social group in a traditional society consisting of linked families or communities sharing customs and beliefs'. In ordinary conversation, tribe is often understood as a brotherhood or a community of belonging. While the term in this sense can perhaps be safely used for communities who lived in the past, it may cause offense if used for contemporary people. The use of the adjective 'traditional' in the dictionary definition will become clear in the course of the chapter when we discover that the term was often used in a derogatory sense and associated with 'primitiveness' and lack of civilisation. In most countries, the term 'tribe' has been replaced by others such as 'indigenous people' (the United States), 'First Nations' (Canada), 'ethnic groups' (China), 'natives' and 'aborigines'. In countries colonised by Europeans, the term 'indigenous' is often used to refer to those who were native to the land before European occupation, like the Native Americans of the US, the indigenous people of the Amazon, the Maori of New Zealand and the Aboriginal Australians.

The *Compact Oxford Dictionary* (2001) defines a tribe as a 'social group in a traditional society consisting of linked families or communities sharing customs and beliefs'.

In India, today, when we talk about 'tribe', the meaning is derived from a context other than colonisation. In relation to the colonisers, everyone living in India was 'native'. The category of tribes has been seen as distinct from that of caste by social scientists as well as administrators, colonial and postcolonial. Tribes were also distinguished from the followers of universal religions for both heuristic and academic purposes. In this sense, the term 'tribe' may be seen as an internal distinction rather than one created by colonial rule. It refers to a category that is seen as outside of what is understood as mainstream India. It conjures up visions of people who differ significantly from the urban or even peasant populations of India. To many lay persons, this term is often associated with being backward and not quite 'civilised'. With regard to governance, especially of the category of Scheduled Tribes (ST), the term also implies people with special needs of a social and economic nature.

The term tribe, however, is also viewed by many as having been introduced by the British colonial government as an administrative strategy to distinguish between those already incorporated within the hierarchical feudal system and those situated outside of it. The British viewed tribes as those practising animistic religion, racially distinct and not part of the Hindu civilisation. The term has a racial connotation, and in India it became an adjunct of the Aryan myth, whereby an invading pastoral people of Euro-Central Asian origin (with fair skin and chiseled features) had conquered or 'pushed back' autochthones of dark skin and broad noses. The Vedic or Aryan civilisation was the forerunner of the present-day peninsular Hindus, and the tribes, now located in forests and on mountains and hilltops, were the 'pushed back' (hence inferior) people (Trautmann 1997). These constructs imply that tribes were weak and less equipped to deal with the advancing Aryans, who had a more developed technology and superior culture. Such myths have now been demolished; yet they continue to live in the collective imagination of the people of this subcontinent and lead to the creation of stereotypes about the tribal 'other'.

Ethnicity and Ethnic Groups

In the postcolonial period, the term 'tribe' was either replaced or supplemented with the concepts of ethnic group and indigenous people, both of which are also contested and come with their own agendas and contexts.

The term 'ethnic group' was a replacement for the concept of race, which was charged with negative connotations because of not only the slave trade, but also the Holocaust that saw unprecedented dehumanisation on the basis of racial markings. Today, however, the term 'ethnic group' is rarely used for those otherwise known as tribes or indigenous people. It is mostly applied to communities that may be in a less dominant position in the social hierarchy, and who may consider a social boundary or closure in relation to others as desirable, both politically and socially. The term 'ethnicity' was first used by the American sociologist David Riesman. As pointed out by Glazer and Moynihan (1975: 3), the term arose in the context of the danger of identities being lost in a world where people were being thrown together in new places and situations. Reisman, in his book *The Lonely Crowd* (1950), had conceptualised the 'inner directed' individual and, as pointed out by Lemert (2014: 16), created the 'I' of personal identity that could be contextualised to a social identity. Moran (2014: 180) identifies two main reasons for the rise of this concept: First, new nations and democracies were careful in the allotment of resources in socially just ways so that ethnicity became one criterion for judging the fair representation of all kinds of people. Second, the term came to be deployed in claims for social equality under conditions where some groups were likely to dominate culturally and socially over certain other groups. In such a scenario, the disadvantaged tried to gain political mileage through collective representation under the label of ethnic groups or ethnicity.

The term 'ethnic group' was first comprehensively defined by Weber (1958 [1904–05], 1968 [1922]) in terms of the subjectively held belief that certain groups may have about their common descent and similar physical appearance. Weber was careful to mention that the ties of blood are often putative rather than real. What is important is the belief, and this too is conditioned by circumstances, often of a feeling of exclusion and dominance by a powerful other. Thus, particular segments of the population in India have taken recourse to the label of 'ethnic group' to press forth their claims for social justice or equitable distribution of resources, a case in point being the people of the Northeast. While the northeast of India is largely constituted of tribes with differing identities, it has nonetheless acquired an identity in interaction with what is known as the Indian mainland or what, for most people from this region, is 'India'. This separation of identity may be traced to historical factors that kept this region away from direct contact with mainland India and the 'historical accident' (Maxwell 1980: 3) that merged this area with the Indian nation. Ethnic group, in this sense, is both an externally and a historically situated identity and, in the context of the subjective consciousness of the people of this region, a self-sustaining one that draws a boundary around itself and what it perceives as the 'other'. Biswas and Suklabaidya (2008) have pointed out that the ethnic nature of such an identity is derived from the notion of a 'lifeworld', where certain cultural, ritual and even racial characters are used to separate the self from the 'other'.

The term 'ethnic group' was first comprehensively defined by Max Weber in terms of the subjectively held belief that certain groups may have about their common descent and similar physical appearance.

To a large extent, the 'ethnic' nature of such identities has been a product of British attempts to create uniformity for the sake of administration. As described by Biswas and Suklabaidya (2008: 195), 'The colonial policy of bringing together disparate groups of people through certain interventions, such as settlement, propagation of a common language and the creation of a uniformity through abolition of practices obstructive to normalizing such identities, mobilized signifiers like "Naga" or "Kuki" as names for some groups of people.' Such identities were then used for further negotiations with others, and these formed concepts of self-realised ethnicity in a different historical and political context, like the present relationship with the postcolonial Indian state. The logic and rationale of the creation of collective identities such as that of Naga, which actually combines several smaller and distinct units, were set in motion by what may be called 'colonial modernity'. Colonisation and its administrative regulations created a sense of imposition of outside authority that led to an awareness of the coming of a new era, where there was a felt need to group together in order to deal with the unwanted external interference. Many of these collective identities, including the Naga movement, acquired their own momentum in the postcolonial political arena to form a new platform for negotiation. These forged umbrella identities were invested with greater political power by their larger numbers and, therefore, could exert more pressure. Ethnicity, with its connotation of primordialism and a shared historical past, as well as some kind of symbolic 'blood' connectivity, is most of the time an identity evoked with all these characteristics to negotiate a position, a power or simply an identity, which a group feels it requires. It functions like a boundary, which is evoked to emphasise difference and exclusiveness.

The term 'ethnic group' was often used for tribes to get around the stigma that the term 'tribe' evoked. But the category of ethnic group has a range and scope far beyond that of tribe, which is why 'indigenous people' is the more frequently used alternative for 'tribe'. As compared to tribe or indigenous people, the term 'ethnic group' does not convey any notion of oppression or marginalisation. In fact, the term is used in contexts that are not inherently characterised by dynamics of oppression and domination. For example, the term is often applied to migrant communities in the US like the Italians or the Europeans, while Native Americans are designated differently.

Glazer and Moynihan (1975) argue that the term 'ethnicity' as opposed to the term 'ethnic group' has political implications—the term came into being in the new conditions of competition that arose as more people from diverse origins came to occupy contiguous spaces as a result of global forces of migration and occupation. Ethnicity implies a closure of boundaries for the specific purpose of excluding others from resources coveted by the in-group. It is also often evoked to exert a sense of separation, or it arises from a fear of getting swamped in dominant identities as more people occupy a space that may be termed 'multicultural'. Ethnicity may be compared to the term 'tribalism' as opposed to 'tribe', where it implies political action as against a static identity.

The Notion of Being Indigenous

The term 'indigenous' needs to be examined more critically when applied to Indian tribes (Béteille 1998). Historically, this term is a by-product of colonisation and was used for the native populations of countries such as the US, Canada, New Zealand and Australia. It refers largely to the Western occupation of these countries and refers to the original non-White people who lived there, such as the Aboriginal Australians, the Native Americans, the New Zealand Maoris and the Cree of Canada. Thus, indigenous here means the original people in these regions. It also has the specific connotation of being non-European. But the term is difficult to use in Africa, where the continent still belongs more or less to the original people, who have their own divisions that are called tribes, to identify themselves from each other. Although indigenous people have acted politically for centuries as they fought the invaders into their terrain, the identity 'indigenous' was given a concrete shape by the International Labour Organisation (ILO) in its 1953 report *Indigenous Peoples: Living and Working Conditions of Aboriginal Populations in Independent Countries*, and later in its Indigenous and Tribal Populations Convention (1957, convention no. 107) concerning the protection and integration of indigenous and other tribal and semi-tribal populations in independent countries. Indigenous

The identity 'indigenous' was given a concrete shape by the ILO in its 1953 report *Indigenous Peoples*, and later in its 1957 Indigenous and Tribal Populations Convention on the protection and integration of indigenous and other tribal and semi-tribal populations in independent countries.

as an identity bestows power and creates linkages with more powerful and widely situated identities.

In India, the situation is different from the two aforementioned contexts, with the country being divided into hierarchies of people on the basis of physical characteristics, religion, language and a host of cultural traits that vary geographically. In Hindi, the term 'Adivasi', meaning 'the original people' or the indigenous, is used for people designated as 'tribes'. However, Government of India has refused to acknowledge the existence of indigenous people, saying that all people on this continent are indigenous and that India does not suffer from external colonisation as is the case with the US, Australia and New Zealand. The Indian government's stand is based on the historical condition of a different kind of Western colonisation in India, where the colonial outsiders withdrew completely from the colonised territory. Since all the people of the Indian subcontinent were residents prior to the European invasion, that left only the so-called natives to rule their own country. The term 'indigenous' has been used in the context of those regions where the Europeans had driven out, exterminated or pushed back the native populations and usurped the land as their own. The indigenous were the original inhabitants, and the Europeans the colonisers, and subsequently the rulers. Scholars such as Roy Burman (1998) have argued that the condition of the tribal people of independent India is as bad as those suffering external colonisation. The term 'indigenous' should then be reinterpreted to include the conditions of existence and historical marginalisation of a people and not simply have external colonisation as a referral. The term marginalisation is understood in many parts of the world as internal colonisation also. As it stands, the recognition of the term 'indigenous' by the ILO and United Nations (UN) has given it a lot of political leverage. Yet, the tribes of India continue to suffer because they have not been able to make legitimate use of this leverage.

The distinguished Indian scholar Roy Burman (1998: 145) pointed out that while the Indigenous and Tribal Populations Convention highlighted the plight of indigenous people, it had a certain ethnocentric bias, especially as it considered the indigenous to be less advanced than other populations. Later, there was an amendment and the ILO drew up a new convention, namely, Indigenous and Tribal Peoples of

Independent Countries (Convention 169 of 1989). In this, the earlier evolutionist bias was removed and the terms 'tribe' and 'indigenous' were treated as separate but analogous. Roy Burman (1998) critically analysed these two conventions and asserted that while tribes have been referred to as 'peoples' all through, it is mentioned that the indigenous were 'populations' in the pre-colonial era, becoming peoples only in the postcolonial phase, which, according to him, has grave legal implications and protects the interests of the colonising countries. As populations, the pre-colonised indigenous peoples had no particular legal rights; they could only acquire these rights when they became peoples. Roy Burman also pointed to huge discrepancies in the definition of the indigenous by UN sources, which largely decline from naming the indigenous, leaving it to the people to categorise themselves [see, for example, United Nations (1953, 2007)]. These sources view Europe as not having any indigenous population because it was never colonised, but at the same time, they consider China and Thailand, which too were never colonised, as having indigenous people, which once again points to a Eurocentric bias.

The Indian subcontinent and Asia are occupied by mostly native people, that is, those occupying these regions for centuries and having a distinct ethnic identity from the European colonisers. These countries also have an internal division of the mainstream populations that control power and the subjugated populations, mostly referred to as tribes (and also the lower castes in the case of India). This division between the dominant and the tribal has had a long history, some aspects of which will be discussed later in this book. In view of this internal hierarchy, the indigenous tribal people of India made an appeal to the United Nations Working Group on Indigenous Populations, Geneva, held during 3–7 August 1987. The five signatories on behalf of the Indian Council of the Indigenous Tribal People (ICITIP) were Samar Brahma Chowdhury (member of Parliament, Lok Sabha), a representative of the Bodo tribes of the plains of Assam in east India; Nirmal Minz, a representative of the Oraon tribes of Chotanagpur in south Bihar; Sharad Kulkarni from Centre for Tribal Conscientisation, Pune, western India; Ram Dayal Munda, Vice Chancellor, University of Ranchi, representing the Munda tribe; and A. K. Kishku, a professor from West Bengal, representing the Santal tribe.

In their appeal to the UN, the representatives of the indigenous tribal people of India cited historical, anthropological and sociological evidence to say that they were the primal population of India, even before the advent of the Aryan and the Muslim peoples who occupied India. They asserted that in spite of being called by various names, they wished to assert themselves as Adivasis (indigenous people) and forge solidarities with indigenous peoples across the world. They also stated that although the Constitution of India has overtly safeguarded the interests of tribes through the Fifth and Sixth Schedules, as well as the Tribal Advisory Council, the real needs of the tribal people are far from being attended to. They also mentioned that the Panchsheel put forward by India's first prime minister, Jawaharlal Nehru, was honoured neither in spirit nor in action. Industrialisation and mining in the heart of the Adivasi areas has created conditions of internal colonisation, displacement and dispossession, reducing the Adivasis to penury and converting the once proud and independent people into beggars. The Indian appeal to the UN Working Group on Indigenous Populations in Geneva in 1987 specifically stated, 'Today the Adivasis, i.e., Indigenous Tribal People of India are *reduced to a colonial situation* and are completely dominated by a system of values and institutions maintained by the dominant ruling group' (emphasis added). Thus, the aspect of internal colonisation comes out clearly in the statement. In the end, the tribal representatives reiterated their appeal for the right to self-determination and economic, social, cultural and political identity.

The category 'indigenous' confers a lot of political mileage and connectivity to a huge global network. The tribes of India have suffered because they have not been formally recognised as indigenous by the Indian government as they are, according to the government, no more indigenous than the rest of the Indian population. The appeal made by the tribal representatives is in view of the political, and not ontological, interpretation of the term 'indigenous'. The tribal leadership and others in their support want the term 'indigenous' to be used synonymously to refer to the existential conditions of the indigenous in some countries and to that of tribes in regions such as India. However, the appeal of 1987, as well as a subsequent one made in April–May 2017 to the 27th session of the Human Rights Council by tribal activists, have not been accepted by the Indigenous People's Committee of the UN. The second appeal was made by the Joint Stakeholders' Submission on the Situation of the Rights of Indigenous Peoples in India and signed by 11 tribal organisations. These organisations represented both the central and the northeast regions of India.

The use of the term 'peoples' for the indigenous confers considerable rights to them as the term implies a distinct identity as a community and some kind of a structure. One of the most fundamental rights that a people may have is the right to self-determination. Once designated as indigenous and a people, a group can claim the right to self-determination. But this right comes up in direct confrontation with the right to sovereignty of the nation state of which these particular people may be a part. Thus, Hector Gres Espiel, who in August 1988 submitted the Country Report on Human Rights Practices on self-determination to the UN, clearly reserves the right to secession only for those people who are ruled by an external source or for a situation of 'external colonisation'. Here it is pertinent to quote Rehman (1998: 74):

> The inevitable movement towards decolonization was built around a consensus that the right to self-determination was only permissible if the State and its "colonial peoples" were geographically distinct. The plea by many indigenous people and minorities that "colonization is no less colonization, if it is made by territorial contiguity, than by overseas expansion" was ignored for it provided a threat to the sacrosanct principles of territorial integrity and State sovereignty on which the post-colonial world order was established.

In spite of the complete aversion to any form of threat to the territorial integrity of sovereign countries, the United Nations Special Rapporteur to the Sub-commission on Prevention of Discrimination and Protection of Minorities, Martinez Cobo (1986: paragraph 379), laid down some definitions that are widely quoted and put in practice.

> Indigenous communities, peoples and nations are those which, having a historical continuity with pre-invasion and pre-colonial societies that developed on their territories, consider themselves distinct from other sectors of the societies now prevailing in those territories, or parts of them. They form at present non-dominant sectors of society and are

determined to preserve, develop and transmit to future generations their ancestral territories, and their ethnic identity, as the basis of their continued existence as peoples, in accordance with their own cultural, social institutions and legal systems.

In addition to Martinez Cobo's definition, Article 1.2 of the ILO convention 169, adopted in 1989, is also significant for its mention of a key factor in the characterisation of people as indigenous: 'Self-identification as indigenous or tribal shall be regarded as a fundamental criterion for determining the groups to which the provisions of this convention apply' (International Labour Organisation 2003: 8). This particular convention moves forward from the earlier ones in addressing many pressing issues. Article 2.1 of this convention urges governments to take responsibility for ensuring the participation of these peoples in the process of governance, to protect their rights and to ensure the protection of their ways of life, customs and institutions. Article 3 prohibits discrimination in the enjoyment of human rights and fundamental freedoms. The other articles too enjoin the rights of people to live according to their own wishes and to enjoy their territorial and cultural freedoms. Articles 6 and 7 are of special importance as the former requires governments to consult people in matters affecting them, while the latter states that the people concerned shall have their right to decide on their course of development in as much as it affects their lives, beliefs, institutions and spiritual well-being. The convention, however, makes it clear that its use of the term 'peoples' has no bearing on how it is used in international law. Thus, all through, we find a tightrope walk between granting people their rights and upholding the sovereignty of the nations of which they are a part.

An ILO convention adopted in 1989 regards self-identification as indigenous or tribal as a fundamental criterion. It also urges governments to ensure participation of indigenous people in the process of governance, and to protect their ways of life, customs and institutions.

Scheduled Tribe

The reluctance of the governments of India, Pakistan, Bangladesh and Indonesia to grant the status of indigenous people to their tribal populations is understandable, as all these nation states are encroaching on the lands and resources of their tribal populations to a very large extent in their push for so-called development. However, through the official category of Scheduled Tribes and the principles of positive discrimination, the Constitution of India has given recognition to the historical marginalisation of these people from the mainstream. Article 341 of the Indian Constitution authorises the President of India to specify 'castes, races or tribes which shall for the purposes of the constitution be deemed to be scheduled tribes'. There also exists a special Commission for Scheduled Castes and Tribes, and both these categories are granted many privileges and affirmative policies of the Indian government. The inclusion and exclusion of some peoples into this category has always been fraught with problems, for the labels are often shifting and many so-called peoples may have an ephemeral existence. It has been difficult to identify specific groups of people as 'a tribe', and to the confusion of many government officials assigned to this task, they find that identities and claims keep shifting.

Since the inclusion of a community within a category [Scheduled Caste (SC), Scheduled Tribe or Other Backward Classes (OBC)] has entitled it to the official policy of positive discrimination, from 1950 onwards, when the Constitution of India provided these safeguards, the matter of being included or not in one or other of the categories has become more of a political than an academic project. Thus, Béteille (1986) maintained that in this process of 'identification' of tribes, the actual process of defining them has been thrust aside. The question being posed is 'who' rather than 'why'. Thus, officials have been under political pressure to recognise certain communities as tribe and not locate them by using any defined characteristics. Consequently, the same community may end up having different official statuses in different places. For instance, the Girasia community is a Scheduled Caste in Rajasthan but not in the neighbouring state of Gujarat. Also, many people were recognised under names that were imposed on them by external power-yielding groups, rather than in terms of their self-identification. In Uttar Pradesh (and now in Uttarakhand also), among the tribes recognised is that of the Bhotiyas, which is not by any means a single tribe (Channa 2013). Even subcategories like the Jad Bhotiyas of Uttarkashi (not recognised as such in official records, where they only appear as 'Bhotiya') are not a bounded category at all.

As pointed out by Maharatna (2005: 10), a systematic effort to prepare a list of groups that could be called tribes began from the 1931 Census by the then colonial administration. Even then, the ostensible purpose was to give these groups some kind of benefits in recognition of their marginal position. Initially these groups were identified primarily on the basis that they did not belong to any major religion of India. Initially, they were categorised as animistic and then put into the 'tribal religion' category after the 1931 Census. With the adoption of the Constitution of India in 1951, a formal list of Scheduled Tribes was prepared, where the number came to 212. This was based, 'in a large measure, on the list of Backward Tribes promulgated in 1936 by the British administration' (ibid.: 13). Under the recommendation of the Backward Classes Commission formed in 1953, the number of Scheduled Tribes rose to 427, further increasing to 432 by the 1971 Census. Kulkarni (1991: 205–08) comments that the 'political forces released over the decades since Independence have not only disrupted the historical process of tribal absorption, but have indeed reversed it'.

The share of tribes rose from around 3 per cent of the total population in pre-Independence India to more than 5 per cent in 1951. With the inclusion of more and more groups under this category, the proportion rose to more than 8 per cent in 1991. 'A remarkable higher growth rate of the tribal population during 1971–81 was largely fueled by the inclusion of new communities under the scheduled tribe category' (Maharatna 2005: 25). However, there still remain many anomalies, for example, the tribes of the upper Himalayan region such as the Bhotiyas and the Kinnauries regard themselves as upper caste Hindus (Kshatriya). Others are contesting this very Hindu identity imposed on them. During the colonial period, the motivation for identifying tribes as Hindus was 'more nationalist and political than scientific or academic' (ibid.: 10). At that time, tribes were also interested in emulating Hindus. But since then, with transformations in political identity, the move towards establishing a separate indigenous identity has become a greater driving force for tribes, especially larger groups like the Mundas.

Many tribes are no longer interested in identifying themselves as Hindus, and processes like Sanskritisation and Hinduisation are being replaced by more revivalistic trends. Within tribal groups, there is also a clamour for the separation of smaller groups from larger ones, thereby leading to a rise in the number of tribes. At the moment, despite the number of Scheduled Tribes having crossed the number 500, the bulk of the tribal population is composed of only nine major tribal groups that account for nearly half of the tribal population of the country. The National Policy on Tribes mentions 67.8 million members of Scheduled Tribes, constituting 8.08 per cent of the Indian population and numbering 698 tribes. They are spread all over India, with the exception of Chandigarh, Delhi, Haryana, Puducherry and Punjab. Odisha has the largest number of tribes, numbering 68. The major tribal groups are as follows in terms of their regional distribution:

According to the National Policy on Tribes, Scheduled Tribes constitute 8.08 per cent of the Indian population. They are spread all over India, except in Chandigarh, Delhi, Haryana, Puducherry and Punjab. Odisha has the largest number of tribes, numbering 68.

1. Bhil (Gujarat, Madhya Pradesh and Rajasthan)
2. Gond (Madhya Pradesh, Odisha, Andhra Pradesh, Telangana and Maharashtra)
3. Santal (Bihar, Jharkhand, Odisha, Tripura and West Bengal)
4. Oraon (Bihar, Jharkhand, Madhya Pradesh, Odisha, West Bengal and Madhya Pradesh)
5. Meena (Rajasthan)
6. Munda (Bihar, Jharkhand, Odisha, West Bengal and Madhya Pradesh)
7. Kond (Andhra Pradesh and Odisha)
8. Ho (Jharkhand and Odisha)
9. Naga (Nagaland, Manipur, Assam and Meghalaya)

These tribes have large populations, and several of them like the Santal, Munda, Gond and Ho have their script and written languages. The smaller tribes such as the Tharu, Raji, Korwa and Nayakan, spread across India, are not only lesser known but also have much less political and cultural impact. But even with the nine large tribes, the total share of the population of tribes is only 8.6 per cent of the Indian population as per the 2011 Census, up from the earlier figure of 8 per cent in the 2001 Census, thus making them politically less important than Scheduled Castes and Muslims, whose numbers are much larger. There has also been a Hindu pressure on tribes to declare themselves as Hindus and thus lose much of their cultural identity.

Tribal areas still suffer from infrastructural inadequacies: lack of medical facilities, roads and schools. The privileges granted to them have only worked partially in making a difference. It has made possible the education of the youth and the absorption of some of them in government jobs, but this too has resulted in internal stratification, thus obscuring the chances of those at the bottom of their own societies.

Under the Fifth and Sixth Schedules, tribal areas are exempt from some of the civil laws of the country and can follow their own customary laws. It may be mentioned that the Fifth and Sixth Schedule provision of the Indian Constitution followed from the Excluded and Partially Excluded Areas clause of the British colonial administration, under Government of India Act, 1935. The rationale behind these provisions was to shield the vulnerable tribal areas as well as the tribal people from exploitation and usurpation by outsiders. The Sixth Schedule gives partial autonomous status to the tribal areas of the northeast of India, covering Nagaland, Meghalaya, Mizoram and Arunachal. Under these provisions, tribes can follow their customary laws and ensure protection of their land and resources. The Fifth Schedule covers the tribal areas throughout the country, but it still remains up to the states to declare some of their areas as falling under this provision. As pointed out by B. D. Sharma,

The rationale behind the Fifth and Sixth Schedules was to shield vulnerable tribal areas and populations from exploitation by outsiders. The Sixth Schedule gives partial autonomous status to the tribal areas of the Northeast, covering Nagaland, Meghalaya, Mizoram and Arunachal.

the last Commissioner for Scheduled Castes and Scheduled Tribes (1986–91) of Government of India, many of the areas that should have been protected as scheduled areas have been conveniently left out, to serve the vested interests of developers and industrialists. As he points out, only two-and-a-half *tehsils* (administrative units) out of eight in the Bastar district are scheduled, and the entire excluded area of Sombhadra in Uttar Pradesh is not scheduled because the tribes of this region were wrongly listed as Scheduled Castes. There is no scheduled area in West Bengal, Tripura, Kerala, Karnataka, Tamil Nadu and Goa. Thus, scheduled areas do not cover even one-third of the actual tribal areas of the country (Sharma 2010: 25).

The Manmohan Singh government initiated the National Tribal Policy in 2006, with a view to correcting some of the mishaps and lapses of the earlier policies, especially as the Red Corridor, areas with concentration of Naxalite-Maoist insurgency, spread through the entire tribal belt of India, posing a threat to the very integrity of the country. The overt goal of this policy is to bring tribes into the mainstream. The policy mentions the Nehruvian Panchsheel as abstract and claims to now focus on specificities—like formal education, traditional wisdom, health, displacement and resettlement issues, forest villages, shifting cultivation, land alienation, intellectual property rights, tribal languages—as areas that need special attention and specific action plans. The policy also focuses on Primitive Tribal Groups (PTGs, since then revised to PVTGs or Particularly Vulnerable Tribal Groups), Scheduled Tribes and scheduled areas. It emphasises both administration and research, identifying methodologies for both in terms of participatory research. However, the final point is of assimilation, which leaves a big question mark for the future of tribes in India. The policy reflects clearly the primary goal of the then government, which was to assimilate tribes as much as possible into urban and mainstream society, to convert them into settled agriculture and to promote formal education that will employ them in the market economy, in effect, slowly eroding their traditional livelihoods and ultimately the tribal ways of life. Lip service to forest rights and indigenous knowledge is not evident in the consequent policies of the state, irrespective of the political parties in power.

PERSPECTIVES ON TRIBE

Let us now examine some of the philosophical underpinnings and the academic backdrop of the concept of tribe. We will see how the term 'tribe' has been constructed and understood over the years, and how it has undergone several paradigm shifts.

Classical Evolutionary Theories

From the sixteenth century onwards, Europe was the fountainhead of enlightenment philosophies and critical thought that gave more importance to social rather than theological perspectives. Society was no longer viewed as divinely ordained and created, and hence a given; instead, social relations and political organisations were understood as human creations and as capable of change and transformation. With industrialisation and improved technology, the volume of trade and travels from European countries to other parts of the world increased manifold as the emerging capitalist economy demanded more and more resources. Coming in contact with a diverse range of people and cultures, Europeans were faced with questions about human diversity and cultural differences. The establishment of positivism as a definite philosophy that looked upon society as something external and objective, capable of academic scrutiny laid the foundation of subjects such as social philosophy, sociology and, later, anthropology. A distinction between sociology and anthropology developed in the colonial context, whereby sociology came to be the study by Europeans of their own society and anthropology the study of 'other cultures'. While philosophers and social theorists like Auguste Comte, Henri de Saint-Simon, Herbert Spencer and Voltaire studied European societies (Aron 1965), they also became interested in how European societies had come to be in their present stage of development, and what could have been the past of their own society.

A central concern of European scholars was a critical appraisal of their own societies and of their cultures and ways of life. If they were not created *in situ* by a divine hand, how did they come to be the way they were? Why were other people different? What did this difference signify?

This was also the time when Europeans had already begun their colonisation of the non-Western world. The Americas were already colonised, the native populations devastated and their cultures destroyed; South and Southeast Asia, and Africa, were also being dominated by White people. The Europeans had no doubt that they were superior as a 'race'. They had the power of guns and they had more cunning than the simple folk they encountered and overpowered in the colonies. For Europeans, people who exchanged gold for glass beads appeared child-like and undeveloped in intellect.

Europeans, therefore, speculated that perhaps these people represented the 'childhood' or early stages of human social development and that by some criteria or circumstances (never really understood), Europeans had evolved into a superior stage that they self-designated as 'civilisation'. Seen from the European or Eurocentric point of view, the natives or original inhabitants of the continents that they were conquering were 'primitive', a word modified from its original meaning of 'early' or 'initial' to designate contemporary people. These were people who lived in the present but were seen as representing the early stages of human evolution or, more specifically, the past of European civilisation. The word 'native' with its innocuous meaning of being born in a particular place assumed quite a different connotation when it was applied by the colonising Europeans to the people of the colonies they had acquired. It meant something derogatory, something that implied someone who was less than human, a 'savage', a word unfortunately used by anthropologists of the classical era to people they did not consider 'civilised'. The word 'tribe' too emerged in such a context, applied again to people who were seen as being far away from civilisation and urbanisation. This word also created a rift between people of the same continent, where there were evidently various different modes of adaptation and forms of culture.

From a Eurocentric point of view, the natives or original inhabitants of the continents they were conquering were seen as 'primitive', representing the early stages of human evolution; the word 'tribe' emerged from such a context.

In India, for example, those who did not belong to the *varna* (four-fold division of the Hindu universe) categories of Hindu society and those who were not part of the agricultural economy on which the caste system was based were relegated to the category of 'junglee' or uncivilised and then designated as 'tribes', under both the colonial and postcolonial administrations. In continents like New Zealand, Australia and America, the label 'tribe' became a legitimate tool for not only the acquisition of land and resources but also all-out genocide. The geographical regions occupied by non-Europeans were often declared as *terra nulis* (vacant land) and the people occupying these lands were likened to animals that could be exterminated (Shanklin 1994).

Beliefs such as these were strengthened by theories of biological evolution (race theories that deemed that some races were superior than the others and that there was a connection between race and mental development) and also by theories of psychological evolution. Sigmund Freud (1919 [1913]), the nineteenth-century father of psychoanalysis, in his popular thesis, equates the totemic rituals of the so-called primitives with the regressive behaviour of immature adults whose psychological development, he argues, is similar to that of pre-adolescent children or of adult neurotics in the European civilised world. However, most intellectuals of the European Renaissance were against racist theories that attributed the so-called less developed cultures of non-Europeans to their racial inferiority. They believed that there is a psychic unity of mankind, and people have different levels of cultural development due to circumstances external to their biological or racial attributes. Yet the belief in racial inferiority was what sustained the slave trade, and led to the building of the European empires and to the establishment of the Americas as a White country. The native populations of countries such as the US, New Zealand, Australia and Canada were subjected to genocide and the remaining peoples put into Reservations (bounded territories where the tribes were secluded and confined) outside of the mainstream of national life, where they still live (Shanklin 1994).

The intellectual belief forming the foundation of evolutionary theories is that human society goes through stages of evolution and that some societies get arrested at an early stage of development (represented by tribes or natives) while others move on to the next stage. However, no clear-cut explanation for this evolved till anthropology was established in the early part of the twentieth century to explain human diversity and evolution. The biological theory of evolution is a general theory, while anthropology is a discipline specifically oriented towards explaining human evolution in all its specific dimensions. In terms of social evolution, anthropology based itself solidly on the concept of the primitive, and we find that much of the early literature in anthropology is replete with the repeated use of this term.

True to their initial goal of explaining human origins and development, anthropologists applied themselves to the study of the so-called primitives—the people they encountered in their colonies and who appeared farthest away from Europeans in terms of their appearance and lifestyle. It is interesting to note what kind of people they considered the most primitive. The Australian Aborigines were one such people—with their short stature, thick lips, broad noses, minimal clothing and stone tools, they became an immediate favourite to be designated as 'primitive', and formed the material for the study of primitive religion and rituals by Freud and also Émile Durkheim in his search for the most original religion in his work *Elementary Forms of Religious Life* (1947). In other words, it was clear that those who were farthest away from the Europeans in looks, clothes and ways of life were dubbed the most primitive. Thus, matrilineal societies were more primitive than patrilineal ones; polytheistic religions were more primitive than monotheistic ones; and hunters and food-gatherers were more primitive than agricultural societies.

The term 'tribe' could not be applied to all 'natives' uniformly—there were very apparent differences within the natives, and while some of them approximated quite closely to Europeans, others seemed miles away. Hindus practising a complex caste system were quite different from the people inhabiting the Andaman Islands; the headhunting Nagas were different from the Vaishnavites of Manipur. The stage-by-stage theory of evolution put forth by the early anthropologists was aimed at explaining the vast differences within non-Western people who differed greatly in terms of their social organisations, political systems, and religious ritual and other practices.

Classical evolutionists conjured up several schemas, the early ones focusing upon religion and marriage/kinship as key variables to explain stages of evolution. Their methodology was based upon speculative thinking, deductive reasoning and secondary sources of data. They had little exposure to the real societies they wrote about, and they provided explanations on a mega scale, encapsulating practically the entire humankind. The term 'tribe' was used by them without any specific qualification. Morgan (1910 [1877]) used the term to describe Native American political organisation. He was among the first to identify tribe as designating a level of political organisation, differentiating it from sib (a kin group) and the higher order of the confederacy of tribes.

The Functionalist School of Anthropology

As anthropology relied more and more on fieldwork as a method, and participant observation as a technique, the discipline shifted towards a functionalist approach. The main difference of this approach as compared to the earlier evolutionist approach was that it relied more on empirical, first-hand data, and less on speculation. The universal concept of culture as first defined by Tylor (1871) was replaced by a more particularistic and situated definition of cultures in the plural along with the dictum of cultural relativism. Instead of grading cultures on a scale, functionalists believed that all cultural practices have their relevance in a specific context. Hence, the term 'primitive' was rescued from its evolutionary significance. Yet, it remained in use to designate a specific kind of organisation and continues to be used in the planning process of so-called development.

The concept of an absolute 'culture' was replaced by a more particularistic definition of 'cultures'. Instead of grading cultures on a scale, cultural relativism put forward the idea that all cultural practices have their relevance in a specific context.

As anthropologists went to the field to do their research, the term 'tribe' was extensively used to designate the people they studied. This choice of the field area also marked the difference between sociology and anthropology, and even till recent times, anthropologists have been associated primarily with the study of tribes and indigenous peoples. The functionalists put forth the paradigm of isolated, bounded and homogenous entities designated as tribes. 'It came to be assumed that each tribe in the ethnographic present was a single homogenous entity, a single pattern of institutions and ideas, and that those who were "in" it shared this pattern uniformly and participated in no other pattern' (Leaf 1979: 148). During the early colonial period, many anthropologists claimed to have 'discovered' one of these entities, which they fondly referred to as 'my tribe'. These tribes were viewed as having a definite identity, often enclosed by the practice of endogamy and having some definite characteristics like a body of beliefs that were unique enough to be designated by the name of the tribe, like in the case of the Nuer (Evans-Pritchard 1940). They were also believed to be endowed with a structure of relationships that was bounded, in equilibrium and unchanging. Tribes were believed to not have a history. Changes in them were mostly attributed to the postcolonial phase and to external agents. Anthropological studies in social change focused upon specific agents of change and on their impact upon specific institutions.

In the popular usage of the term 'tribe' and the official designation of a group as a tribe, the concepts of isolation, backwardness and homogeneity continue to be deployed. However, as Leaf (1979: 148) points out, methodologically the concept has always been an enigma as one could never study a 'tribe' in its pristine state, as the very act of studying would contaminate it. Therefore, at best, the anthropologist could conjure up what would have been the original state: 'One therefore had to infer or deduce its traditional order from what one could see, by assuming that some sort of uniform pattern existed' (ibid.).

Durkheim is revered as the father of the functionalist approach. In his study of Australian Aborigines, Durkheim transformed from an evolutionist to a functionalist when he realised that the most 'elementary' religion that he had come to study was a set of beliefs and practices that, far from being a set of superstitions, played a key role in the maintenance of society. The initial studies by anthropologists (including the one by Durkheim) focusing on small and well-knit communities led to the concept of the bounded tribe or the tribe as a social system. Each tribe was seen as and referred to as a specific society so that there were studies of Nuer society, Andamanese society, Toda society and so on.

As the functionalist school established itself, studies were conducted to create elaborate typologies of tribes, where they were classified according to their political organisations, kinship systems or modes of subsistence. Anthologies were published, such as *African Political Systems* (Fortes and Evans-Pritchard 1940) and *African Systems of Kinship and Marriage* (Radcliffe-Brown and Forde 1950). However, such neat classifications were not always possible. In South Asia, for example, it was realised that although some so-called tribes could be seen as isolated and distinct, many others were integrated within the larger Indian civilisation. Thus, while Africa yielded a conglomeration of 'tribes' of various kinds, India was a civilisation incorporating many different kinds of social types. Terms like 'great tradition' and 'little tradition' were invented to explain and classify these gradations.

> **While Africa constituted of a conglomeration of 'tribes' of various kinds, India was a civilisation incorporating many different kinds of social types. Terms like 'great tradition' and 'little tradition' were invented to explain and classify these gradations.**

In America, the entities called tribes had almost lost their structures of relationships. The American way of colonisation, with guns in the hands of a militant set of people, led to the extermination and dispersion of the indigenous communities, and an almost total destruction of their habitats and ways of life. Often these cultures and associated ways of life existed only in the memories of a few last remaining members of a tribe. The surviving few had been put in reservations, losing much of their heritage and relational structures. The focus in this part of the world, therefore, shifted from the study of structures to that of cultures, seen in a more ephemeral manner in terms of folklores, myths, material cultures and oral traditions. Tribes were here seen more in terms of a set of cultural practices, traditions and memories than as real people. The American anthropologist Kroeber (1952) defines culture as 'super-organic', something that has an existence beyond the culture bearers for that was how tribes or the Native American people were to be studied.

American anthropologists, faced with a disappearing scenario, could not deny that history and processes such as acculturation and cultural transformation were integral to the study of anthropology in the US. Rather than study individual bounded entities, they devised methodologies such as culture area theory. The German school of diffusionism continued its influence through the intellectual heritage of the father of American anthropology, Franz Boas. Culture was always a less-bounded concept than structure and, therefore, the flexibility of viewing tribes as more diffused, and as in a process of transformation, was inherent in the American cultural tradition.

We can take as an instance the classic study by Kluckhohn (1944) of the witchcraft beliefs of the Navaho, whom he studied in their reservation. Here, unlike the well-adjusted Zande, studied in their own habitat by Evans-Pritchard, the Navaho were living in miserable conditions, uprooted from their traditional life by the impact of colonisation. Kluckhohn studied witchcraft as it was practised under conditions of mental instability and tension. He demonstrated how it was used as an adaptive measure by people to combat the highly stressed and unhealthy lives they lived within the reservations.

The functionalist school faced criticism for the neatness and closure of their analyses. It could always be pointed out that actual situations are rarely so harmonious and so symmetric in their arrangements. But some of these classifications, although ideal in conception, did provide a means of understanding variations in the kinds of societies that were classified as tribes.

BAND, TRIBE, CHIEFDOM AND STATE

A comprehensive definition often accepted by anthropologists is the socio-political typology provided by Service (1962), in which he placed 'tribe' on a scale of evolving organisational complexity, without attaching any developmental or progressive significance to the stages on the scale. His schema was 'band, tribe, chiefdom and state'.

The first category 'band' refers to societies that have fluid and small organisations, for instance, hunting food-gathering communities. Bands are characterised by their small size, bilateral kinship ties or little emphasis on kinship except ties between parents and children, which often tend to be fluid. We shall discuss these kinds of communities in greater detail in Chapter 2. At present, it is best to understand them as based on a situational logic, an adaptive strategy of people who have to directly live off nature and who do not have a technology of storage and accumulation. The lack of technology does not reflect a lack of capacity to develop technology but a lack of motivation to do so. Again, this is a debate that needs more discussion, and we shall do it in a more appropriate place.

Cultural anthropologist Elman Service placed 'tribe' on a scale of evolving organisational complexity, without attaching any developmental or progressive significance to the stages on the scale. His schema was 'band, tribe, chiefdom and state'.

The second level, namely, that of tribe, refers to all those societies that are based on relations of kinship, especially of descent groups. In his seminal paper in *American Anthropologist* (1953), Fortes described in great detail societies that use unilineal descent to define group boundaries and also social and political identities. A person becomes a member of society by being born into a descent group and carries that identity for purposes of marriage, ownership of resources and also for maintaining and negotiating political relationships. Kinship relations form the basis for economic and religious functions, and according the Godelier (1972), kinship plays the role of both relations of production and of reproducing human beings; the former he referred to as the outer relations of kinship and the latter, that is, the familial one, as the inner relations of kinship. Fortes (1969) referred to them as the politico-jural and affective functions of kinship, respectively. Since kin groups or descent groups are politically and socially equal in principle, societies based on these are also referred to as segmentary societies, as each descent group forms a horizontal segment at level with other such segments. In many anthropological usages, the term 'tribe' refers to this kind of society.

A chiefdom is a hierarchical political organisation, unlike the ideally equal segmentary organisation of the tribe. A segment may for some historical reasons become more powerful than others, and the elders of that lineage may exert more power than others and be designated as chiefs. It is not necessary that such a chiefdom is stable and enduring, as Leach (1954) shows through the concepts of *gumsa* and *gumlao* in his book *Political Systems of Highland Burma*. Gumsa refers to the stage where the tribe is organised under a chief and gumlao to one where the people rebel and return to chaotic conditions.

It is important to note that a chiefdom depends on a person's ability to gather and keep followers attracted to them. Economically, it is often a redistributive rather than an accumulative system. A chief is a chief on the basis of what he can do for his followers, like organising rituals and throwing feasts. Followers may give the chief tributes and gifts, which need to be returned in a public and ceremonial fashion. It is the public display of wealth and generosity that marks out the power of the chief. A chief rarely has coercive authority and has the moral responsibility to be answerable for his actions. A chief can be removed by collective sentiments and action. Thus, Leach (1954) demonstrates that the swing from gumsa to gumlao is dependent upon the ability of the chief to gather and then keep together the followers. Disgruntled followers may push a system towards anarchy. In writing about Mundas, Roy (1912) argues that the so-called chiefs in these societies were firsts among equals; they had only administrative but no coercive powers.

There are many theories of the evolution of chiefdoms and states. These mainly focus on the conversion of an egalitarian society into a hierarchical one. Real hierarchy in terms of inequality is found only at the stage of proper state formation. Chiefdom, like that of the Burmese highlanders, is not a real system of hierarchy as the chiefs rarely have the power of coercion. They are only able to maintain a certain position of prestige and status by the redistribution of the goods that they either produce or receive as tribute. What Service (1962) has referred to as chiefdom is a tribe that has transited from a segmentary system based on equal descent groups to a stage where one descent group or even an individual manages to gain a higher position. But again, as documented by Leach (1954) in his study of highland Burma, such chiefdoms may revert to an egalitarian state, or even if they continue, they rarely have the structural organisation of a proper state. The classification given by Service (1962), like any other classification, is only a heuristic device, approximating to but never actually describing a real lived reality. These remain ideal types.

A kingdom, unlike a chiefdom, is based on a real concentration of power in the person or persons (a family or a lineage) who head this political organisation. This form of society is based on territorial rather than kinship considerations and has a complex organisation as compared to the other three modes discussed earlier. While the term 'tribe' is often used for all these three kinds of socio-political organisations, there are only specific instances of what may be called tribal kingdoms (for example, the Gond kingdom in India and the Zulu kingdom in Africa). For a kingdom to emerge requires an economic base that can produce enough surplus to support a non-producing elite. This elite should have both coercive and legitimate rights for the extraction of this surplus.

At this point, let us clarify the difference between tribe and peasant. A tribe is usually politically independent and does not pay tribute to higher authorities, although as seen in the case of pastoral nomadic societies, they often rely on chiefs or kings to support and protect their ways of life. Yet tribes can exist without the patronage of kings and chiefs. Peasants, on the other hand, are seen as a necessary condition for the existence of a centralised power like a king. Peasants produce food that supports this centralised structure; yet they are always subordinate to it. This hierarchy is necessary for the extraction of surplus—it provides legitimacy to the transfer of the fruits of one's labour to another, making this process peaceful and more or less voluntary. Redfield (1961) refers to peasants as part society, part culture, as he views them as one half of a whole, that is, a kingdom or a state.

A tribe is usually politically independent, even if it may rely on chiefs or kings to protect its ways of life. Peasants, however, are necessary for the existence of a king: they produce food that supports power; yet they are subordinate to it.

Peasants are often coerced into producing a surplus that they must transfer to the higher authority. Thus, in the anthropological imagination, tribes have been seen as free and independent and peasants as dependent on a superior segment to which they owed allegiance. In India, however, the distinction between who the peasants, and consequently castes, are and who are tribes has never been clear-cut. Thus, the discourse about 'tribe' has often been about distinguishing a tribe from a caste and also about determining whether tribes are Hindus. As we shall see, none of these identities were clearly demarcated and fuzzy boundaries continue to exist.

TRIBE AND CASTE IN INDIA

The term 'tribe' is not an indigenous one. The indigenous term 'jati' encompasses both caste and tribe. Jati is a generalised term with a wide range of referents. The term 'janjati' is used for those 'jatis' that are located in the forests. But in the Indian languages, there is no specific separation of anything like caste and tribe. Castes are actually jatis within the larger system of varna, and 'Adivasi', the term that is most close to tribe, would mean just another kind of jati. In other words, this lack of linguistic separation indicates that in India, there were no such distinct entities socially speaking.

The term 'jati' encompasses both caste and tribe; 'janjati' is used for jatis located in the forests. Indian languages, thus, do not differentiate between caste and tribe. This lack of linguistic separation indicates that there were no such distinct social entities.

Ethnographically, tribes and peasants (caste societies) are rarely dichotomous categories, and as we examine field studies of various tribes and communities in India, we shall find that these neat classifications are often problematic. According to Mandelbaum (1970: 574), there are many groups at the intersection of tribes and castes, whose identities are difficult to pinpoint as they appear like both a tribe and a caste: 'At the middle of a range there may be very little difference between a group that considers itself a tribe and one that claims to be a jati.' Mandelbaum uses criteria similar to that given by Service to define a tribe, that is, in a tribe, 'the principal links for the whole society are based on kinship' (ibid.: 576). For a jati, on the other hand, it is not just kinship but the presence of other jatis of unequal rank that enables it to continue as a particular jati group.

> The crucial difference is that jati members on the one hand believe they must have non-kinship relations with others in their society and that these relations must be arranged in an order of dominance and deference. Tribesmen, on the other hand, tend to see their society

> as held together by kinship bonds and do not insist on hierarchical ordering. Further, jati people expect their village society to be culturally heterogeneous, each jati following a unique combination of customary practices; tribesmen expect their society to be homogeneous or, at least, not necessarily heterogeneous. (Ibid.: 578)

Mandelbaum finally designates tribal societies as more 'segmentary' and jati societies as more organic (ibid.: 579).

According to Béteille (1986: 311), 'One often sees a certain homology between individual castes and tribes in the sense that both perpetuate collective identities in strikingly similar ways.' Similarly, Majumdar (1972: 265) argues that, 'No clear cut definition of the term "tribe" can be found.' Majumdar then goes on to define tribes on the basis of cultural and linguistic homogeneity, and points out that these groups do not follow any of the major religions of India. However, he corrects himself when he admits that, 'The main difficulty with the present definition is that it excludes all the Christians from the connotation of the term tribe' (ibid.). However, Majumdar is also of the opinion that those who have begun to resemble or 'have raised themselves to the level of surrounding non-tribal populations' (ibid.) should no longer be termed as tribes. 'I feel very strongly that these sections are regarded as tribes due only to the general misconception that once a group is considered as a tribe, it should remain as such forever' (ibid.). Majumdar is recognised for his conceptualisation of the tribe–caste continuum, a theory that is based on the basic paradigm that 'tribe' refers to a level of socio-economic and cultural standards (much like the classical evolutionary school), and that this level can be transformed so that the particular group can transcend the level to qualify for the next. He uses the concept of Sanskritisation to identify this transformation. The term, originally coined by Srinivas (1966) to describe upward social mobility within the caste system, is defined by Majumdar as 'the elements by accepting which a non-caste group (tribal group) gets acceptance in the Hindu society and which give vertical mobility to a group which has already been accepted in the Hindu society' (ibid.).

Focusing on the Garo Hills district of Meghalaya (then Assam), Majumdar (1972) has identified two communities: the Songsarek Garo, a tribe showing no signs of Sanskritisation, and the Dalus, who claim a Hindu identity and say they belong to a Bengali Vaishnava sect. According to Majumdar, these two groups occupy the two extreme points on the tribe–caste continuum. The other three groups in this region—the Rabha, the Koch and the Hajong—occupy intermediate positions on this axis. Each group also contains within itself a vertical continuum of different sub-groups. Thus, the Rabha contain within its ranks the Pati/Kocha, Dahori, Maitori and Rongdani, where the Pati are the most Sanskritised and the Rongdani, the least. To complicate the situation further, some Garos have also converted to Hinduism. They are similar to the Dalus and claim Hindu Vaishnava identity, and are served by Brahmin priests. Thus, there are two groups of Garos, the Songsarek or non-Hinduised ones and the Garos who are Sanskritised.

The three main activities that a group must give up in the process of Sanskritisation are beef-eating, keeping pigs and fowl, and eating pigs and fowl. In the next step, the group partially or totally abandons its non-Hindu deities and accepts Hindu deities. The rituals pertaining to these Hindu deities have to be performed by Brahmin priests, who agree to do so only if the group in question has already given up the eating of beef (absolutely necessary) and that of pig and fowl (desirable). In Majumdar's opinion, the final step in tribal Sanskritisation and also assimilation into the Hindu fold is abandoning the clan and social organisation of the respective tribe and accepting Hindu patriarchy. However, not many tribes have shown a tendency towards this step.

Scholars like Majumdar were strongly influenced by the classical evolutionary theory and believed that tribes belonged to a 'lower stage' than caste Hindus, and that they actually aspired to a higher status. In other words, they attributed the acceptance of Hindu traits as something voluntary and even desirable, from the point of view of tribes. Influenced also by the structural-functional school, these scholars could not visualise how the domination by outsiders and the political hierarchy would have influenced this process. This does not mean that scholars like Majumdar were prejudiced against the tribal way of life; they simply had a perspective that was rooted in their own times and influenced by the then prevalent theories.

The intensive fieldwork that was done by scholars of the stature of D. N. Majumdar also led them to identify some exceptions to the neat labelling that was characteristic of those times. Majumdar (1972) found that while tribes also follow the practice of linguistic endogamy, as is common among Hindu castes, such rules of dialectical endogamy are not very strict if the languages are similar; the greater the similarity, the more frequent the intermarriage, for instance, as between the Rongdani Rabhas and Maitori Rabhas.

There have been eminent Indian scholars who moved beyond a given theory to see the dynamics of interaction between Indian tribes and the society at large. Just like Majumdar who was able to identify the interaction between tribes and caste groups and some of the processes of transformation in a historical perspective, another eminent scholar of those times was N. K. Bose, who applied a nuanced approach to the entire history of Indian civilisation in order to analyse the present. According to Béteille (1992: *xiii*), 'Very few anthropologists have brought to the study of the Indian tribe the historical imagination that guided Bose's observations.' Bose integrated anthropology with Indology and social history, thus moving way beyond the restricted approach of evolutionism/functionalism followed by most others of his times. He also introduced a uniquely Indian approach to theory instead of following what Western scholars had written. By contextualising tribes within the Indian civilisation and foregrounding their centuries of interaction with non-tribal people of the continent, he was not looking at them as isolated or bounded, which was the norm those days. The Juangs, a hill tribe studied by him, were relatively untouched at that time by Brahminical Hinduism; yet both the tribe and the Hindu population in its vicinity were well aware of each other. Bose uses an interesting term—'non-Aryan'—to refer to tribes, indicating that he too subscribed to the 'Aryan theory' or the racial theory of caste, which was popular in his times.

Anthropologist N. K. Bose integrated anthropology with Indology and social history. He focused on the centuries of interaction between tribal and non-tribal people of the continent, looking at them not as isolated or bounded, which was the norm those days.

In his book *The Structure of Hindu Society* (1992 [1975]: 39), Bose raises interesting questions as to why hill tribes such as the Juang, who had an almost independent subsistence base, sought to establish economic ties with caste Hindus, even though they always occupied the lowest rank in such interactions. To this end, he collected ethnographic data from tribes such as Munda (now in Jharkhand). Bose (1992 [1975]) describes the *khuntkatti* system whereby persons who originally cleared the land and established villages are known as *khuntkattidar*s, and their rights over all the resources such as land, water and trees are taken as uncontested. The villages are owned by the collective of the khuntkattidars but not by individual families. The land is redistributed according to the requirements of each family. The eldest of each lineage or *kul* was known as the *munda* or the leader. The present-day Mundas have emerged out of the Kol tribe as elders kept taking on the name 'Munda'. The religion of the Munda is centred round the sacred grove of *saran* trees and the cremation stones known as *sasan-diri*. Several villages come under the jurisdiction of the *manki* (local headman) who also takes care of the *akhra*, a place for the performance of dance and rituals. The Mundas are not totally egalitarian, and have a two-fold division of the khuntkattidars, and the artisans and cattle keepers, on one hand, and people who are not part of the original landownership, on the other. Such two-fold divisions are also seen among other tribal groups such as Bhotiyas and Kinnauries.

Bose discusses how the khuntkattidar system of the Mundas, which had given them independent land rights, was gradually absorbed within the *jagirdari* system imposed from above. The Mundas were subjected to external authority and made subservient to local kings. The coming of the East India Company and the establishment of its financial administration over the region of Bengal, Bihar and Orissa brought further oppression of the earlier independent tribes and they rose up in revolt several times. The oppressions increased with the coming of the *thekadar*s, a merchant class whose only aim was economic gain.

The only help to the tribal people came from the missionaries who genuinely tried to help them and petitioned the then British government (in place after 1857) to help the former retain their land rights. In 1869, the Bhuinhari Act was passed, but it did not help the illiterate tribals much, as the cunning outsiders such as the thekadars prevented them from doing so, taking recourse to several devious means. In Chapter 6, we will learn more about the revolts that took place among the Mundas and other tribal groups against this oppression from the outside.

Bose tries to answer the question of why the Munda and the Oraon took the path of imitating caste Hindu society rather than turn towards Christianity by identifying three factors. The first was the better technology and lifestyle of the Hindu peasants who surrounded them; second, they lacked confidence in the Christians who failed to give them support when they revolted; and third, Christianisation led to the formation of classes among them, which they found disruptive. The tensions between the Christian and non-Christian tribals continue in this region of Jharkhand even today, although in terms of identity politics, the tribes no longer wish to be identified as Hindus, an aspect we shall take up later, in Chapter 4.

Since there are many tribes in India that claim caste status, terms such as 'Sanskritisation' and 'Hinduisation' have been used to denote attempts at upward mobility on the part of tribes. Some scholars are of the opinion that some upper castes may have been reduced to a so-called marginal status as they lost their political power, and the term 'tribalisation' (Chauhan 1966) has been used for such a process. It has been recorded by Brown (1990) that the Bhotiya tribes on the Indo-Tibet border were actually Rajputs who preferred to accept a non-Hindu lifestyle, for instance, eating beef, in order to form long-term trading relationships with the Tibetans, which involved living in each other's houses. They sacrificed their upper-caste status for the sake of economic benefits. Again, once the trade was discontinued and the Bhotiya communities found themselves forging greater economic and political relations with the Indian mainland, they attempted to move towards their original Hindu upper-caste identity (Channa 2013). However, Unnithan-Kumar (1997) is in disagreement with the notion that tribalisation means a loss of civilised ways, and is more supportive of

Since there are many tribes in India that claim caste status, terms such as 'Sanskritisation' and 'Hinduisation' have been used to denote attempts at upward mobility on the part of tribes.

the idea that communities like Girasia have been able to maintain their original ways of life to a greater extent than the Bhils, who had more intimate contacts with caste communities. Thus, the identity of being a tribe and the identity of being a caste are, as suggested by Unnithan-Kumar, a matter of historical and political process, and may change over time depending upon the context.

COLONIAL ETHNOGRAPHIES

The holistic description of peoples, known as an ethnography, became the vogue from the colonial period onwards, especially as the functionalist and structural-functional schools established themselves as major theoretical paradigms. Beginning with Malinowski's qualitative in-depth study of the Trobriand Islanders, in his now classic work *Argonauts of the Western Pacific* (1922), many excellent ethnographies were crafted. Although these works detailed the everyday lives and various aspects of culture and society of the people studied, they were later criticised for being too concerned with function and harmony, equilibrium and stability, when the actual field situation was never as simple as depicted.

During the colonial period, anthropologists were reluctant to recognise the real impact of colonial rule on the lives of tribes. Beautifully written ethnographies described serene and functional societies without even mentioning the real conditions of misery in which they were living. A case in point is Radcliffe-Brown's (1932) description of the Andaman Islanders, where the entire society is described as in equilibrium and as timeless. The reality was that most of the Andamanese had died out by the time they were studied by Radcliffe-Brown, who studied them as an agent of the British Raj, calling informants into his tent to take down their narratives. No actual marriage took place while he was in the field and no baby was born. The Andamanese were dying out by European-borne diseases like measles and syphilis, a fate suffered by many tribes, who had no immunity to foreign infections. But Radcliffe-Brown's ethnography does not reflect this. The ethnographies of Indian tribes written during the colonial period by Indian anthropologists such as Roy were also informed by schools of thought such as classical evolutionary and diffusion theories, and, in addition, followed a strictly positivist approach, where the field was treated as a scientific 'object' of study.

Taking a close look at Roy's now classic work, *The Mundas and Their Country* (1912), we find that he is influenced by 'scientific' theories such as those of the Aryan invasion of India and the related racist theories that explained the variations in the Indian population. Like Bose and others, Roy also located the tribes of central India, as a pre-Aryan people, who were later displaced by the Aryans from their territory. However, Roy had a very different vision of the tribes than was the popular image of 'primitive' people at that time. It goes to the great credit of Indian scholars that some of them like Bose and Roy did not consider tribes to be 'ahistorical' and 'static', but rather contextualised them in a historical perspective, trying to assess how they came to be in their present condition. Roy (1912: 26) has combined both evolutionary and diffusionist perspectives in coming to the conclusion, 'Thus, we have grounds for inferring that the Mundas and other Kolarian tribes originally lived in the hilly regions along the Aravalli and Vindhya ranges and gradually spread further to the North and occupied the valleys of the mighty rivers of Northern India.' He was also reluctant to treat tribes as 'primitive' and with no cultural developments, 'Herdsmen and farmers by occupation, these aborigines of the soil could build houses for themselves, erect castles of stone, make flint weapons fitted for all uses, and understand the benefits of law and order' (ibid.: 59). In fact, Roy was unhappy with the way conservative historians had treated Indian tribes. He commented that these historians had dismissed tribes as if they were the same as the dense forests cleared by the later agricultural people to build the so-called Indian civilisation: 'A total absence of historical traditions regarding the antiquities of these tribes is tacitly assumed to exist by writers of Indian History' (ibid.: 2).

Some Indian scholars did not consider tribes to be 'ahistorical' and 'static', but rather contextualised them in a historical perspective, trying to assess how they came to be in their present condition.

Roy, who was also well conversant with the languages of the middle-Indian tribes, used all kinds of material, mythical, pseudo-historical (based on ancient scriptures and classical texts), archaeological, prehistorical and racial (from biological anthropology) theories, to reconstruct the 'origin' and later spread and development of these tribes. He certainly did not believe that tribes were 'ahistorical', and he recognised that identities evolved and consolidated over time.

Roy's work is particularly rich in documentation with respect to the historical period and how tribes were slowly deprived of their independence by the feudal system of the local rulers and the unscrupulous moneylenders and traders. He provides a graphic description of the tribal uprisings and the effects of the 'Mutiny' (First War of Independence) of 1857. However, while being extremely critical of the 'outsiders' who exploited and tortured tribes, Roy takes a benign view of the missionaries and, to some extent, even of the colonial administration. He is critical of the colonial administration's efforts to regularise land tenancy without paying any heed to tribal systems of collective ownership, including their relationship with their sacred land and groves. Criticising the Chotanagpur Tenures Act of 1869 for disregarding the khuntkatti system of the Mundas, Roy observes how this facilitated the transfer of unmarked land from tribes to 'outside' land-grabbers. 'It was not till late in the year 1903 (August) that by Bengal Act V of that year, special provisions were made to protect the Mundari Khuntkatti tenancies', but as rightly observed by Roy (1912: 279), it was too late and much of tribal land had already changed hands.

Roy praises the efforts of the missionaries to educate and 'civilise' tribal people, thus indicating his evolutionary bias and his acceptance of the definition of 'civilised' as concurrent with the conceptualisation of Western scholars. The missionaries opened schools to teach tribals the crafts of masonry, carpentry, weaving and ironworks, efforts that Roy lauds as an outcome of the 'self-sacrificing zeal' (ibid.: 323) of the missionaries. Not once did it occur to Roy that these efforts to 'educate' tribals were only turning them into low-paid labour serving the upper castes and classes of society, robbing them of their pride and independent lifestyle. It is also to be noted that the missionaries did not impart any real education to tribes, but only as much as was enough to make them enter the cash economy at the lowest level. This again reflects how strongly the scholars of those times were influenced by the stereotyping of tribes as 'primitive' and also as incapable of higher levels of thinking.

> For one thing, it has been their long contact with the Hindus that has raised the Mundas of the eastern paraganas of the Ranchi District in the scale of civilization. In fact, at the census of 1901, as many as 1,64,162 Mundas described themselves as Hindus. Many of the Hinduised Mundas of the Panch Parganas are, in their manner and intellectual capacity, now hardly distinguishable from other Hindus of equal social status and intellectual culture. (Ibid.: 352)

From this statement it becomes clear that initially even Indian anthropologists, in spite of their immense scholarship, were strongly influenced by the schools of thought that believed tribes to be less developed than other people.

In his extremely exhaustive and detailed account of the Birsa Munda movement, Roy likewise takes an unsympathetic attitude, favouring the British administration. His account differs significantly from that of K. S. Singh and the deification of Birsa Munda by later tribal activists and sympathisers.

The second part of Roy's ethnography is based on first-hand empirical data. He describes the various institutions of the Munda in a descriptive style. It is to be noted that his description of the day-to-day life of the Munda only begins in the seventh chapter, the first six being devoted to determining the origin and evolution of the Munda as a tribe. The ethnography covers most aspects of Munda day-to-day life, including material culture, rituals, folklore, agriculture and taboos. The ethnography is modelled along the same lines as that of eminent ethnographers of those times, which often included British administrators, for instance, J. P. Mills (1937) and J. H. Hutton (1921). In spite of the later criticism of these colonial ethnographies, they were accurate and honest works by persons who were dedicated to recording as minutely as possible the tribal ways of life. Even today, they are sources of knowledge and provide comparative material to understand the present times.

By the middle of the twentieth century, scholars like Elwin (1959) studied tribes from a completely different perspective. They were of the opinion that the original ways of life of tribes were harmonious, balanced and actually examples of a superior way of living. As acknowledged by most chroniclers of tribes, the suffering brought upon them by outsiders, the market economy and external political agents led to a perspective that tribes were better off left to themselves. Elwin was one of the major influences on the early development of the policy of the Inner Line as it was applied to the North-east Frontier Agency (presently Arunachal Pradesh). The functionalist school inspired works such as the ethnographies written by Fürer-Haimendorf (1975, 1981), Vidyarthi (1963), Srinivas (1966), Nakane (1967) and others. This trend continued till about the 1970s, when a paradigm shift occurred as a more critical perspective developed.

POSTCOLONIAL PARADIGM SHIFTS

There was criticism of the functionalist school over its emphasis on equilibrium, and several scholars brought out the dark side of the colonial impact on tribes. For example, ethnographies based on this perspective rarely brought out the facts of depopulation, violence and epidemics; the devastation caused by colonial rule; or the symbolic violence of the imposed categorisation of 'peoples' who never existed as they were represented.

The designation of tribe as 'ahistorical' has also been criticised in light of the evidence that non-Europeans were in contact with each other for centuries before Europeans set foot on their soil. There is archeological evidence of long-distance trade in most of the Old World. The merchants of Mohenjo-daro were trading with those in Mesopotamia thousands of years back. The Ivory Coast of Africa was the centre for flourishing sea trade, and in India, aborigines and peasants lived side by side for centuries without the former giving up their identities.

Wolf (1982) provides a detailed study of the world from 1400 AD to show that war and kingdom expansions, long-distance trade and the communicative and binding forces of religion and political ideologies had spread and bound many societies. The pastoral societies had also spread themselves all across the globe. Ancient migrations had taken place even across the seas and there was interaction at many levels, but the Europeans only considered contact with them as a mark of civilisation. They also created stereotypes of static traditional non-Western societies that contrasted with a dynamic modern West.

Morrison (2006) observed that the forest dwellers of the Western Ghats of India have been far from isolated, and that the forest life and the identity that they assumed were part of an economic and ecological strategy. The hunters/foragers and the agricultural groups had trading relations extending far back in antiquity:

> These relationships were marked by a high degree of variability and flexibility, with specific groups altering their strategies in relation to ecological, demographic, and political imperatives, such that it is difficult, and at times misleading, to use labels such as "hunter-gatherer" or "agriculturalist" as if they described an exclusive or stable strategy. (Ibid.: 45)

The opening up of coastal spice-trade routes and the integration of this region into the world economy from 1400 to 1700 AD may have encouraged many groups to move into the highlands and into the forests. Many other anthropological studies indicate strategic adaptations and the movements of people between different forms of adaptation. The existence of cross-border traders identified as Bhotiyas has been described by authors such as Fürer-Haimendorf (1975, 1981) and Channa (2013), thus providing evidence that such trade was centuries old.

Another fallacy of the functionalist school has been the postulate that a tribe is a bounded entity with a definite identity, an assumption that has now been negated by many scholars. Black-Michaud (1986) discusses how the Lurs of Luristan claim that they have an identity that sets them apart from the Arabs and the Persians, who flank them on both sides. Yet 'no two Lurs, unless very close agnates, ever share the same frame of genealogical or even geographical reference' (ibid.: 23); in other words, the identity is based more on an assumption than any material or factual criteria. As Black-Michaud makes clear, the tribes were identified on the basis of the princely lineages to which they owed allegiance, and when the feudal system declined, their identities were diffused. The identity of a tribe is neither fixed nor based on endogamy, but is shaped by ecological conditions and resource-use strategies (Channa 2013).

The debates on environment and sustainable development put a completely different perspective on tribal ways of life. From being regarded as ignorant and superstitious, tribes are now being regarded as wise, having a sustainable relationship with the environment, and indigenous knowledge systems have become linked with wisdom and the conservation of the environment. Tribal medicines, healing systems and even philosophies of illness and health are now regarded as worthy of attention. There have been reappraisals of tribal world view (Mathur 2001) and the works of scholars such as Bodding (1986), who, even as early as the eighteenth century, made a complete scientific analysis of the Santal medical system. Thus, many scholars have focused on one aspect of tribal life rather than provide a comprehensive account, although even these focused works have been contextualised in the total framework of the particular tribe's society and culture.

The debates on environment and sustainable development have put a completely different perspective on tribal ways of life. From being regarded as ignorant and superstitious, tribes are now considered wise, having a sustainable relationship with the environment.

A considerable proportion of the works are now revisited for the life situation of tribes and the conditions of their marginalisation and oppression. Later in this book (Chapter 6), we shall examine some of these debates and the critical appraisal of terms such as 'development'. Nathan and Xaxa (2012: 1) proposed that development that leads to deprivation should be called as 'adverse inclusion'. They were commenting on the ongoing process of integration of tribes into the mainstream of Indian politics and economy. Normally, the concept of exclusion is used to describe the conditions of marginalisation and deprivation suffered by groups that fail to benefit from nation-building processes. But according to these authors, exclusion would mean isolation, when, in reality, the processes of development thrust upon tribal areas have not isolated these people, but included them in deprived and disadvantaged ways. For example, the tribes displaced by the building of dams or by industrialisation get incorporated into the monetary economy as low-paid wage labour or fringe workers in the informal sector of the economy. Thus, there has been a significant change in perspective from the time when tribes were regarded as 'primitive' specimens of humanity in need of civilisation to the contemporary times where they are regarded as repositories of knowledge for a sustainable lifestyle, but also as victims of capital growth and neoliberal economics.

In India, debates around the processes of development have also raised questions of 'national interest' and 'regional development', issues that we will take up for discussion later, in Chapter 6. What is significant to reiterate here is that the theoretical basis of the term 'tribe' is now being replaced by the concept of identity. While terms such as 'tribe' are closed and bounded, referring as they do to structural entities, the concept of identity, which is now more frequently in use, is more flexible and operates at multiple levels.

SUMMARY

In the end, one can pick up the threads of the long discussion on the concept of tribe, and identify some of the key points. First, it must be realised that tribe is neither a definable term nor does it refer to anything tangible and clearly identifiable. Like most social categories, it is a product of the time and space, of its use, and reflects the dynamics of power relations and historical specificities that provide its background.

Second, the term is contestable, as it was used mostly in a derogatory sense of the uncivilised 'other' during the colonial period. Today it has been replaced by more politically correct terms such as indigenous, First Nation (Canada), Native Americans (US), ethnic minorities and so on. The term indigenous, having been adopted by the UN, provides a political platform and opportunities for networking among the largely marginalised communities that are covered by this term. However, as discussed in this chapter, the Indian state denies this identity to its tribal population. Scholars and the tribals themselves have opted for this identity, which is also contained in the Indian word for tribes, namely, Adivasi. Therefore, a large number of scholars of India prefers to use 'Adivasi' instead of 'tribe' (Dasgupta 2012: 3; Hardiman 1987: 15). As Karlsson and Subba (2006: 2) have pointed out, all three terms, 'tribe', 'Adivasi' and 'indigenous people', have been used at different times and also for different purposes.

Third, there is considerable internal variation among the people designated as tribes, or Scheduled Tribes in India, which will be illustrated through ethnographic examples throughout this book. In the South Asian context, this term has also been evaluated and compared to terms such as ethnic groups, but with somewhat different definitional paradigms. The phenomenon of the tribe–caste continuum also has been the centre of much theoretical discussion, and indicates that at least in some parts of India, the tribes and castes are not clearly distinguishable and also have a dynamic relationship with each other (Bailey 1961; Nathan 1997; Veluthat 2004). Many communities cannot be clearly distinguished as either one or the other. This is truer for those communities that live in close proximity to each other.

Finally, the important point to emphasise is the political situation of most communities termed as tribes, to the extent that political marginalisation has quite often been taken as a definitional paradigm for tribes (Dasgupta and Basu 2012; Hardiman 1987; Roy Burman 1994). The term 'indigenous', which is traced to the situation of colonisation, is therefore extended to the situation of internal colonisation, and has been found apt for Indian tribes. Scholars have emphasised that Indian tribes can be called indigenous (Karlsson and Subba 2006; Sen 2018) as they are in the same situation of marginalisation and oppression as experienced by indigenous communities in the situation of external colonisation (Bates and Shah 2014; Misra and Das 2014). This is a view shared by the tribal communities themselves.

Contemporary Indian tribal people vary considerably in terms of urbanisation and integration with the dominant sections of the Indian population. Yet tribal communities continue to face discrimination and remain marginal to most of mainstream India. They are stereotyped as backward and, at best, exotic; they are economically both exploited and marginalised; and are considered dispensable in the face of mega developmental projects that are directed towards the mainstream. Understanding tribes, therefore, requires an empathetic approach and ethnographic accuracy.

REFERENCES

Aron, Raymond. 1965. *Main Currents in Sociological Thought* (Vols 1 and 2). Harmondsworth: Penguin.

Anthias, F. 2006. 'Belonging in a Globalizing and Unequal World: Rethinking Translocations', in Nira Yuval-Davis, Kalpana Kannabiran and Ulrike Vieten (eds), *The Situated Politics of Belonging*, pp. 17–31. London: Sage Publications.

Bailey, F. G. 1961. '"Tribe" and "Caste" in India', *Contributions to Indian Sociology*, 5: 7–19.

Bates, C., and Alpa Shah. 2014. *Savage Attack: Tribal Insurgency in India*. New Delhi: Social Science Press.

Bayart, Jean-Francois. 2005. *The Illusion of Cultural Identity*. Chicago: Chicago University Press.

Béteille, André. 1986. 'The Concept of Tribe with Special Reference to India', *European Journal of Sociology*, 27: 297–318.

———. 1992. 'Preface', in N. K. Bose, *The Structure of Hindu Society*. New Delhi: Orient Longman.

———. 1998. 'The Idea of Indigenous People', *Current Anthropology*, 3 (2): 187–93.

Biswas, Prasenjit and Chandan Suklabaidya. 2008. *Ethnic Life-Worlds in North-East: An Analysis*. New Delhi: Sage Publications.

Black-Michaud, Jacob. 1986. *Sheep and Land: The Economics of Power in a Tribal Society*. Cambridge: Cambridge University Press.

Bodding, P. O. 1986. *Studies in Santal Medicine and Connected Folklore*. Calcutta: The Asiatic Society (originally published by the Asiatic Society in three parts between 1925 and 1940).

Bose, Nirmal Kumar. 1992 [1975]. *The Structure of Hindu Society*, revised edition Hyderabad: Orient Longman.

Brown, Charles W. 1990. 'What We Call "Bhotiyas" Are in Reality Not Bhotiyas', in M. P. Joshi, Allen C. Forger and Charles W. Brown (eds), *The Himalayas Past and Present* (Vol. 2), pp. 147–71. Almora: Sri Almora Book Depot.

Channa, Subhadra Mitra. 2013. *The Inner and Outer Selves*. New Delhi: Oxford University Press.

Chauhan, B. R. 1966. 'Tribalization', *Tribe*, 2 (1–2): 5–11.

Compact Oxford Dictionary, Thesaurus and Word Power Guide, Indian edition 2001. Oxford: Oxford University Press.

Dasgupta, Sanjukta and Raj Sekhar Basu (eds). 2012. *Narratives from the Margins: Aspects of Adivasi History in India*. Delhi: Primus Books.

Dasgupta, Sanjukta. 2012. 'Introduction', in Sanjukta Dasgupta and Raj Sekhar Basu (eds), *Narratives from the Margins: Aspects of Adivasi History in India*, pp. 1–16. Delhi: Primus Books.

Durkheim, Émile. 1947. *The Elementary Forms of Religious Life*. Glencoe, IL: The Free Press.

Elwin, Verrier. 1959. *A Philosophy for NEFA (North East Frontier Agency)*, published on behalf of Advisor to Governor of Assam, Shillong by P. C. Dutta.

Evans-Pritchard, E. E. 1940. *The Nuer*. Oxford: Clarendon.

Fortes, Meyer. 1953. 'The Structure of Unilineal Descent Groups', *American Anthropologist*, 55 (1): 17–41.

Fortes, Meyer. 1969. *Kinship and the Social Order*. London: Routledge.

Fortes, Meyer and E. E. Evans-Pritchard (eds). 1940. *African Political Systems*. London: Oxford University Press.

Freud, Sigmund. 1919 [1913]. *Totem and Taboo: Some Points of Agreement between the Mental Lives of Savages and Neurotics*, trans. James Strachey. London: Routledge and Kegan Paul.

Fürer-Haimendorf, Christoph von. 1975. *Himalayan Traders: Life in Highland Nepal*. London: John Murray.

———. 1981. *Asian Highland Societies in Anthropological Perspective*. New Delhi: Sterling Publishers.

Ghurye, G. S. 1959 [1943]. *The Scheduled Tribes of India*, second edition Bombay: Popular Book Depot.

Glazer, N., and D. Moynihan (eds). 1975. *The Ethnicity Reader: Theory and Experience*. Cambridge, MA: Harvard University Press.

Godelier, Maurice. 1972. *Rationality and Irrationality in Economics*. London and New York: Verso.

Hardiman, David. 1987. *The Coming of the Devi: Adivasi Assertion in Western India*. Delhi: Oxford University Press.

Hutton, J. H. 1921. *The Angami Naga*. London: MacMillan.

International Labour Organisation. 2003. 'A Manual', ILO Convention on Indigenous and Tribal Peoples 1989 (No. 169). Available at http://pro169.org/res/materials/en/general_resources/Manual%20on%20ILO%20Convention%20No.%20169.pdf (accessed 25 December 2019).

Karlsson, B. G., and T. B. Subba (eds). 2006. 'Introduction', in *Indigeneity in India*, pp. 1–17. London: Kegan Paul.

Kluckhohn, Clyde. 1944. 'Navaho Witchcraft', *Papers of the Peabody Museum of Archaeology and Ethnology*, 22: 2. Cambridge, MA: Harvard University Press.

Kroeber, Alfred E. 1952. *The Nature of Culture*. Chicago: University of Chicago Press.

Kulkarni, Sharad. 1991. 'Distortion of Census Data on Scheduled Tribes', *Economic and Political Weekly*, 26 (5): 205–08.

Leach, Edmund R. 1954. *Political Systems of Highland Burma: A Study of Kachin Social Structure*. Cambridge, MA: Harvard University Press.

Leaf, Murray J. 1979. *Man, Mind, and Science: A History of Anthropology*. New York: Columbia University Press.

Lemert, Charles. 2014. 'A History of Identity', in Anthony Elliot (ed.), *The Routledge Handbook of Identity Studies*, pp. 3–29. London and New York: Routledge.

Maharatna, Anup. 2005. *Demographic Perspectives on Indian Tribes*. New Delhi: Oxford University Press.

Majumdar, D. N. 1972. 'A Study of Tribe-Caste Continuum and the Process of Sanskritization among the Bodo-Speaking Tribes of the Garo Hills', in K. Suresh Singh (ed.), *The Tribal Situation in India*, pp. 263–70. Delhi and Simla: Motilal Banarsidass and Indian Institute of Advanced Studies.

Malinowski, Bronislaw. 1922. *Argonauts of the Western Pacific*. London: Routledge and Kegan Paul.

Mandelbaum, D. G. 1970. *Society in India* (Vols 1 and 2). Berkeley: University of California Press.

Martinez Cobo, José. 1986. 'Study of the Problem of Discrimination against Indigenous Populations', UN Document E/CN.4/Sub.2/1986/7Add.4.

Mathur, Nita (ed.). 2001. *Santhal Worldview*. New Delhi: Indira Gandhi National Centre for the Arts and Concept Publishing Company.

Maxwell, Neville. 1980. *India, the Nagas and the North-East*, Report No. 17. London: Minority Rights Group Ltd.

Mills, J. P. 1937. *The Rengma Nagas*. London: MacMillan and Co. Limited.

Misra, K. K., and N. K. Das (eds). 2014. *Dissent, Discrimination and Dispossession: Tribal Movements in Contemporary India*. New Delhi: IGRMS and Manohar.

Moran, Anthony. 2014. 'Identity, Race and Ethnicity', in Anthony Elliott (ed.), *Routledge Handbook of Identity Studies*, pp. 170–85. London: Routledge.

Morgan, Lewis H. 1910 [1877]. *Ancient Society*. Chicago: Charles H. Kerr.

Morrison, Kathleen. 2006. 'Environmental History, the Spice Trade, and the State in South India', in Gunnar Cederlöf and K. Sivaramakrishnan (eds), *Ecological Nationalisms: Nature, Livelihoods and Identities in South Asia*, pp. 43–64. Ranikhet: Permanent Black.

Nakane, Chie. 1967. *Garo and Khasi: A Comparative Study in Matrilineal Systems*. The Hague: Mouton.

Nathan, Dev (ed.). 1997. *From Tribe to Caste*. Shimla: Indian Institute of Advanced Studies.

Nathan, Dev and Virginius Xaxa (eds). 2012. 'Introduction and Overview', in *Social Exclusion and Adverse Inclusion: Development and Deprivation of Adivasis in India*, pp. 1–32. New Delhi: Oxford University Press.

Padel, Felix. 2011. *Sacrificing People: Invasions of a Tribal Landscape*. New Delhi: Orient BlackSwan.

Pfaff-Czarnecka, Joanna and Gerard Toffin (eds). 2011. 'Introduction: Belonging and Multiple Attachments in Contemporary Himalayan Societies', in *The Politics of Belonging in the Himalayas: Local Attachments and Boundary Dynamics*, pp. *xi–xxxviii*. London and Los Angeles: Sage Publications.

Radcliffe-Brown, A. R. 1932. *The Andaman Islanders*. Glencoe, IL: Free Press.

Radcliffe-Brown, A. R., and Cyril Daryll Forde. 1950. *African Systems of Kinship and Marriage*. London: Oxford University Press.

Ramirez, Philippe. 2014. *People of the Margins: Across Ethnic Boundaries in North-East India.* Guwahati: Spectrum Publications in Association with CNRS, France.

Redfield, Robert. 1961. *The Little Community and Peasant Society and Culture.* Chicago: University of Chicago Press.

Rehman, Javaid. 1998. 'Indigenous Rights at Risk: A Survey of Indigenous Peoples of South Asia', in B. K. Roy Burman and B. G. Verghese (eds), *Aspiring to Be: The Tribal, Indigenous Condition*, pp. 72–122. London: Commonwealth Human Rights Initiative and Minority Rights Group, and New Delhi: Konark Publications.

Reisman, David. 1950. *The Lonely Crowd: A Study of Changing American Character.* New Haven: Yale University Press.

Roy, S. C. 1912. *The Mundas and Their Country.* Calcutta: Kuntaline Press.

Roy Burman, B. K. 1994. *Indigenous and Tribal Peoples: Gathering Mist and New Horizons.* New Delhi: Mittal Publications.

———. 1998. 'Tribal and Indigenous Rights and Wrongs', in B. K. Roy Burman and B. G. Verghese (eds), *Aspiring to Be: The Tribal, Indigenous Condition*, pp. 1–20. London: Commonwealth Human Rights Initiative and Minority Rights Group, and New Delhi: Konark Publications.

Sen, Asoka Kumar. 2018. *Indigeneity, Landscape and History: Adivasi Self-fashioning in India.* London and New York: Routledge.

Service, Elman R. 1962. *Primitive Social Organization: An Evolutionary Perspective.* New York: Random House.

Shanklin, Eugenia. 1994. *Anthropology and Race.* Belmont, CA: Wadsworth Publishing Co.

Sharma, B. D. 2010. *Unbroken History of Broken Promises: Indian State and the Tribal People.* New Delhi: Freedom Press.

Srinivas, M. N. 1966. *Social Change in Modern India.* Bombay: Allied Publishers.

Trautmann, Thomas. 1997. *Aryans and the British India.* California: University of California Press.

Tylor, E. B. 1871. *Primitive Culture* (Vols 1 and 2). London: John Murray.

United Nations. 1953. 'Indigenous Peoples: Living and Working Conditions of Aboriginal Populations in Independent Countries', ILO publication.

———. 2007. 'United Nations Declaration of the Rights of Indigenous Peoples (UNDRIP)', adopted by the General Assembly, 13 September.

Unnithan-Kumar, Maya. 1997. *Identity, Gender and Poverty: New Perspectives on Caste and Tribe in Rajasthan.* Oxford: Berghahn Books.

Veluthat, Kesavan. 2004. 'From Tribe to Caste?: The Koragas of South Canara', in B. B. Chaudhuri and Arun Bandopadhyaya (eds), *Tribes, Forest and Social Formation in Indian History*, pp. 51–63. Delhi: Manohar.

Vidyarthi, L. P. 1963. *The Maler: A Study in Nature-Man-Spirit Complex of a Hill Tribe.* Calcutta: Bookland.

Weber, Max. 1958 [1904]. *The Protestant Ethics and the Spirit of Capitalism*, trans. Talcott Parsons. New York: Scribner's.

———. 1968 [1922]. *Economy and Society*. Los Angeles: University of California Press.

Wolf, Eric W. 1982 *Europe and the People Without History*. Berkeley: University of California Press.

SUGGESTED READINGS

Behara, M. C. (ed.). 2018. *Revisiting Tribal Studies: A Glimpse after Hundred Years*. Jaipur: Rawat Publications.

Bodley, John H. 1994. *Cultural Anthropology: Tribes, States, and the Global System*. London: Mayfield Publishing Company.

Channa, Subhadra Mitra. 2015. 'State Control, Political Manipulations, and the Creation of Identities: The North-East of India', NMML Occasional Paper, History and Society, New Series No. 72, Nehru Memorial Museum and Library, New Delhi.

Diamond, Stanley. 1974. *In Search of the Primitive: A Critique of Civilization*. New Brunswick: Transaction.

Guibernau, M., and J. Rex (eds). 1997. *The Ethnicity Reader: Nationalism, Multiculturalism and Migration*. Cambridge: Polity Press.

Kuper, Adam. 1988. *The Invention of Primitive Society*. London: Routledge.

Moran, Anthony. 2014. 'Indigenous Identities: From Colonialism to Post-colonialism', in Anthony Elliott (ed.), *Routledge Handbook of Identity Studies*, pp. 347–63. London: Routledge.

Smith, A. D. 1986. 'State-Making and Nation Building', in J. A. Hall (ed.), *States in History*, pp. 228–63. Oxford: Basil Blackwell.

2

SOCIAL LIFE OF TRIBES

Marriage, Family, Kinship and Gender

HIGHLIGHTS

- Identity
- Social reproduction
- Social exchange
- Domestic power relations
- Gendered perspectives and critiques

INTRODUCTION

In Chapter 1, we saw that the term 'tribe' encompasses many different kinds of societies and several levels of organisational complexity. In its anthropological usage, tribe refers largely to those societies where kinship is the basis of most social operations and relationships. However, among communities that are primarily forest-dwelling and that are engaged in hunting and gathering, there are some that put more emphasis on the husband, wife and children unit (the nuclear family) than on any kind of descent group. There are also tribes that have become urbanised or follow some universal religion like Christianity or Islam. They may change their marriage practices and inheritance rules to suit those of the new religion, for example, most tribes of the northeast region are Christian and have church weddings, although they retain some of their original cultural practices as well. Similarly, tribes may have their own world view or may adopt foreign ones or may even subscribe to an amalgamation of different kinds of beliefs and practices.

Unlike popular perception, tribes are internally stratified and have the prevalence of some forms of patriarchy, which may not be of the same level as that in more 'complex' societies. The internal power relations in tribal societies indicate interesting equations and raise questions regarding stratification and gender relations.

This chapter will familiarise students with some key concepts and the variations in social forms that one may find among communities recognised as tribes. We will examine the institutions that are responsible for social reproduction, namely, kinship, marriage and family; social inheritance; and gender. These are the institutions through which the identity of any social unit is reproduced, whether caste, tribe or ethnic group, and the basic social characteristics of a group are passed down over generations. Tribal institutions are not necessarily different from those found in non-tribal societies, being based on many general universal characteristics, some of which form an inherent part of being human. So the student will first be introduced to some basic concepts, which will then be applied to specific tribal communities. This chapter has also been written with a gendered lens as it is an accepted paradigm that all human relations and institutions follow a gendered pattern. In many tribal societies, access to resources, livelihood and social power are all vested in one's kin relations. Even as kinship continues to play a significant role in tribal habitats and social settings, it has also been undergoing transformations, and its role is not as pervasive in the twenty-first century.

MARRIAGE AND KINSHIP

Although human beings constitute a single species, capable of biological reproduction with any member of the opposite sex, yet all human societies are bound by rules of marriage and more specifically by rules of incest, which translate into rules of endogamy and exogamy. Mating in all human societies has been elevated from the various forms of pair bonding found among non-humans to a social institution with several levels of complexity. The main purpose of the institutionalisation of marriage is to reproduce the socially created groups that we know of as communities, societies, tribes, etc. Every society recognises a category of people that its members cannot marry—these could be both those who are too 'close' and those who are very 'far'. A basic rule of kinship that applies to all societies known, of the present or of antiquity, is that there should be a clear separation between those who are recognised as 'blood' kin and those who are related by marriage or are marriageable. The former are known as consanguines and the latter as affines. In the interest of not causing social confusion, these two categories are always kept separate, although there is no universal rule for regarding any particular related person as marriageable or not marriageable. Blood is a purely putative concept, which varies considerably from society to society (Beattie 1964a, 1964b; Graburn 1971). However, Fortes (1969: 52) conceptualised kinship in terms of 'irreducible genealogical connections'. Also, as indicated by Fortes (1949), the rules of sexual relationships and of marriage need not coincide, and in many societies like the Tallensi, while marriage may be forbidden with certain relatives, sexual relations are not.

The most universal rule of incest is applicable to what is regarded as the nuclear family, composed of husband, wife and their children. This unit contains only one married couple; all other possible pairings, namely, parents and children or siblings, are prohibited from marrying each other. However, even this rule is not absolutely universal. For instance, in ancient times, the royal families of Egypt allowed, or rather preferred, brothers and sisters of royal lineage to marry each other in order to preserve the purity of the royal blood. A few other exceptions are also known. Thus, there is the identity of close brethren, people who are so close that they cannot marry each other; yet they form close bonds of putative and real siblingship. The others are somewhat far but not too far. These are people who are not related by blood and yet have enough similarity to be married. Such similarities can have different names—jati, clan, caste, ethnic group, tribe, racial identity, national identity and so on. Most tribes are characterised by the rules of clan exogamy as clans form the most functional social groups among them. Thus, through marriage, the boundaries of social identities are reproduced and maintained.

The rules of marriage are also known as rules of exogamy and endogamy, and these tend to fix the social identity of a group as a whole and its members in relation to each other. Marriage does not imply sexual relationship as much as it implies the production of socially recognised children. It is the legitimising aspect of marriage that is the most important, and it is here that rules of marriage and principles of exogamy and endogamy are applicable. Any social unit of kinship is best reproduced if the children are born of parents who share an identity. However, rules of lineality can also determine which parent is more important in fixing the identity in case of mixed marriages, for instance, all children born to Khasi women belong to the Khasi clans of their mothers, irrespective of who the father is.

The rules of marriage are also known as rules of exogamy and endogamy, and these tend to fix the social identity of a group as a whole and its members in relation to each other.

There are two broad categories of exchange systems, prescriptive and preferential. In the prescriptive system (also referred to as closed societies), the rules of marriage require a person to marry someone who is already a part of his/her kinship group. The most common form of prescriptive marriage known is cross-cousin marriage, that is, marrying the child of one's parents' opposite-sex sibling. The implication of such prescriptive rules is the reinforcement of already existing kin ties and also a regulation of the direction of flow of women. For example, if a girl marries her mother's brother's son, then the direction of flow of women is reversed in the second generation and the bride receivers of one generation become bride givers in the next. It is not necessary, however, that all tribes have such prescriptive marriages. There are wide variations in marriage rules. Many tribes follow preferential forms of marriage where one has a wider choice limited only by rules of endogamy and exogamy, that is, tribal endogamy and clan exogamy. However, there is almost no society that is fully open or preferential in its marriage practices. All preferential systems also become prescriptive in the long run, for as Bourdieu (1977: 70) put it, most marriages tend to reproduce their own conditions of existence. Thus, even in societies that appear to be open, class and power stratifications tend to be reproduced through marriage. For instance, apparently open societies like American society reproduce class and race divisions. People tend to marry those they consider as alike to them, even by choice, thus closing in the boundaries of class, race and ethnicity. However, kinship is also related closely to how personhood is constructed in any society and these constructions of personhood may vary considerably across cultures. According to Maybury-Lewis (1982: *vii*), 'The problem is that all societies recognize, and many attach huge importance to the relationships anthropologists have loosely called kinship. Yet these relationships are so embedded in their cultural contexts that they cannot usefully be analyzed separately from their context.'

WHAT INFLUENCES TYPES OF MARRIAGE?

Let us look into a few ethnographic examples to illustrate how types of marriage and kinship relations are embedded in specific historical and ecological contexts. Property relations, ecological resources and inheritance patterns also play a crucial role in shaping the types of marriages that take place. Circles of endogamy are influenced by the ability to communicate and have a similar world view. People with different ways of life and world views may live next to each other for centuries and yet never marry. For example, the Paliyans of Tamil Nadu never marry the peasants in their vicinity, even though they have had sustained economic and even social relationships with each other. Thus, pastoral and foraging communities have historically lived for centuries next to each other and next to settled cultivators, yet they have managed to keep their identities separate. On the other hand, neighbouring groups, especially if they share a common lifeworld, may intermarry, and individual identities may easily change over a lifetime. There are pastoral societies like the Nuers and the Lurs (see Chapter 3), where social identities are not necessarily related to birth but rather criteria like location and ecological relations. Persons from one tribe may get absorbed into another through marriage and adoption like the various pastoral communities of the central Himalayas who graze sheep in common pastures.

Economic and ecological factors are only few among the conditions that determine the nature of marriage, gender and kin relationships. There are other constraining factors such as regional cultures, historical circumstances and even traumatic events like displacements and environmental disasters that may influence marriage rules, family types and gender relations that are never rigid. The following typology provides ideal types that will help contextualise actual field-based data and give the students an idea of possible diversities in tribal social organisations.

Simple Band Organisations

Hunting and gathering people are marked by the absence of property and have a different cosmology than cultivators and landowners. They mostly live in bands that are small in size and fluid in structure (Leacock and Lee 1982). The hunting and gathering people are bound to a territory but in a manner in which they do not consider their land to be their property. The foraging way of life is devoid of any sense of property or possessiveness. Rather than the land and its resources belonging to them, hunting and gathering people are more habituated to believing that it is they who belong to the land. It is the forest that nurtures and keeps them alive. Since they do not have a conception of material possessions, there is nothing to inherit or pass down to the children. Marriage for them is a personal matter of liking and living with each other. The husband–wife relationship, more than any other consideration, plays an important role in both negotiation and continuation of marriage. In this respect, forest dwellers are more like the urban individualistic persons of the West, where marriage is a matter of free choice and personal happiness alone. Children among them are seen as a group asset and precious for the continuation of the group as a whole. Men and women often remarry and move to another band, leaving the children behind, who are collectively taken care of. Since there is nothing concrete to inherit, the children are not the jealous possession of a single couple. They are loved and cared for irrespective of who their biological parents may be. Bride price or bride wealth and other kinds of marriage prestation are usually unknown in band societies. The marriages are not elaborately ritualised and remain more or less a personal affair.

The residence after marriage, an aspect that finds attention in the anthropology of kinship, is based on choice. Couples locate themselves according to resource availability and the convenience of becoming a part of a band. As shown by most studies of band societies, the composition of these bands is flexible, adjusting to the needs of the group's relation to its environment. Since resource availability is not fixed, the size and composition of bands may have to be continually readjusted to meet the requirements of survival. Any rigid descent principle is rarely a possibility. Steward (2008), in his study of the Shoshone Indians, postulated that bands have a patrilineal and patrilocal organisation, but later studies have shown that bands are flexible and individuals relocate themselves according to the availability of resources, mainly food and water. Bilateral kin relations are often evoked for such relocations. Since descent does not play any role in such societies in the absence of inheritance and property relations, some scholars such as Meillassoux (1981) have also referred to them as pre-kinship societies.

But not all foragers have identical social organisations. Some like the Paliyan described by Gardner (1988) take on Tamil characteristics while in the village but revert to their egalitarian relations in the forest. When away from Hindu peasant villages, they show greater gender equality, free movement and interaction between spouses, and general disregard for strict norms binding men and women. In terms of kinship terminology, they do not distinguish between wife givers and wife takers, and in terms of marriage age, there is no pattern at all; the husband and wife may have any kind of age difference. It is interesting to note that Gardner clearly demonstrates that outside influence may drastically affect gender relations and marriage practices, and compares the forest-dwelling Paliyans with the ones that live in close proximity to peasants.

The Paliyans provide a typical example of what is known as an 'enclaved' foraging community, meaning one that is in close proximity to an agricultural settled village. The 'enclaved' Paliyans under influence of the settled Tamils have taken on some characteristics of the latter, like a large settlement (much larger than a normal band structure) and a tendency towards virilocality (residence with the husband). However, the transformation is not total, and uxorilocality (residence with the wife) is also present in significant proportion. The most significant character of Paliyan social organisation is sibling preference, where the entire settlement can be seen in terms of having a core composition of sets of siblings. All members of the settlement prefer to stay close to siblings of either sex—brother and sister are equivalent in terms of kinship and affective relations. With respect to gender roles, Gardner (1988: 97) reports a minimum division of labour and a culture of mutual respect: 'Neither partner has authority over the other in any regard; neither has greater property rights, greater rights to divorce, and greater freedom in sexual matters. Male and female may do something with a different style, but it is symmetry that really matters in a field of rights and privileges'. However, verbal abuse and ridicule by Hindu neighbours has forced Paliyans to change some of their practices, at least overtly for outsiders. Those in a settlement near the Tamil village showed practices that were closer to the Tamils than the forest Paliyans, for instance, the comparatively low frequency of remarriage of women as compared to those living in the forest. They also exhibited an explicit deference to patriarchal traits and gender-based division of labour, which approximates to the ones found in Tamil society, thereby putting pressure on the accepted egalitarian relationship between spouses.

Thus, we find that gender relations may change under cultural pressure from a group with an overt higher rank and power. Such transformations of tribes under pressure from outside groups and upper-caste neighbours have been seen in many parts of India and described in terms of Hinduisation (Chauhan 1978; Sinha 1962) or Sanskritisation (Srinivas 1972).

Descent Group-Based Societies

Moving ahead from band societies that have no or a minimal concept of lineality, we come to those societies that are primarily aligned through the concept of descent and where traditionally most social functions like collective ownership of property, village organisation, and political and ritual powers have been vested in these lineage groups. Marriage in these societies is seen primarily as a means for the perpetuation and reproduction of these descent groups. The major differences then from the foraging band societies are, one, the emphasis on descent group (mostly clan) exogamy and, two, the birth of children to the lineage. Lineality refers to the transfer of identity and resources to one's descendants.

From the study of societies across the world and in historical times, anthropologists have identified four kinds of lineal transmission: (i) patrilineal, where property, identity, name, ritual objects, etc., pass down the male line, that is, from father to son; (ii) matrilineal, where transmission is in the line of women, that is, from mother to daughter; (iii) bilateral, where the transmission is equally distributed along both lines of descent, and (iv) ambilineal, where there is choice regarding whose identity and inheritance the offspring take on or parents pass on.

There has been a debate as to the location of power in these systems and many scholars, including feminist ones, have been of the opinion that men hold power in almost all societies and that even matrilineal societies tend to be patriarchal because the property of a woman is managed and controlled by her father or brother instead of her husband or father-in-law. Lewis (1981: 241) has written about how fathers manipulate the marriages of their sons in a matrilineal society so that the property passes to the son and not the sister's son. Richards (1971) has described the conflict that arises when a person of the 'dominant sex' finds himself in subordination in his wife's village because of matrilocal residence combined with matrilineal descent. The major tension in matrilineal societies, according to her and other scholars of kinship, is the division between the power of administration of resources (always in male hands) and the inheritance of the same. The men, in other words, are always taking care of and managing someone else's resources. Richards has provided possible solutions such as visiting husbands or matrilineal heirs, that is, the sister's sons being claimed at puberty (like among the Trobrianders). However, the real contention lies in that the earlier scholars, such as Richards, had assumed universal male domination when they had used terms such as 'dominant sex' for the men. More recent feminist scholars such as Caldwell (1999) have critiqued this androcentric perspective and shown that matrilineal Nayar women as well as other women of matrilineal groups in Kerala possessed real power, both secular and sacred.

Lineality refers to the transfer of identity and resources to one's descendants; it may be patrilineal (identity and inheritance passed down the male line), matrilineal (female line), bilateral (equally distributed along both lines of descent), and ambilineal (open to choice).

Some societies combine both principles of descent and are known as double unilineal societies, where some resources may pass in the male line and others in the female line of descent. The Todas of Nilgiris have a double unilineal system where productive resources pass through the male line, while some ritual and social resources pass down the female line. The Dimasa (Danda and Danda 2004), one of the Kachari tribes of Assam, also have a double unilineal descent system. A man primarily reckons descent from his paternal grandfather and secondarily from his maternal grandmother, and a woman reckons primary affiliation from her maternal grandmother and secondary descent affiliation from her paternal grandfather.

In some tribal societies, the principle of unilineal descent may give rise to what are known as unilineal descent groups that Fortes (1953) defines as corporate, resource-holding groups. One characteristic of a unilineal descent group is that all its members are equivalent, divided only by sex and age. All females and all males in the same generation are socially equivalent and may replace each other. Thus, a woman can be replaced by her real or classificatory sister—one sees this in the practice of sororate, where a man can marry his wife's younger sister. Sometimes such marriages can also take the form of polygyny, that is, two or more sisters can be married to the same man at the same time. This often happens if the first wife is childless. However, most of the time, monogamy is the widely prevalent form of marriage in all tribal societies in India. Polygyny is more common among shifting cultivators, where women play an important productive role. Having more than one wife increases a man's ability to create surplus, and he can continue to do so, especially if it allows him to establish himself as a chief. Among Indian tribes, polygyny is a rare occurrence, though it is found in some tribes of the Northeast.

Polyandry, where a woman is married to more than one man, exists in a few enclaves in the tribal world. The most prevalent form of this marriage is that of fraternal polyandry where a set of male siblings marry a single woman. In some parts of the central Himalayas like in Kinnaur and Jaunsar-Bawar, the practice of fraternal polyandry has been quite common. During fieldwork in this area in 2008, I found that fraternal polyandry was prevalent and the elders praised the system saying that if there is only one wife between brothers, there is less likelihood of the family breaking up.[1] Even if the husbands go to work in distant places, the wife continues to live in the village and takes care of the land and animals, and also the elders in the family. If there is one wife per husband, they have a tendency to set up house in the city all by themselves. However, fearing stigmatisation by outsiders, few men overtly declare that they have one wife in common, and women also keep quiet about their multiple husbands.

Levine (1988: 9) has recorded statements of her Nyinba (a Himalayan border community) informants about polyandry, which argue 'how it prevented the dispersion of property and fragmentation of limited landholdings and how it supported a higher standard of living'.

Levirate is the substitution of a younger brother in the place of a dead husband. It is a different form of brothers marrying the same woman. This usually happens when the lineage has paid a bride price for a woman and it does not wish that her fertility lies unused because of the untimely death of her husband. So for the same bride price, another brother is substituted. This practice becomes necessary if the earlier husband dies childless. It may also take place if there is a general shortage of women in the community.

Such compulsory marriage practices have often been seen as against the principles of individual choice, but one must remember that here one is considering not individuals but categories. By the very principle of what Radcliffe-Brown (1950) calls the Unity of the Sibling Group (one of his rules of kinship), there can be a larger number of persons to be found in one category than simply those related directly, for example, the term 'brother' can be used for those born of one's own parents as well as those born of the siblings of one's parents, that is, extended to all others in a similar structural position. Thus, siblings in a tribal society based on descent principles would include a wide range of collateral relatives (called cousins in the West) and would enable the exercise of choice within a larger range of possible candidates rather than being confined to just a few individuals.

The principle of bilateral kinship is found among all foraging societies that also have the least prescriptive marriage rules as already discussed. Bilateral kinship means the absence of lineality and the equal placement of siblings from both parents, which dilutes the concept of descent. Bilateral descent is to be distinguished from double descent that takes into account both sides of descent, patrilineal as well as matrilineal. While bilateral kinship is usually associated with a fair amount of gender equality, this may not be

Bilateral kinship is the absence of lineality and the equal placement of siblings from both parents. Double descent, on the other hand, takes into account both sides of descent, patrilineal as well as matrilineal.

the case for double unilineal descent. The Toda are an Indian tribe that follow the double-descent principle. A Toda person's identity is composed of a mixture of traits borrowed from the patriline and the matriline. All productive resources are passed down the patriline, but some important rituals are assigned to the matriline. But this recognition of the matriline is not translated into equality for women.

Most societies that have communal ownership of property place a great deal of emphasis on descent groups, and membership in descent groups is usually the most recurring mode of accessing common property resources. Pastoral communities and shifting cultivators tend to have two kinds of property. For pastoral people, their animal herds may be owned by individuals as among the Himalayan pastoral communities such as the Bhotiyas and Bakkarwals, or they may be owned by lineage groups, as among the Todas of Nilgiri who herd buffaloes. But even in the latter case, the animals are allotted to individual households for daily care and rearing. At another level, pastoral communities require large and immovable resources in the form of pasture land and water. These are not owned directly but access to them may be regulated by virtue of group membership. Since these are vast resources, they are usually held by the local feudal lord or by the centralised state, and the pastoral people need to get access to them through their allegiance with the centre of power (Black-Michaud 1986). But such access is usually mediated by the tribe or descent groups within the tribe. Thus, even if the pastures are held by the local chief, access to them would be through tribal lineages, and a person has to be the member of a lineage by birth or marriage to access the resources. At times, adoption may also take place to incorporate new members. Thus, marriage in such communities serves the purpose of reproducing the descent groups and also keeping their identities distinct through the principles of clan exogamy. Let us examine a few examples to make this point clear.

The Todas of Nilgiris (Walker 1986), who are a pastoral and patrilineal people, are divided into two endogamous groups. While all Todas marry within their own group, they also have a secondary spouse in the other group, for whom death rituals are observed. If a tribe is divided into two exogamous groups, then these are called moieties, but the Todas have two caste-like endogamous divisions.

These are further divided into resource-holding descent groups that may be called lineage groups as they trace their descent from known ancestors. The Todas access their resources through membership of their lineages which passes in the male line. The women are exchanged between lineages and are required for reproduction of the male line. Bride price is paid for them in acknowledgement of their reproductive powers and ability to produce male heirs. The Todas in the past also practised wife capture, and it was common practice for a man to capture another man's wife through a show of strength. The negotiations for bride price and also for compensation for a captured wife were done by men among themselves, and women were only seen as property.

The Todas are also well known for their institution of fraternal polyandry, where a group of brothers marries a single woman. This is done both to save on bride price and also because of the paucity of women, possibly caused by the prevalence of female infanticide. When a child is born to a Toda woman, one of the brothers claims paternity by presenting her with a small bow and arrow. The social position of the Toda woman is largely connected only to her sexual and reproductive roles, which has led to the society being patriarchal. However, with the adoption of Christianity on a large scale and also with changing times, such practices are disappearing among the Todas.

The shifting cultivators and horticulturalists, like the tribes recognised as various Naga communities, also have social organisation based on patrilineal descent groups, and the land is collectively owned by the lineage groups. In such a social formation, women are ritually and socially disadvantaged to the men, but because they contribute significantly to the economy, they have more agency than the women in those communities where land is privately owned. Community ownership means that women and men have equal access to the resources, and if women do most of the work, as they do in shifting-cultivation societies, then they have the agency of movement and enjoy more liberties in comparison to non-tribal women. In such communities, bride price is often paid and polygyny is practised. Marriages are often negotiated by elders by paying bride prices to continue the lineages.

Naga societies are organised around clans, which are descent groups where the members are supposed to have descended from some remote ancestor, often mythically located at the beginning of time and rationalised in the origin myths. Clan exogamy can also be linked to prescriptive forms of marriage. The Tangkhul Nagas have clan exogamy and also practise cross-cousin marriage. A boy may marry his mother's brother's daughter (MBD).[2] Prescriptive marriages are found among other tribes also. Sarkar (2004) mentions that the Khamti of Arunachal Pradesh prescribe MBD marriage (from the perspective of a male ego) while preventing marriage with the father's brother's daughter (FBD), as it leads to women travelling in the opposite direction such that the bride-givers and bride-takers are not distinguishable from each other. He has tabulated the practices of many other tribes belonging to the Manipur, Nagaland, Arunachal and Meghalaya regions (ibid.: 121). Most tribes are divided into wife-giving and wife-taking lineages, giving rise to the rule of the non-reversible direction of brides between two descent groups. Usually, these are the segments like the minimal lineages that are operative on the ground. According to Longkumer (2010), even under the impact of Christianity, the rules of clan exogamy are strictly enforced among the Ao Naga. Even though the converted Ao do not observe any of their earlier rituals of marriage and have church weddings, the rules of exogamy are maintained and even required by the pastors of the church.

Not all communities with collective ownership have well-defined descent group organisations, nor do they necessarily have well-defined boundaries based on descent group membership and well-defined marriage rules. In fact, even the tribe as an entity may not have clear-cut boundaries, and in the absence of strong values of lineality and endogamy, the marriage practices also vary from being clearly rule-bound to being more flexible and egocentric.

Although it was believed earlier that a tribe is necessarily an endogamous unit—in other words, all those who belong to a 'tribe', of necessity, marry each other—ethnographic realities indicate that the rule of endogamy may not be so rigid. Thus, Das and Das (2017: 1) are of the opinion that although traditionally a tribe was seen as a 'self-reproducing "life-world" of stable organisations and shared histories', and also 'territorially bound and culturally distinct', such parameters may not be applicable to all tribes in the present context.

In the context of the Jad Bhotiyas of Uttarakhand, Channa (2013) has shown the fallacy of the concept of 'endogamous tribe'. These people—who refer to themselves as Rongpa and have the self-identity of being people who graze sheep—marry with all those with whom they share pastures. Other Bhotiya groups from the nearby regions of Chamoli and Kinnaur used to come down, just like the Jads, to graze their sheep in the lower latitude pastures, mostly near Dehradun. In the lower altitudes, because of paucity of grazing land or forests, they shared pastures with each other. Although they spoke different dialects, there was enough similarity in their cognitive worlds and their ways of life for them to be able to communicate with each other.

Marriages were negotiated in these shared pastures and friendships were fostered so that whenever a young man became frustrated with this own surroundings, he migrated to some other village, in another part of the Himalayas, and often married and settled down there. Thus, the Jads were not bound by endogamy as much as by a shared way of life and shared resources. Since they do not have well-defined descent groups, children are not considered important to a marriage, and if none are born, that is no reason for the dissolution of a marriage. A woman who has no child is not stigmatised. Children are seen as gifts of god and cherished. Children are brought up without their parents by other relatives as a normal routine. The village provides a secure and closed social space for the rearing of children and is primarily ruled by women.

Thus, we find a contrast to other pastoral communities like the Todas, who are also herders and pastoralists but with very different marriage rules and gender relationships.

PERFORMING MARRIAGE

Tribes have often been distinguished from non-tribes, especially caste Hindus, because of the absence of certain Hinduised rituals among them, in particular life-cycle rituals like marriage and death. But there has been a strong influence of powerful Hindu caste neighbours, which has led to changes in the marriage patterns of some tribes, especially those who have had long-term political and social relations with their Hindu neighbours. As reported by Longkumer (2010), changes in marriage performances have also been influenced by changes in religion. The Ao and other Naga groups of the Northeast, who have become Christians, have church weddings officiated by pastors. But they may still retain some of the minor ritual elements of tribal culture, in terms of feast-giving and decoration of the bride. For example, even though the bride may wear a Western wedding outfit, she may put on a traditional head-dress, or the groom may wear a neck-tie with the traditional clan emblem.

Many central Indian tribes like Santals and Konds still practise bride capture. Young men and women go the village market or *haat*, where there is plenty of opportunity for young men and women to mingle, and a young man may carry off a young woman, sometimes even with her consent, to marry her. In tribes where bride price is given, this may be one way to circumvent the giving of bride price or at least to reduce its magnitude. Tribes are also marked off from caste society by the prevalence of bride price instead of dowry. There is usually no economic exchange during marriage. For instance, the Bhotiyas of Uttarakhand have no exchange of gifts, except that the bridegroom's family is honour-bound to gift the bride with a gold nose ring. The size and weight of the nose ring symbolises the prestige and economic status of the bridegroom's family. Sometimes, even married women may be captured, and in such a case, the husband has to be compensated. As mentioned by Mishra (2007), in many tribes who pay bride price, the children belong to the husband's lineage and the mother has no rights over them if she chooses to leave and marry again.

Most forest-dwelling tribes and those who are pastoralists have no or very minimal rituals for weddings. Even where there are elaborate and extended rituals, the marriages remain largely secular without a priest officiating the occasion. The priest or shaman, if present, is a local religious functionary. In the upper Himalayan region of the central Himalayas, there is the prevalence of sovereign village deities who rule over the villagers. For example, in Kinnaur, the boy and girl intending to get married have to seek permission of the village deity, without which they cannot marry. However, most couples persist if they are refused the first time, and they carry on various rituals and ways to appease the deity to give them permission.

Many tribes, especially those living in proximity to Hindus, may call in a Hindu priest for the performance of marriage rituals. Sachchidananda (1987: 53) writes about the Gonds of Bihar, 'Except in Sighbhum and Palamau, Gond in all areas call the Brahman priest for officiating in their marriages'. The transhumant Jad Bhotiyas do not observe any Hindu rituals in their upper-altitude village but do perform marriage rituals imitating the Hindus in their lower-altitude village near Uttarkashi. A similar situation has been described for the Paliyans of Tamil Nadu, and this is a likely occurrence in most parts of India. Unlike the relatively rigid caste societies, the negotiation of marriages among tribes, even if they are relatively Hinduised, is for the boy and girl to choose their own partners, although marriages can be arranged by elders as well. Among the patriarchal Nagas, parents may play a significant role in the choice of a spouse for their daughter. As Zehol (2003: 303) notes,

> Parents among the Angami and Konyak Naga tribes and even among the Nishi tribe of Arunachal arrange marriages. The girl's parents demand huge property as bride-price for their daughter. She does not have any option to choose her life partner. If she refuses her parent's choice, she is discarded by her family.

All the tribes mentioned are dominant, land-holding and politically powerful. Thus, the class system among tribes also affects their attitudes—the more economically and politically powerful a tribe, the greater the patriarchy it exhibits. Marriages among the Bhotiyas are largely a matter of personal choice although some kind of exogamy avoiding clans is required. These clans are identified by the names of their respective lineage god or *kuldevta*. A similar practice exists among other tribes like the Bhils, who also do not marry those who have the same clan deity. As already described, they do have marriages with other similar groups, and the consideration for marriage is in terms of a likeness of livelihood patterns and world view. Men and women have equal agency in getting married, although the proposal must come from the boy's side. Often friends or elders are roped into acting as go-betweens on behalf of the boy as the girls have the choice to refuse a match, which they often do, leaving the men in a vulnerable position. The consent of family members is also required, and a stubborn prospective mother-in-law may put a spanner into a romance. A boy and girl may also elope into the forest and then their match has to be accepted by everyone. Marriage is not sacred and separations take place often.

Most tribes permit widow remarriage, especially if the woman is young and fertile. However, it is also a matter of choice and it is not known that women are forced into marriage. Child marriage is an unknown phenomenon among tribes, but nowadays because of factors of marginalisation and insecurity, some tribes like the Lodhas of West Bengal have teenage marriages and motherhood at a high level of frequency. The Bondo highlanders of Odisha were known for the marriage of full-grown women to child bridegrooms. The Bondos, who traditionally engaged in frequent warfare, were always at the risk of losing the young men. The practice of marrying a pubescent boy to a fully mature woman ensured that she would conceive and have a child, even if her husband was always at the risk of being killed. In most tribes, however, women are married only when they are fully capable of doing all the work that is required of them and also producing children. Tribes do not have the luxury or inclination to support child brides. There is also no undue concern with virginity or sexual conservativeness among them. Marriage is seen first and foremost as a pleasurable union of man and woman, whereby they set up a family, have children, and also support each other in work, rituals and social activities. The Hindu ideal of the bridegroom's side being superior to the bride's side is also unknown among tribes, even the Hinduised ones.

Marriage customs for all tribes are prescribed in their customary laws, and even the Christian tribes may retain certain elements historically derived. Ningshen (2014: 129) describes Tangkhul Naga (of Manipur) marriages, as sanctioned by their traditional religion Ameoyan, as a mixture of sacred and secular elements. The term for marriage is *lakhot*, which means the settling down of an adult man and an adult woman, so that they have the sanction to cohabit. Marriages can be of the valid and of the non-valid type: the former is also known as a 'holy marriage'. Such a marriage takes place between two never-before-married persons and is solemnised through the payment of a bride price and with the approval of the parents.

A voidable marriage is one that takes place by elopement and without approval from parents. Such a marriage can also be made valid by taking the approval of the parents within a reasonable period of time after elopement. The children born of a valid marriage are legitimate and such marriages are rarely dissolved. A truly valid marriage has to take place between two adults, following the rules of clan exogamy and other socially prescribed incest taboos. Matrilateral cross-cousin marriages are desirable, and the daughter of one's mother's brother is regarded as the most suitable spouse for a boy. But the opposite, that is, a girl marrying the son of her mother's brother is not permitted. The children of two sisters or two brothers also cannot marry. Although the children of two sisters can belong to two different clans, they cannot marry. This would mean that the blood is returning to the same lineage, and it is considered as incest. It is also required that both parties to the marriage must agree and approval is given by their parents.

A marriage that is not within the rules prescribed by customary law is also possible. In Tangkhul language, it is referred to as *shokhala*. These are the marriages that violate the rules of incest and clan exogamy. Although we find many tribes following prescriptive rules with respect to descent-group affiliations, there are some that are regulated by the ascribed status of the named social groups that have an internal hierarchy. For example, among the Wancho of Arunachal, there are four named social groups that are exogamous (Sarkar 2004: 124). The Wancho practise village endogamy. The exogamous groups are, first, the Wangham (WH), that is, the social group of the chief and their consanguines, and, second, the Wangpam (WP), the social group of the commoners. A third group is formed by the intermarriage of a WH man with a WP woman—Wangsa (WS). Since the WS are considered blood relatives of WH, the two groups cannot intermarry. By the rules of hypergamy, a WP man cannot marry a WH woman, but a WH man can marry a WP woman. Since only WP women can be married to both WH and WP men, society allows the marriage of WP men with WS women to produce more WP men and women, and to keep up the 'supply' of WP women. The marriage of a WP mother with a WS father gives rise to a fourth group, Wangsu (WSu). However, during his fieldwork, Sarkar did not find a single individual belonging to this category. But it remains a possible group. Thus, the WP act as wife-givers to the WH, WS and WSu groups, while they are wife-takers for the WS and WSu, and in case of WH they are only wife-givers. A similar marriage system exists among the Konyak and the Nocte, who are also divided into aristocrats and commoners—the Great Ang and the Small Ang (ibid.: 125).

The rules of marriage in any society are not static. Among the Tangkhuls, there have been changes under Christianity, like the prohibition of polygyny that was permissible earlier. However, the rules of clan exogamy and other prohibitions are not enforceable in the present times, as the punishments such as banishment from the village are no longer seen as punishments, since people are in any case mobile and free to move to different places. Social ostracisation and fines may still work in villages but are difficult to enforce in cities.

THE FAMILY

The family is a unit that is characterised by the core group of the husband, wife and children, known in anthropological language as the nuclear or the basic family. It is this core to which the rules of incest are also most universally applicable. In most tribal societies, it is this group that is the most functional, although, as already discussed, it may be embedded within the larger lineage or descent-group relationships. Tribes rarely live in what is known as the joint or extended family. But they may have households that include members other than those bound by the primary relationships of husband–wife, parent–child and siblings. Among the sheep-herding communities of the Himalayas, there are often young men employed as shepherds who live as members of the family. Relatives, especially children, may be raised by family members, although they do not actually belong there. Thus, the family is distinguished from the household in that the former refers to those who are related to each other, and remain so even if they are not physically located in the same place. Sons and daughters who marry and go away are still family members, and they may come together for what is known as family gatherings like weddings and other rituals. A household, on the other hand, consists of those who live under the same roof and who eat at the same hearth.

As anthropologists like Goody (1973) and Fortes (1970) have theorised, the family or the domestic group is not a static entity. It transforms over time due to the marriage, death and migration of members. Not only children but also older parents may relocate, sometimes going off to live with married sons and daughters. Thus, the composition of the family is dynamic, and it is not always correct to say that a particular form of family is characteristic of a particular community. For example, Longkumer (2010) finds that urban Nagas are deviating from their traditional patrilineal, patrilocal and nuclear families to live in joint families as married sons often continue to live with their parents for various reasons. Earlier all families were practising shifting cultivation, and immediately after marriage, the newly-wed couple were put up in their new home, often built next to that of the bridegroom's father, and were given a plot of land to cultivate. In the city, sons and even daughters-in-law do jobs, and they may prefer to stay on with parents/parents-in-law. Longkumer reports that out of the 30 families she studied in the years 2002–04, there were a total of seven joint families. Such a phenomenon was unknown among the cultivating Nagas.

The composition and power relations within the family are informed to a large extent by the kind of lineality that exists. Patrilineal households are usually ruled by men, although women play important roles in the domestic domain. In describing the family among the matrilineal Khasi, Nongbri (2016: 89) writes,

> The Khasi family stands rather unique in the annals of history in the way in which authority within the household is divided between the dominant males belonging to two sides of the family. Despite the centrality of women in the organization of the clan (kur) and the lineage (kpoh), authority over the family does not lie with the mother but is "shared between the mother's brother and the father".

This is reinforced by the pattern of residence in which the father remains a member of the household and has considerable influence over the children and his wife. He is also seen as the chief provider, although the property does not belong to him.

The household among tribes is also an economic unit (production and consumption). Based on her ethnographic work among the

Konds of Odisha, Mishra (2007: 69) describes the household economy as based on subsistence agriculture practised in forest and plain land, where both men and women play an equal role. However, since the land is held by the men in this patrilineal society, the women only have user rights in the land. Earlier when land was held by the community, the position of women was better as they had equal rights as men to access the land. With subsequent land settlements beginning from the colonial period, the land is now almost exclusively controlled by individual men, so the women are totally dependent upon their status as wives to access the resources. Although widow remarriage is common among Konds, a woman marrying again loses all her rights over her first husband's property including her children. In fact, among the Konds, the children are seen as the property of the husband. When the Konds pay a bride price, it means that they are legitimising their rights over the productive as well as the reproductive powers of the woman. A woman must work in her husband's field, be responsible for feeding the family and bear children for the patrilineage of her husband. A woman has to collect fuel, fodder and water for the household as well as do all other household tasks. Although tribal women are not restricted in their movements and appear more liberated than their non-tribal counterparts, legally and socially they are often disadvantaged within the family. An already married woman may fetch more bride price as she is recognised to have more expertise in doing work and would have also established her fertility by having had children. However, since almost all tribals live in nuclear families, the husband is also dependent upon his wife for all day-to-day requirements, and that may lead to more equality within the household.

Danda and Danda (2004: 150), in writing about the Dimasa, describe the composition of the household as being informed by taboos that make the shifting out of a married son from his natal household compulsory. Among the Dimasa, there is a strict taboo against two women from different matriclans living under the same roof. Thus, since the daughter-in-law and mother-in-law belong to different matriclans, they cannot stay together. To solve the problem of immediate residency after marriage, the newly-weds live for a year with the wife's parents, till they are able to build their own house.

Since mother and daughter belong to same matriclan, they can always stay together. If a man has a second wife who belongs to a different matriclan than his first wife, and if he also has a daughter, the daughter cannot continue to live in the same house as her stepmother and has to be relocated. Thus, we find that the composition of households can be governed by taboos and social restrictions, and the persons who can live under the same roof are also those who can, by the rules of customary law and tribal norms, share the same hearth and live together.

The family is also the seat of learning and education. In earlier times, all the essential social tasks were learnt within the family and the gender-based division of labour was reproduced within the household. Even today, girls help their mothers, and since women are burdened with most of the domestic tasks, girl children are also inducted early into work. Thus, Zehol (2003: 303) describes how the boys among the Naga tribes play and have fun even up to the age of 13–14, but the girls have to begin to work early and take on the 'little mother role'. The boys follow their fathers and learn tasks such as hunting, fishing, house-building and animal husbandry.

In many tribal societies, the family was replaced by youth dormitories for the purpose of education and socialisation. In his classic work *The Muria and Their Ghotul* (1948), Verrier Elwin has described in great detail how boys and girls in a traditional tribal society learn various tasks and also learn about life, sexuality, and family and social values and norms from their peers and older members of the dormitory. The dormitories also taught the arts, crafts and many skills required to live a harmonious life in the forests and the villages. With the advent of formal education, the responsibility for imparting learning has been transferred to schools, but the family still remains the seat for the transmission of values, beliefs and practices of tribes. Because tribal cultures are still transmitted through oral traditions, the myths, stories and songs of tribes are the proud possession of the elderly. As long as tribal families are located in their natural and original habitats, the elderly have a respected place in the family. But as families get displaced or their habitats and traditional modes of livelihood are lost, the elderly are neglected and looked upon as burdens on the family.

Tribal families have suffered the onslaught of displacements and poverty-related migrations, and in some parts of India, they have been ravaged by political violence, and military and political actions. In some parts of India, the impact of violence, drug abuse and the spread of HIV/AIDS is making tribal families increasingly matrifocal, with women playing greater nurturing and responsible roles. Tribal families are embedded within larger clan and village relationships, which often shift the burden of primary childcare from the family to the community. Even in those tribes that do not have the youth dormitory system, there appears to be a collective commitment towards children as towards each other. The social networks of village life, clans and wider kinship ties often act as support groups, and although the household may remain a basic production–consumption unit, economic cooperation extends beyond the primary family.

In tribes practising shifting cultivation or any other form of cultivation, the larger family group always helps. Even married daughters are often involved in helping out their parents. The actual composition of the family thus often reflects situational needs, even though the normative family may be different. For example, in Kinnaur, I met a married woman who was staying with her aged parents to take care of them. She said that her in-laws, who were also aged, were being taken care of by her sister-in-law, the husband's brother's wife; her own parents did not have any daughter-in-law to take care of them as her brothers were elsewhere. So with the consent of her husband and her parents-in-law, she was taking care of her own parents and living with them. In another case, a young female child was being brought up by her mother's parents because her mother had married again and left the village. Among tribes, especially the smaller and close-knit ones like the small communities living in the upper Himalayas, the community is seen as the primary unit and the families are smaller units that are encompassed within the ties of community.

Joint families are not common among most tribes, though they exist among the settled cultivators and landholding tribes like the Badaga of the Nilgiris. The Badagas keep herds of buffaloes as well as practise swidden (shifting) agriculture.

> Both swidden and ordinary plough cultivation also called for the combined efforts of several men (as well as a number of women), and

> so here too Badagas found a good reason for cultivating their fields as a joint family. Many still do today. The point to be noted is that both the buffalo-herding and ox-ploughing and swidden cultivation were economic conditions that favoured patrilocality, the joint family, and brother/sister exchange at marriage—this latter a preference which maintained a balance of manpower between two intermarrying families or small settlements. (Hockings 1999: 78)

The plains cultivating large tribes like the Mundas, Hos and Oraons also sometimes have joint patrilineal, patrilocal families, the rationale being more or less the same. A large group of men and women are able to manage various aspects of settled cultivation and animal husbandry more efficiently. Hockings (1999: 221) also found that the Badaga households pooled in their incomes, so that those not working in the fields and holding low-paying jobs could be supported by the family landholdings.

GENDER RELATIONS

While this chapter does not go into a detailed discussion of gender, it might be useful to examine a few aspects of how gender relations vary among tribes, especially in relation to the concepts of lineality, property relations and economy. It is often found that foraging societies exhibit the least gender inequality. Morris (1982: 180), in describing the Malpantaram (or Hill Pandaram) of south India, talks about their 'pervasive emphasis on sexual egalitarianism' and lack of any organisation above the level of family. What Morris means is that the Malpantaram have minimal or no sexual division of labour, men and women do not have differentiated access to resources, and there is no ritual or cosmological basis to distinguish between them. In fact, from his description, the forest-dwelling Malpantaram exhibit probably the least gender differences as known in any society. The Malpantaram move around the forest doing the same things; they wear each other's clothes and share everything equally. Since nothing is passed down, the concept of generational transmission or lineality is itself non-existent or weak. Inequality cannot be based on differential access to resources as the goods in the forest are traditionally available to all. Thus, there is very little to support gender differences.

In the case of pastoral communities, we can see from the two examples discussed that the Todas and the Bhotiyas show very different kinds of gender relationships. Toda women have a much lower social and ritual position as compared to men, while Bhotiya women have control over all village-level activities as the men are more engaged in trade and animal husbandry. The women in Toda society are regarded as ritually polluting and rank lower than even buffaloes in their ritual hierarchy. Toda women are not even allowed to walk on those paths that pass in front of the sacred dairies that house the sacred buffaloes that are the deities for the Todas. Women do not have any property or inheritance rights. They are not allowed to cook or enter the inner part of the Toda hut where men do the cooking with milk and milk products of the buffalo. Since the bodies of the women are regarded as impure, they are not allowed to touch milk or milk products with their hands, milk being pure, coming as it does from the sacred buffaloes. Women can clean the house, winnow the grains that they obtain from the Badaga in exchange for milk and other dairy products, and are expert weavers of the famous Toda shawls. The Todas, like many other pastoral societies that domesticate large animals, extol the masculinity of strong men and regard women as property, as objects of sexuality and as vehicles of reproduction. This is in sharp contrast to Bhotiya women who have agency and significant control over the wool trade and the affairs of the village. Bhotiya women buy and sell their own handicrafts, like shawls and sweaters, and also keep the money they earn to spend as they like. Even unmarried girls have access to money and have a say in household matters, like buying and selling, cooking and entertaining guests. Although women are considered ritually inferior to men, it does not prevent them from carrying out rituals as men are mostly absent from the village.

Thus, two contrasting gender relationships exist in societies practising herding and pasturing. The difference can be seen to lie both in the nature of animals being domesticated and the nature of property relations. Toda buffaloes are large in size and reputedly aggressive. In fact, among the Todas, a proof of masculinity is in the taming of buffaloes by young men. The sheep, goat and mountain horses domesticated by the Bhotiyas are passive and docile. Although these animals are still herded by the men, there are no particular concepts of masculinity among them. Among the Todas, buffaloes are owned by the patrilines and men inherit land and animals by their membership into the patrilineages that are both named and ranked. The animals and property of the Bhotiyas are individually owned, and there is no strong concept of patrilineages among them. Although property passes in the male line, women also control property through the existence of the practice of resident sons-in-law. In this form of marriage, a woman is married to a man who chooses to reside in his parents-in-law's house and enjoy their property, although de facto it is the wife who controls the property, since it is socially recognised that it is her and not her husband's property. The *magpa* (resident son-in-law) has a low social status, and he is often the target of jokes, for instance, being called a *bahu* (daughter-in-law) by the women.

These examples are enough to caution us that one cannot have a reductive approach in understanding kinship and marriage practices. Just like two pastoral communities can differ in terms of descent and marriage rules as well as gender relations, shifting cultivators and agricultural economies can be very different.

In the northeast of India, we have two contrasting systems of lineality from tribes with similar agricultural practices and community ownership.

The Naga tribes are examples of patrilineal and patriarchal tribes where property and power passes down male lines. Yet their gender relations are not as unequal as in agricultural societies because the nature of property relations is of collective ownership. Since most Naga tribes practise shifting cultivation, the land is held in common and women play a key role in this kind of cultivation. However, with urbanisation and acquisition of private property by many individuals, the inheritance patterns of the Nagas are becoming contentious. Many Naga women in their personal communication to me said that they would prefer if the Nagas accepted the Indian legal system that now gives equal inheritance to women rather than stick to their customary laws in the name of 'tradition'. The men from the Northeast often point to the use of tradition as a way to maintain their identity, and adherence to 'customary laws' is seen as one way to assert tribal autonomy or an independent identity. For instance, when the 53rd Amendment to the

Constitution of India made it mandatory for women to be represented in village councils such as panchayats, the same was not implemented in tribal areas including the Northeast, citing 'customary laws' and the entitlement of tribes to their ways of life. But Naga women have always felt the burden of patriarchy. Naga scholar Hümtsoe-Nienü (2012: 74) writes:

> However as an insider, writing from the "womb" of the Naga context, it is disturbing to assume that retrogression to the past is a readymade solution. This conviction is more intensely felt as a woman member of the Naga community where communitarian principles function against the inclusion of women. Be it in the Morung tradition, the kinship system, land inheritance practice, or the village administrative set-up; all are basically male-biased.

In India, the Khasi and Garo communities of what is today known as Meghalaya are still matrilineal. Property among the Khasis passes to the youngest daughter, known as *kawasdiah*, who inherits the ancestral house and property, though the other daughters too may get a share in parental property. The Khasis and Garos are also regional communities with many subdivisions, such as the Pnar of the Khasi hills. As discussed earlier, problems of nomenclature and identity exist here, but all the groups in this region are matrilineal. The Khasis follow a unilineal principle of matrilineal descent, in which the largest division is known as a *kur*. Whenever two Khasi persons meet, they identify each other by the name of the kur. It is believed that all those who belong to one kur have descended from a common female ancestress. There are two other matrilineal descent groups at two other levels, namely, the *kpoh* and the *iing* (Nongkynrih 2002). The kpoh was in the nature of a corporate resource-holding group.

> The kpoh (literally womb) is an extended kin group that comprises a group of households whose members trace descent from a single great grandmother. Traditionally, members of a kpoh are bound together by shared sentiments of genealogical connectedness, joint landholding, and a shared cromlech where the bones of the dead are deposited. At the present time, however, the corporate character of the kpoh is rather limited. Demographic expansion, spatial mobility, conversion to Christianity, and the ultimogeniture pattern of inheritance continually

> threaten its unity, rendering it functionally ineffective outside the core group of the family. (Nongbri 2016: 87)

Studies on societies with matrilineal inheritance have come out with varying opinions. While classical anthropologists were reluctant to recognise any real power being vested in women, and had suggested that although property passed in female lines, power was wielded by men alone, this was later challenged by feminist scholars. Dube (2001) in her work on the Muslim matrilineal tribes of Lakshadweep who had migrated from Kerala, demonstrated that the women in these tribes have an equal status in society as the men, with men and women negotiating power in different domains. She was of the opinion that patrilineal societies are not any more or less stable than matrilineal societies, being beset with conflicts of interest. Thus, the feminist interpretation of matriliny described it as a more stable and equal system unlike earlier interpretations, which constructed matriliny as inherently unstable because of the ambivalent position of the man, who has conflicting interests between his sister's house and his wife's house. In a matrilineal system, a woman has certain rights, which are often considerable, and she also enjoys full personhood and agency. Among the Pnar-Khasi (Pakyntyne), women enjoy full power in the management of property. Thus, Khasi women manage both economic and ritual resources, while only men have political power, with the position of headman or chief going only to the latter. It is only men who are part of the village councils and who negotiate with each other. When I asked some political leaders from among the Khasis as to why women do not become part of the tribal councils, they replied, 'It is their choice; they have too much work to do and have no time for politics.' But Khasi women often do not agree on these points, even as they admit that their ritual and social duties are quite a handful. Nongbri (2016: 88) is of the firm opinion that Khasi society shows strong social pointers to the ideological inferiority of women:

> In the Khasi conception, men are physiologically and intellectually superior to women. As the "weaker sex", women are expected not only to submit themselves to the control of their brother and mother's brother, and protection of their father and husband, they are also

> excluded from important areas of decision making both within the family and society at large.

Following up on Nakane's (1967) work, which reported that Khasi men have one foot in their wife's house and the other in their sister's house, but feel more at home in the latter, Nongbri points out that the situation remains more or less similar in the present times too. There is a high incidence of divorce among the Khasis, and Khasi men tend to be indifferent to their children, as they feel the children are the responsibility of the mother's lineage. Khasi customary law puts no obligation on the father to maintain his children so that most women are left to take care of their children singly.

There is a myth that tribal women enjoy higher social status generally. This is usually bolstered by the fact they seem to have more freedom of movement than upper caste women. Since in subsistence economies, the household is usually the productive unit, the separation of public and domestic is not clear-cut and women often play an important role in both society and economy. In societies with no property or community access to property, patriarchy and patriliny often exist, but their implications are not the same as in more complex peasant and urban societies, where there is a clear emphasis on individual ownership of property, and a division of labour between the public and the domestic spheres. Thus, even in agricultural societies like the Gonds and the Mundas of central India, the land is mostly held collectively by the village or community. Although the society is patrilineal and follows more or less patrilocal residence, the relationship of women to men is more equal as the men too do not have much power. The economic activities are carried on by men and women together, and nuclear families make husbands dependent on wives. In writing about the Santals, a large agricultural tribe spread over central India, Carrin (2007: 282) describes them as 'strong personalities who enjoyed life despite its hardships'. She describes the Santal women as independent and able to negotiate their own bodies through courtship and labour.

Urbanisation and changing land and property relations are, however, changing the scenario and pushing tribes towards individual landownership. The role of men as primary workers and owners of property leads to a greater tendency on their part to exert control over women and their bodies. The restrictions on women become more stringent. Marriages become more ritualised and rigid. Urbanised and modernised tribal people tend to follow the same norms as the majority populations they come in contact with. As in the case of tribes converted to Christianity or other religions, the marriage practices and rituals are largely modified to suit the new ideology. Christianised tribes do not pay bride price or practise multiple marriages. However, some social rituals may still be observed and identity-markers like traditional dress and cuisine may be proudly exhibited. While clan exogamy and tribal endogamy continue to be largely practised by tribes, several well-educated persons find spouses outside of their tribes or regions and even marry non-tribal individuals (though these are exceptions rather than norms).

As tribes are coming in contact with complex cultures and facing situations of globalisation and integration into the national mainstream, the position of women among them is deteriorating. In many states in the Northeast, women are facing the brunt of violence and the outcomes of military and state oppression. Family relations have been disrupted, and women are often left to fend for themselves when the men become victims of police or military aggression or go underground. As Dzuvichu (2012: 82) writes, 'The conflict ridden region has also affected women and children the most, and they have been the largest victims of the armed conflict that has continued till today'. For instance, insurgency and a flourishing drug cartel have destroyed lives and transformed gender roles in the northeastern states of Manipur and Nagaland. The women of this region have shown courage to care for not only their livelihood, but also peace by protesting and advocating for it.

As tribes are coming in contact with complex cultures and facing situations of globalisation and integration into the national mainstream, the position of women among them is deteriorating.

The introduction of new technology does not always favour women, nor do changes in lifestyle in terms of following Western and modern ways of living. In her study of the Santals of Santhal Paragana in Jharkhand, Rao (2004) points out that traditionally the collection of forest products such as bamboo and fuelwood was the responsibility of women, who used to sell them in the market and keep the money. With the introduction of bicycles, which are used only by men, it is now men who take the produce to sell in the market. With this shift, the women's burden of carrying heavy loads has decreased, but their income too has been curtailed. Rao's study shows that men use the money earned from selling forest produce for buying household provisions, but if there is a surplus, they spend it on drinking. Women, on the other hand, would have used the same surplus for buying goods like trinkets and clothes for themselves, which are luxury items from their perspective.

Liquor drinking was always a part of traditional tribal life, but with the introduction of a monetary economy, the drinking habits fall into a non-sustainable pattern. When liquor becomes a commodity rather than a home product, it is no longer under the control of women, who are normally in charge of brewing in all tribal communities. In the traditional situation, women would brew and distribute the liquor, and hence control the drinking habits of men. Also the men's drinking habits tend to escalate when political and economic conditions deteriorate. Men under conditions of stress frequently get drunk and violent, and out of control. Tribal women in many parts of India have often organised against large-scale drinking habits of the men.

Tribes converting to Christianity has also resulted in a shift from more equal gender relations towards patriarchy. While emulating Christian and Western values, the tribal people believe that they are emulating a higher culture and moving towards civilisation. The shifting-cultivation tribes of the Northeast used to hold resources in common. But with the advent of private property, their patrilineal clans have interpreted property as something that passes in the male line, and individual property, including cash and purchases in the form of houses and land, are seen as the property of the patriline, excluding the inheritance of women. Today, the Naga women decry this so-called tradition of patrilineal inheritance and wish that the Indian (Hindu) law of equal inheritance by men and women be applied to their society. They complain that in the name of preservation of 'tradition', the men are trying to perpetuate patriarchy in the name of 'ethnic nationalism'—a common problem almost universally, where women find that upholding 'tradition' and 'identity' often works against feminine interests. As Dzuvichu (2012: 83) mentions, in 2006, the amendment of the Nagaland Municipal Act was passed, ensuring 33 per cent reservation for women in municipalities and town councils. The act was met with much resentment by male councillors and was implemented with much difficulty after several years in 2012. In Meghalaya, the youth have been demanding a conversion of Khasi society to a patrilineal one, and the movement peaked during 1997–99. The movement was contained only by the passing of the Khasi Custom of Lineage Bill by the Khasi Hills Autonomous District Council in March 1997, which became the Khasi Custom of Lineage Act, subsequent to the governor's assent in February 2005 (Nongbri 2016: 86).

The position of tribes across the states of Madhya Pradesh, Odisha, Maharashtra and Jharkhand is worsening because of their marginalisation by the processes of so-called development that is taking away their livelihoods and resources (Nathan and Xaxa 2012; Padel and Das 2010). The earlier proud kings of the forests are now reduced to being rickshaw pullers and menial workers on the streets of big cities. There is what may be called in Dukheimian terms a state of anomie or collective distress among them. The frustrations and problems of daily life are often directed against the women, often culminating in accusations of 'witchcraft' to which many innocent women are becoming victims (Mishra 2003). These practices are not leftovers of past traditions of the tribes themselves but an expression of their maladaptation in the present circumstances. Thus, contact with the outside world, the pathology of consumerist goals instigated by the modern market and capitalism, is bringing in values that are denigrating women and even the girl child. Some tribes are even practising female infanticide and selling their women under duress. These practices have no roots in their own traditions but are often held as examples by lawmakers and policymakers as signs of their 'backwardness'. Destruction of tribal lifeworlds, including the legitimacy of their knowledge systems and practices, is having its repercussion on gender relations, where women often emerge as the worst victims although men too are affected.

The tribes like the Sabar, a marginalised tribe of the East and West Singhbhum districts of Jharkhand, suffer from malnutrition and high infant mortality. In the frustration and grief of losing their children, the men often turn against the women, accusing them of witchcraft. The more marginalised and poverty-stricken a tribe is, the more likely are women to be victimised as witches. Mishra (2003) recounts horrific stories of starving mothers and children for whom no help comes forth either from the family (which is too poor anyway) or state officials (who could not care less). Thus, poverty, marginalisation, starvation and malnutrition are the most pressing challenges faced by tribal women in many parts of India today. Gender relations are embedded in conditions of life and living, and when life support starts ebbing away, the women and children are the ones most affected.

Thus, gender relations are not givens in any society but have a link with the living world and respond to situations that have current relevance. One needs to analyse gender keeping all historical and present circumstances as a backdrop, while also remembering that no tribe is or has ever been completely isolated or totally self-sufficient. Gender relations are linked as much to the inherited traditions and the history of a tribe or community as they are to the external linkages with and locations within a more extended hierarchy. In today's world, this hierarchy is almost global in nature.

The commonly held belief among scholars is that since tribes have a simpler division of labour and utilise less complex technology, they have not yet developed mechanisms of inequality as sophisticated as those in more complex hierarchical societies. Within the rationale of this argument, it is believed that even if patriarchy exists among tribes, it does so in a more dilute form than in non-tribal societies. But as Zehol (2003) writes about the Naga tribes, there are cultural forms of denigration of women that may, in the absence of actual violence, perpetuate what is called symbolic violence. Many tribes have folklore, myths and popular beliefs in which women are often equated with animals and birds, and there are jokes about their intelligence. For instance, there are Mizo proverbs which say that a woman's intelligence cannot go beyond the banks of a river or 'that a wife and an old fence can be replaced at any time, and an unbeaten wife and an uncut weed of the field are both unbearable' (ibid.: 301).

Further, she points out, 'An irony of the traditional Naga society is the case of Angami Nagas among whom the husband is credited for his extramarital affairs' (ibid.). This flaunting of masculinity is also found among several other tribes including the Todas. The men among the Angami actually publicly carry symbols of their extramarital affairs, and hence of their masculinity, by having an extra row of cowries in their loincloth. A woman in the same community is shamed and punished if she is found to have an extramarital affair, thereby demonstrating the strong patriarchal values among the Angami.

The myth of the absence of patriarchy among tribes is also being demolished as tribal women are taking up the pen and writing about themselves (Dzuvichu 2012; Hümtsoe-Nienü 2012; Nongbri 2016; Zehol 2003). Hümtsoe-Nienü's (2012) essay on the sorrow experienced by Naga women because of headhunting is particularly poignant as she explains the grief of women on losing their loved ones in a game of prestige played by the men. She also writes about Nagas gravitating towards a male deity under Christianity, making a shift from the more inclusive and unisexual/bisexual meaning of divinity in their tribal religion. She is further critical of the interpretation of Biblical meanings as she states that both man and woman were created in god's image (ibid.: 98), but today the interpretation tilts towards the masculine perspective of visualising god as only male. In personal communications too, tribal women have been severe critics of the tribal customary laws that support patriarchy. As sufferers from within the system, they are better able to articulate their own positions.

SUMMARY

In this chapter, we examined the basic institutions that are found in all human societies, which provide and reproduce the key identities of people. The sense of belongingness and identity comes from parentage and family, and is nurtured by kin and community. Political power is vested in both institutions and in the social relationships of kinship and gender. All these relations are not mutually exclusive but are supported by each other, for example, gender constructs and customary law as well as political institutions cannot be mutually exclusive. None of the institutions are static and, as we have seen, they change continuously.

Tribes, as we see them today, are very different from the way they were constructed in the colonial period. The fallacy of most people is to keep to the 'constructs' and not realise that the lifeworlds of tribes have been fast transforming. This chapter has attempted to steer the student through these changes and to provide an idea of how tribes exist in the contemporary times. Since 'tribe' is not a monolithic category, this chapter also draws upon many ethnographic examples to enable students to grasp some of the variations encompassed within this single category.

NOTES

1. I did fieldwork among the Kinnauries in the year 2008, along with my students Dr Antu Saha and Dr Nutan Maurya, with assistance from the Department of Anthropology under its Special Assistance Programme of the University Grants Commission.
2. It must be noted that by changing the sex of the ego, the pattern of marriage changes. What is matrilateral cross-cousin marriage for a boy becomes patrilateral cross-cousin marriage for a girl. In this sense, these are equivalent forms of marriage.

REFERENCES

Beattie, John H. M. 1964a. 'Kinship and Social Anthropology', *Man*, 64: 101–03.

———. 1964b. *Other Cultures*. London: Free Press.

Black-Michaud, Jacob. 1986. *Sheep and Land: The Economics of Power in a Tribal Society*. Cambridge: Cambridge University Press.

Bourdieu, Pierre. 1977. *Outline of a Theory of Practice*. Cambridge: Cambridge University Press.

Caldwell, Sarah. 1999. *Oh! Terrifying Mother: Sexuality, Violence and Worship of the Goddess Kali*. New Delhi: Oxford University Press.

Carrin, Marine. 2007. 'Women, Adivasis, Subalterns: Perspectives on the Empowerment of Santal Women', in Kamal K. Misra and Janet Huber Lowry (eds), *Recent Studies on Indian Women*, pp. 281–301. Jaipur: Rawat Publications.

Channa, Subhadra Mitra. 2013. *The Inner and Outer Selves*. New Delhi: Oxford University Press.

Chauhan, B. R. 1978. 'Tribalisation', in N. N. Vyas, R. B. Mann and N. D. Chaudhury (eds), *Rajasthan Bhils*, pp. 29–40. Udaipur: Tribal Research Institute, Social Welfare Department, Government of Rajasthan.

Danda, Dipali and Ajit K. Danda. 2004. 'On Dimasa Descent System', in Arabinda Basu, Biman K. Dasgupta and Jayanta Sarkar (eds), *Anthropology for North-East: A Reader*, pp. 140–51. Calcutta: Indian National Confederation and Academy of Anthropologists, Indian Anthropological Society and National Museum of Mankind.

Das, Rajat Kanti and Bidhan Kanti Das (eds). 2017. 'Introduction: Contemporary Relevance of Tribal Studies in India', in *Rethinking Tribe in Indian Context: Realities, Issues and Challenges*, pp. 1–20. Jaipur: Rawat Publications.

Dube, Leela. 2001. *Anthropological Explorations in Gender: Intersecting Fields*. Thousand Oaks and New Delhi: Sage Publications.

Dzuvichu, Rosemary. 2012. 'Development and Women: The Discourse in Nagaland', in Dev Nathan and Virginius Xaxa (eds), *Social Exclusion and Adverse Inclusion: Development and Deprivation of Adivasis in India*, pp. 81–93. New Delhi: Oxford University Press.

Elwin, Verrier. 1948. *The Muria and their Ghotul*. Bombay: Oxford University Press.

Fortes, Meyer. 1949. *The Web of Kinship among the Tallensi*. London: Oxford University Press.

———. 1953. 'The Structure of Unilineal Descent Groups', *American Anthropologist*, 55 (1): 17–41.

———. 1969. *Kinship and the Social Order: The Legacy of Lewis Henry Morgan*. Chicago: Aldine.

———. 1970. *Time and Social Structure and Other Essays*. London: Athelone Press.

Gardner, Peter M. 1988. 'Pressures for Tamil Propriety in Paliyan Social Organization', in Tim Ingold, David Riches and James Woodburn (eds), *Hunters and Gatherers, Vol. 1: History, Evolution and Social Change*, pp. 91–107. Oxford: Berg.

Goody, Jack (ed.). 1973. *The Character of Kinship*. Cambridge: Cambridge University Press.

Graburn, Nelson E. 1971. *Reading in Kinship and Social Structure*. New York: Harper and Row.

Hockings, Paul. 1999. *Kindreds of the Earth: Badaga Household Structure and Demography*. New Delhi: Sage Publications.

Hümtsoe-Nienü, Eyingbeni. 2012. 'Women's Experience of "Sorrow": Ending the Saga of "Headhunting"', in Eyingbeni Hümtsoe-Nienü, Paul Pimomo and Venüsa Tünyi (eds), *Nagas: Essays for Responsible Change*, pp. 66–79. Dimapur: Heritage Publishing House.

Leacock, Eleanor and Richard Lee (eds). 1982. *Politics and History in Band Societies*. Cambridge: Cambridge University Press.

Levine, Nancy E. 1988. *The Dynamics of Polyandry: Kinship, Domesticity and Population at the Tibetan Border*. Chicago and London: University of Chicago Press.

Lewis, I. M. 1981 [1976]. *Social Anthropology in Perspective: The Relevance of Social Anthropology*. Hammondsworth: Penguin.

Longkumer, Limanungla. 2010. 'An Anthropological Study of Contemporary Naga Identity', unpublished PhD thesis, University of Delhi.

Maybury-Lewis, David. 1982. 'Foreword', in Akos Ostor, Liza Fruzzetti and Steve Barnett (eds), *Concept of Person: Kinship, Caste and Marriage in India*, pp. *vii–ix*. Cambridge, MA: Harvard University Press.

Meillassoux, Claude. 1981. *Maidens, Meal and Money*. Cambridge: Cambridge University Press.

Mishra, Archana. 2003. *Casting the Evil Eye: Witch Trials in Tribal India*. New Delhi: Roli Books.

Mishra, Arima. 2007. 'Between the Visible and the Invisible: Gender Relations in a Tribe in India', in Kamal K. Misra and Janet Huber Lowry (eds), *Recent Studies on Indian Women*, pp. 63–78. Jaipur: Rawat Publications.

Morris, Brian. 1982. 'The Family, Group Structuring and Trade among South Indian Hunter-Gatherers', in Eleanor Leacock and Richard Lee (eds), *Politics and History in Band Societies*, pp. 171–89. Cambridge: Cambridge University Press.

Nathan, Dev and Virginius Xaxa (eds). 2012. 'Introduction and Overview', in *Social Exclusion and Adverse Inclusion: Development and Deprivation of Adivasis in India*, pp. 1–32. New Delhi: Oxford University Press.

Ningshen, Vareso. 2014. 'Marriage Systems under Tangkhul (Naga) Customary Law', in R. Vashum (ed.), *Encountering Modernity: Situating the Tangkhul Nagas in Perspective*, pp. 127–37. New Delhi and Chicago: Chicken Neck, imprint of Bibliophile South Asia.

Nongbri, Tiplut. 2016. 'Khasi Women and Matriliny: Transformations in Gender Relations', in Nandini Sundar (ed.), *The Scheduled Tribes and Their India: Politics, Identities Policies and Work*, pp. 85–108. New Delhi: Oxford University Press.

Nongkynrih, A. K. 2002. *Khasi Society of Meghalaya: A Sociological Understanding*. New Delhi: Indus Publishing Company.

Padel, Felix and Samarendra Das (eds). 2010. *Out of This Earth: East India Adivasis and the Aluminium Cartel*. New Delhi: Orient BlackSwan.

Radcliffe-Brown, A. R. 1950. 'Introduction', in A. R. Radcliffe-Brown and Daryll Forde (eds), *African Systems of Kinship and Marriage*, pp. 1–85. London: International African Institute and Oxford University Press.

Rao, Nitya. 2004. 'Enhancing Women's Mobility: Transport and Gender Relations in the Santal Parganas, Jharkhand', in Sumi Krishna (ed.), *Livelihood and Gender: Equity in Community Resource Management*, pp. 248–74. New Delhi: Sage Publications.

Richards, Audrey I. 1971. 'Matrilineal Systems', in Jack Goody (ed.), *Kinship*, Penguin Modern Sociology Readings. Harmondsworth: Penguin.

Sachchidananda. 1987. 'Tribe–Caste Continuum: A Case Study of the Gond in Bihar', in Maheshwari Prasad (ed.), *Tribes: Their Environment and Culture*, pp. 43–79. Delhi: Amar Prakashan.

Sarkar, Jayanta. 2004. 'Marriage Systems in North-East India', in Arabinda Basu, Biman K. Dasgupta and Jayanta Sarkar (eds), *Anthropology for North-East: A Reader*, pp. 120–28. Calcutta: Indian National Confederation and Academy of Anthropologists, Indian Anthropological Society and National Museum of Mankind.

Sinha, Surajit. 1962. 'State-formation and Rajput Myth in Tribal Central India', *Man in India*, 42 (1): 35–80.

Srinivas, M. N. 1972. *Social Change in Modern India*. New Delhi: Orient Longman.

Steward, Julian. 2008. 'The Great Basin Shoshone Indians: An Example of a Family Level of Sociocultural Integration', in Michael R. Dove and Carol Carpenter (eds), *Environmental Anthropology: A Historical Reader*, pp. 168–80. Malden, MA: Blackwell Publishing. (This chapter is a condensation of 'Basin-Plateau Sociopolitical Groups', *Bureau of American Ethnological Bulletin*, 120 (1938): 1–346.)

Walker, Anthony. 1986. *The Todas of South India: A New Look*. Delhi: Hindustan Publishing House.

Zehol, Lucy Vashum. 2003. 'Status of Tribal Women', in T. B. Subba and G. C. Ghosh (eds), pp. 293–306. *The Anthropology of North-East India: A Texbook*. New Delhi: Orient Longman.

SUGGESTED READINGS

Balandier, George. 1972 [1967]. *Political Anthropology*. Harmondsworth: The Penguin Press.

Bird-David, Nurit. 1999. '"Animism" Revisited: Personhood, Environment, and Relational Epistemology', *Current Anthropology*, 40 (1): 567–92.

Kelkar, Govind and Dev Nathan. 1991. *Gender and Tribe: Women, Land and Forests in Jharkhand*. New Delhi: Kali for Women.

Nongbri, Tiplut. 2014. *Development Masculinity and Christianity: Essays and Verses from India's North-East*. Simla: Indian Institute of Advanced Study.

Padel, Felix and Samarendra Das. 2012. 'Bauxite Business in Odisha', in Nandini Sundar (ed.), *The Scheduled Tribes and Their India: Politics, Identities, Policies and Work*, pp. 223–53. New Delhi: Oxford University Press.

Redfield, Robert. 1956. *Peasant Society and Culture: An Anthropological Approach to Civilization*. Chicago: University of Chicago Press.

Wolf, Eric. 1966. *Peasants*. Englewood Cliffs, NJ: Prentice Hall.

3

LIVELIHOODS AND ENVIRONMENT

HIGHLIGHTS

- Adaptation and technology
- Foraging, pastoralism, shifting cultivation and agriculture
- Industrialisation and the global economy

INTRODUCTION

The human species is unique in that it wrests its livelihood from the environment by modifying the habitat it dwells in. Over the centuries of human existence, this modification is intensifying, leading to greater and greater transformations, which have now led the present age to be labelled as the Anthropocene by geographers. This term implies that we are now living in a world almost totally transformed by human interventions. Humans have been referred to as tool-using animals, and in this chapter, we shall discuss the various stages that human adaptation to the environment has gone through. Adaptation is a complex of traits, including a technology, a habitat and a way of life by which humans transform their environment into a secondary environment, which is more conducive to their bodies that lack innate capacities for survival. Humans are the only animal species almost totally dependent upon extensions of their bodies by the use of tools; for example, they use knives and sickles to cut as they do not have claws. They use clothes because they do not have fur, hair or scales covering their bodies. The human capacity for tool-making and for technology, probably developed at the expense of their bodies, is the story of human evolution that students can read elsewhere. In this chapter, we shall discuss the various techno-economic systems by which the species Homo sapiens has made its home in the various habitats of the world. The communities we call tribes belong to all these modes of adaptation, but more to the ones we designate as pre-industrial. This divide between the pre-industrial and the industrial is also one way, though not the only way, of defining a tribe. The modes of adaptation have appeared at different points in the course of human evolution, one by one and not all at the same stage. However, when we talk of different stages, it does not imply that an evolutionary, progressive point of view is being endorsed. The earlier scholars of evolution had presumed that each stage is naturally superior to the previous one, but this is a point of view that is no longer acceptable.

The different types of adaptation that humans have achieved are all effective in their own ways and have functionality and viability according to their historical and geographical presence. The present-day industrial age has put many of the earlier forms of technology in jeopardy, but this is not desirable. Each technology and the way of life associated with it have contributed to the conservation of certain kinds of bio-forms and are endowed with knowledge systems that have their own functionality. Students must learn to examine each way of life for its own merits and demerits and not think that anyone is superior or inferior to others. It is the contemporary times that are the most dangerous, and we need to have a rational and pragmatic attitude towards what technology is, what adaptation is, and what works well for the conservation and future of the earth.

ADAPTATION AND TECHNOLOGY

The foraging tribes, represent the earliest modes of adaptation of the species Homo sapiens, a reason why they were earlier designated as 'primitive'. However, the contemporary tribes with pre-industrial technology have evolved over millions of years, and the hunter-gatherers of today are as contemporary as our industrial civilisation. They are constantly improvising and adapting to new conditions. One does not need to do much research to understand that flora and fauna are changing all across the world and have been doing so since the beginning of life on earth. The earth's surface itself has been transforming because of both human interference and natural causes. Rivers change their course, volcanoes erupt, earthquakes take place, forests disappear and new species appear as old ones die out. Even as people hunt and gather, they need to react to what is transforming in their habitats. Contemporary communities are adapting to climatic changes as never before. Humans are constantly innovating and adapting to changed environmental conditions. Even cultures do not stagnate but reinvent and persist in different guises.

The terms 'adaptation' and 'technology' are important to understand before we go into a detailed discussion of various modes of livelihood. Adaptation for the human species means that they are not only able to reproduce their numbers but also their social relationships and cultural practices to such an extent that there is no severe disruption of life ways. In case such a disruption occurs because of external causes such as war, colonisation or natural disasters, a human society can also physically die out. There are many recorded instances of an aboriginal population losing its culture and meaning of life under Western colonisation, and also being unable to reproduce physically, and eventually dying out. Cosmology and meaning are as important to a human population as food and physical security. Thus, a well-adapted population is one that is able to maintain the continuity of its social life and find continued relevance for its systems of meaning.

Adaptation for the human species means that they are not only able to reproduce their numbers but also their social relationships and cultural practices to such an extent that there is no severe disruption of life ways.

A mode of livelihood is dependent upon the relationships that emerge from the technology and environment in which the human group concerned is embedded. Technology is an aspect of the group's history as also its conscious adaptation of certain knowledge systems and ways of life. It is a trait of culture, being a system of knowledge. But technology is equally embedded in systems of meaning and ways of life. Thus, many groups practising hunting and gathering as a mode of living are not doing it because they do not have access to other kinds of technology but because they have a way of life and world view that is more compatible with foraging than with the production of food, that is, agriculture. There are many reported instances of the coexistence of hunting-gathering people and agricultural peasants living in close cooperation with each other for centuries. In this sense, there can be no evolutionary or progressive classification of different kinds of technology. Even today, people often talk of a superior technology when they are referring to industrial technology as compared to pre-industrial ones. But even the earliest technologies are as sophisticated as the most recent ones; take, for example, the boomerang or some of the traps that were used by Australian aborigines, which are so evolved that scholars have not been able to decipher how to use them. One would still be amazed by the skill by which an Old Stone Age tool is made. Very few of us would be able to craft a hand axe from a piece of solid stone.

Technology is an aspect of the human group's history, and a conscious adaptation of certain knowledge systems and ways of life. It is a trait of culture, embedded in these systems of meaning and ways of life.

The difference is between a simple and a complex technology rather than between a lower and higher form. The former has fewer steps between the raw material and the finished product, while the latter may have so many steps that the links between them are almost invisible to the ordinary person. Thus, one can pick up a piece of stone and directly shape it into a hand axe, but to make a motor car, one needs to go through innumerable stages of production of its various parts before the final product is put together. Yet, at each step of production, the task performed by a specific technician may be much simpler than the crafting of a hand axe.

In the case of a simple technology, there is a direct link between the producer and the product, but in the case of a complex technology, this link is lost. A person making a stone tool can take pride in the finished product, invest his or her mind to it, is most likely to be its proud possessor, or may gift it to someone for the sake of an intimate social relationship. If one takes a look at even the simplest utility items that a person makes for herself, one would be struck by the aesthetic quality and the striving for perfection in that work.

On the other hand, in a factory, workers toil mindlessly and are given only fixed tasks. Most do not even know what contribution they are making to the 'whole' (product) and what the whole looks like. It is likely that the object they produce serves as a component of many different items. In any case, none of the workers have any sense of pride in what they do but are only involved as wage labour. This process of disjunction of the worker from the finished product has been referred to as 'alienation'.

In today's globalised economy, everything has a market, and the kind of objects that were made for personal use among tribes are now being increasingly marketed. But once produced commercially, the process of production of objects becomes mechanised and objects lose their essential aesthetics. Let us compare the manufacture of a car by industrial technology with the manufacture of a canoe by a tribal. In the first case, there are numerous parts that are mostly manufactured separately and then assembled, but none of the persons involved, including the ones on the assembly line, has any idea of the totality. Each person is but a mechanical link in a much larger process. In the case of a person making a canoe, he (it is always made by men) has the entire picture of the canoe, and from choice of a tree trunk to the final decorations, he and his associates (if any) exercise their personal choice and agency. In the case of the industrial product, there is neither pride nor ownership in the final product, but in the case of simple manufacturing, a person has an enduring bond with the product. A woman weaving a basket will put her own creativity and imagination in the pattern that she weaves. The design will also incorporate the emotions and sentiments of the maker, and its value will lie more in the social bond or responsibility that it embodies than in its gross material value. Thus, industrial production is only evaluated commercially and does not have any personal content.

Wolf (1966) divided technology into two broad categories: 'paleotechnic' and 'neotechnic'. Paleotechnic technologies are those that are dependent on organic forms of energy—that is, animal or plant products, such as dung or wood—and simple devices like farming with a plough and draft animals. In this type of technology, humans are directly engaged with their environment, and hence have an intimate relationship with it. Each adaptive system that is based on the paleotechnic form of technology presupposes a special kind of human–environment relationship, which is mutual rather than exploitative, and involves its own kind of relational organisation and cognitive world view.

Neotechnic technologies make use of non-organic forms of energy like machines and chemicals. Today, the world has evolved many different sources of energy beyond the conventional ones, but coal and natural gas remain the most prominent, with electrical, nuclear, wind and other forms remaining alternative forms of energy. With industrialisation, humans became dissociated from their natural environment, and today many live in completely secondary environments that are far removed from nature. Social and cultural life are thus not conditioned by or in sync with natural processes, but have created their own rhythm and style that is called urban or city culture, which is also often equated with civilisation. A prime example is that our sleep cycles are no longer synchronised with daylight as humans make extensive use of artificial light. It is in this very context that tribes have been called 'primitive' or uncivilised, because they live closer to nature.

Eric Wolf divided technology into 'paleotechnic' and 'neotechnic'. The former is dependent on organic forms of energy (animal or plant products), while the latter makes use of non-organic forms of energy (such as machines and chemicals).

Societies can be classified, if at all, using different criteria and along many different axes. One way to do it is use Steward's (1955) concept of 'culture core'. This core of a culture comprises not only its technology and economy, but also a conglomerate of traits that is directly linked to these two aspects. We can create a typology of tribes using the techno-economic criteria only if one whittles down all the aspects that are not essentially linked to economy and technology. Essentially, it involves taking into account all those parameters that are directly relevant for livelihood and make the survival of the human group possible. Based on this understanding, the following typology of livelihood patterns and productive relations is generally used.

1. Hunting and gathering
2. Pastoralism
3. Shifting cultivation
4. Permanent cultivation
5. Urban and industrial

Tribes are found in all these categories, but the first three categories refer mainly to tribes as they form the defining criteria for classifying certain groups of people as tribes. We shall examine each of these categories, but it should be kept in mind that these do not form exclusive categories and should be treated as 'ideal types' rather than corresponding to real societies. Another point to be kept in mind is that tribes are found at any point of time and are not fixed within any historical or evolutionary time frame. This applies even to modes of subsistence. Unlike the popular view informed by evolutionary theory, there is no one unilineal line of development—in other words, those who are hunter-gatherers today may have been agriculturalists or pastoralists in the past. People may shift from one mode of livelihood to another, just as they may change their name and group identity.

It has been demonstrated by ethnographers from across the globe that tribal identities are fluid, and tribes are rarely bounded and static as imagined. In describing the hunters and gatherers of Rift Valley in Kenya, Chang (1982: 269) has argued that the creation of bounded tribal units is largely an outcome of colonial rule and that the past history of these people reveals fluid boundaries. He pointed out (ibid.: 273) that according to a Kikuyu elder, Muriuki, the 'ancestral immigrants to Mount Kenya consisted of horticulturalists, pastoralists and hunters gatherers who had intermarried extensively, despite heterogeneity in both language and mode of subsistence'. She further argues that the only thing common that the Kikuyu people, also known through various self-identities such as Dorobo, Asi, Okiek, Il Torobo, Aggiek, Oggiek or Ogiehue, is that they are uniformly impoverished and looked down upon by the surrounding people. Chang argues that 'at least from the mid-1800 onwards, Rift Valley hunters and gatherers have consisted largely of disenfranchised pastoralists and farmers, rather than being descendants of ancient populations who have hunted since "time immemorial"' (ibid.: 271). This means that the typology being provided is a theoretical rather than an empirical one. It helps to identify *different modes of subsistence* rather than *different people* as such. As argued in Chapter 1, and taken up for discussion in subsequent parts of the book, the notion of 'tribe' is a fuzzy one and actual people may move between subsistence types, regions and names with ease, and have historically been doing so over time.

HUNTING AND GATHERING

Hunting and gathering as a mode of adaptation is also called foraging, as it is based on a direct dependence on the environment, making use of materials as these exist in nature and making very little modification to the raw materials before consumption. Ideally it refers to a manner of livelihood where wild animals are hunted, and naturally growing fruits, berries and tubers are collected for food. Such groups may live in natural shelters like caves or live out in the open with log fires for warmth and protection. In India, we have such groups in the southern part of the country, such as the Malapantarams, the Paliyans and the Nayakas. The Birhors were proud occupants of the forests of Jharkhand and Chhattisgarh, but are now mostly displaced from their original habitats. The Irulas and the Kotas of the Nilgiri Hills of Tamil Nadu were also forest dwellers and foragers.

Hunting and gathering (or foraging) is a mode of adaptation based on direct dependence on the environment, making use of raw materials as they exist in nature with very little modification before consumption.

The primary character of communities that do not produce their own food is, first, that they are small in size, as their population adjusts to the minimum availability of food in the environment. Second, they usually are nomadic or itinerant rather than settling in one place. The reason for the latter is to save on energy as, after a time, the availability of game and locally grown herbs and berries tends to diminish. The animals move away perceiving danger, and seasonal fruits may disappear. Moreover, any human settlement produces its own share of refuse, and it is better to move away than attempt a cleanup. The very presence of humans changes an environment, and as one place gets somewhat degraded, these communities move to a new place.

This is not to say that foragers have no sense of territory. They do have a designated region within which they move. Therefore, we have differently named tribes belonging to different regions. But these peoples do lack the notion of private property as much of their resources are in the nature of free goods. The air that they breathe,

the water that they drink, the game that they hunt and the fruits that they pick are given to them by nature, and so most of them have a sense of belongingness to the place where they are located, and in most cases such belongingness may span many centuries. As described by Bird-David (1999), the Nayakans of southern India believe that the forest is their father and mother, and it is nature that gives them everything. The forest does not belong to them; it is they who belong to the forest. Most of their belongings are things they make themselves, like tools and weapons and, in earlier times, even clothes and ornaments. These things are gifted and shared with others, and rarely subjected to any definite form of possession.

Anthropologists studying such small-scale and close-knit communities have found that they cherish values of sharing and cooperation as these are the values that are most adaptive in their circumstances. They do not have any technology of storage and their productive activities are not regular. A person going for a hunt may not be successful on every occasion, and women also differ in their daily capacity for work, for instance, a pregnant or lactating mother may not be able to work as much as a young and active one. Yet, no one goes hungry in the camp as long as food is around. These communities practise what Sahlins (1972: 193) has called 'generalised reciprocity'. It means that people give what they have without any calculation of what they might get in return. Yet, there is a check on the behaviour of people as a principle, and miserliness or refusal to share is not tolerated. No one is seen as having more rights than the others, except those related to needs.

The size of the camp and the distribution of persons in a band are flexible and adjusted according to the needs of the members and the availability of food, water and other resources. Natural resources are variable and so is human demography. The size of bands will shrink or expand by the natural processes of birth and death. If no person leaves or enters the band consciously, it is possible that some bands may dwindle and die out, while others may expand to unmanageable sizes. However, there are many mechanisms by which adjustments take place to keep the bands to an optimum size, which means that the population is distributed evenly across the habitat to make the natural resources available to all. For example, in a desert, where water is the most important resource, the people will be evenly distributed around the water holes as shown by Wiessner (1982) in her ethnography about the !Kung San. She has shown how a flexible system of inheritance and institutionalised fictive kinship ties make a rational distribution of the people around the water holes and food resources possible.

Most band societies have bilateral rather than unilineal descent. Residence after marriage is flexible—a couple can take up residence in a camp that may be linked to the husband or to the wife, or to any other relative, depending upon where they find the conditions to be most favourable. Children are highly valued but seen as a collective rather than individual responsibility. Anthropologists who have taken their children to the field find that they become everyone's responsibility and cease to be a burden on just their own parents.

It is sociability and investment in social relations that are seen as worth accomplishing than success in individual productive activities, which become meaningless in these communities as they get submerged in group relations. People spend more time visiting each other and gossiping than in actual work. There have been various myths regarding hunting-gathering people that were busted once field studies on them began. For long, the people in the West had a caricature image of cave dwellers, with the men as hunters seen as strong and patriarchal and the women as dependent and weak. There can be nothing further from the truth. Field studies have shown that the major part of the staple food that was brought to the camp was procured by the gathering activity of the women, and although women rarely hunted big game, they did set traps and hunt small animals around the camp. The big game hunted by the men was not a regular source of food but had a more symbolic value. Thus, women provided the basic subsistence and were responsible for the daily requirements of calories, while men earned more prestige by occasionally getting more valued items of food (Lee and Devore 1968).

There is little hierarchy in an ideal band society, and men and women are more or less independent producers, although the latter do more in terms of subsistence and everyone depends on sharing. The women form more closely knit work groups than the men who may hunt alone or in groups, but the work of men certainly lacks the more cooperative work structure of the women. Among some groups like the Paliyans studied by Gardner (1988), the husband and wife form a team and there is hardly any division of labour. Other groups may have a more specified division of labour and may be more structured.

Another myth about hunter-gatherers has been regarding the lack of time and leisure among them as their level of technology requires labour-intensive work. This again is far from the actual facts. As shown by ethnographers, the average time for work in these societies is far less than that in advanced complex societies. The main reason for this is that there are very few needs. Since society is not stratified, there are hardly any items of prestige, the only requirements being for subsistence and of this there is always plenty. The environment of hunter-gatherers gives enough for them to live on and also reproduce. Referring to the ethnographic work done by Richard Lee on the Bushmen, Sahlins (1972: 23) points out:

> The daily per-capita subsistence yield for the Dobe Bushmen was 2,140 calories. However, taking into account body weight, normal activities, and the age-sex composition of the Dobe population, Lee estimates the people require only 1,975 calories per capita. Some of the surplus food probably went to the dogs, who ate what the people left over.

In the absence of any hierarchy based on accumulation, foragers did not have to work more than the minimum that was required for subsistence. Even if they worked less and gossiped more, they still had greater security for procuring food. Children and older people rarely needed to work, especially if they lived in favourable environments. Describing the Hadza of Africa, Woodburn (1968, 1988) pointed out that the men spent most of their time gambling and rarely engaged in strenuous big-game hunting, while the women too did not work hard and collected vegetables at a leisurely pace. 'Over the year as a whole probably an average of less than two hours a day is spent obtaining food' (Woodburn 1968: 54). As described by Sahlins (1972: 35), 'Hunter's subsistence labours are characteristically intermittent, a day on and a day off, and modern hunters at least tend to employ their time off in such activities as daytime sleep.'

The foraging people do vary according to the nature of the environment and the harshness of the climate, but overall they work much less than people who have productive technologies, as they have adjusted their lifestyle to very minimal consumption and greater human sociability. They entertain themselves by telling stories, writing poetry, singing and being in each other's company. Since they have no sense of property and no sense of hierarchy based on accumulation of physical goods, they feel no need to work beyond a point where they are assured of food and shelter. Protection from animal predators and human enemies is a collective activity, and the group norms require that people do not engage in conflict and stay close to each other. The demarcation between in-group and out-group may also (though not always) translate into categories of kin or enemy. Decision-making is also collective, though some individuals may have more voice and command respect because of their age or reputation.

A third myth about foragers has been about their isolation. Earlier scholars thought that such groups stagnated in their 'primitive' technology because they lacked contact with the outside world, but this too is far from the facts. Hunter-gatherers and agricultural groups have had trading relations extending far back into antiquity:

> These relationships were marked by a high degree of variability and flexibility, with specific groups altering their strategies in relation to ecological, demographic, and political imperatives, such that it is difficult, and at times misleading, to use labels such as "hunter-gatherer" or "agriculturalist" as if they described an exclusive or stable strategy. (Morrison 2006: 45)

Many anthropological studies have drawn attention to the strategic adaptations and the movements of people between one form of adaptation and another.

The greatest blow to the hunter-gatherers has been the loss of their habitat. This happened because of many reasons: massive deforestation to make way for agricultural and urban developments, the clearing of forests for making dams and industries, and the ill-informed recourse to commercial forestry, which destroys the natural biodiversity of forests and leads to a massive loss of species and lifeworlds. Contemporary hunter-gatherers have lost much of their traditional resources to outsiders who wish to exploit the forest and what lies beneath it as resources. Outsiders do not have the same world view as forest dwellers and do not perceive the forest as 'animated'. Following a misplaced notion of environmental protectionism, the state has made efforts to remove forest dwellers from their traditional habitats (Radhakrishna 2012: 147, 149). In February 2019, the Supreme Court directed that all forest-dwelling communities that could not prove their legal rights to the forest were to be evicted. According to the Supreme Court's order dated 13 February 2019, the total number of claims to land rejected under the Forest Rights Act currently stands at 11,27,446 households. But this does not include the several other states that have not provided details to the court, though they have been asked to do so. When all data is made available, the numbers can go up sizeably. The plea of 'eminent domain', as used in this verdict, is one that has been strategically used to favour the corporate exploitation of forest resources. The tribal people to whom eviction notices have been served have been inhabitants of these forests for centuries, and naturally they have no evidence of formal ownership.

From the perspective of environment protection, the eviction of forest dwellers has always proved to be counter-productive, as those coming from outside, say, the forest guards, have little knowledge of the forest as compared to the people who inhabit the forest and sustain themselves through it, and who know it like the back of their hands. They are the ones who have lived there for centuries. Since they are deprived of their livelihoods and often forcibly displaced, they become easy victims of exploitation and are often used as poachers by unscrupulous traders in animal products. Also, as indicated by Radhakrishna (ibid.: 151), they are forced to hunt in the forest, often endangered species, to fight hunger. And they end up in jails as habitual offenders and are continuously harassed by forest officials. They thus become doubly stigmatised and are further removed from forests. In more sustainable programmes, the tribals inhabiting forests are involved in its protection and also encouraged to make a living by trading in minor forest produce like honey, wild fruits and berries. Singh (2004) describes the practice of Community Forest Management (CFM) in Odisha, where forests as well as adjoining areas are largely occupied by tribes. The CFM was taken up by people in the late 1970s and early 1990s, against the backdrop of the rapid degradation of forests and the lack of effectivity of the Joint Forest Management (JFM) programme initiated by the state. It included patrolling of forests to prevent illegal harvesting of timber and other forest goods. As Singh (2004: 309–10) points out, the most effective forest management has been shown by women's groups when they have been given charge. Women are the single-most intense users of minor forest produce like fuels, fodder and edible/medicinal plants. Singh describes how the *mahila samiti* (women's group) of Baghamunda, a small village of the Gondi tribe, protects 500 acres of forest that includes 80 acres of teak plantation. This activity in the Badatalla Reserve Forest was taken up by women when other male agencies failed. But women—the main collectors of non-timber forest produce such as *tendu* leaves (for rolling *bidi*s) and other produce like *sal* seeds, *mahua* and honey—are exploited by the state and other agencies that usurp most of the profit, giving a pittance to the actual collectors. The foraging tribals across the world, and very much so in India, are taken advantage of because of their lack of formal knowledge and understanding of market exchange. This is even more prominent in the case of women, who are even less adept at handling outsiders.

There have been three major theoretical approaches to the social organisation of hunter-gatherers. The first approach is the patrilocal band model given by Steward (2008), which emphasises the environmental variables and the process of environmental adaptation as the key to understanding foraging social organisation. The second approach, elaborated by Lee (1976) and supported by Meillassoux (1981), also emphasises the environmental and technological aspect. Lee (1976) put forth the model of a flexible band where there is little emphasis on rituals and lineal kinship, and he was able to show with respect to the Bushmen that he studied that this flexibility, bilateral kinship and lack of investment in accumulation were adaptive traits to the environment and technology.

However, Morris (1982) argues that it is also not valid to suppose that hunters and gatherers comprise a monolithic category and that their social organisation is a dependent variable of environment and technology. He puts forward his thesis that other factors, both historical and cultural, can also play a role and that there can be at least two broad types of variation in the social organisation of foragers which depends on the historical condition of the extent of intercultural interactions and of the degree of pressure from an external source with superior powers. The presence or absence of trade with others makes a significant difference. Therefore, there are those who live in comparative isolation or at least in comparative freedom, and in a culturally homogenous situation, and those who live under political and economic pressures from an external source (ibid.: 174).

Another dichotomous division has been suggested by James Woodburn (cited in Morris 1982: 174–75): between those communities that do not invest in productive technologies, those who do not make any tools or equipment worth keeping and do not invest in the preservation of resources; and others like the Ainu and the northwest-coast Indians, who accumulate tools, equipment and resources, and invest in delayed return from labour. The latter are closer to agricultural communities. The Australian Aborigines are seen as exceptional in that they invest both time and energy in rituals and marriage patterns even though they have little investment in productive technology. According to Woodburn, here the men invest in gaining control over the productive and reproductive resources of the women.

The parameters that lead to variations among hunter-gatherers in terms of their levels of social organisation are possibly dependent upon the following five factors that can be summarised from Morris (1982: 175–76):

1. *The size and nature of the resource-holding group as well as the type of resource that is held.* For example, among the Ainu of Japan, the core resource-holding group is that of male agnates holding a territorial unit. Among the Australian Aborigines, it is the totemic clan or a sibling group, or there can be no ownership at all and everything is in the nature of a 'free good' like among the south Indian foragers living in forests.
2. *The type of local group or residential aggregate.* The social group could be a clearly bounded one that resides and lives together, known in anthropological literature as a band. However, foragers may also move around as nuclear families and not necessarily as

bands. Sometimes, as among the Bushmen, there can be dispersal and reaggregation depending upon seasonal supply of food and water.

3. *The type of marriage regulations*. Goodale (1971) has shown for the Tiwi that 'land ownership was associated with a patrilineal sibling set, matrilineages were the recognised units of marriage exchange, and residential aggregates were bilateral' (Morris 1982: 176).
4. *The unit of commensality*. Although in the discussion of band societies, families are not always given recognition, in some groups like the Paliyans studied by Gardner (1988), the nuclear family is the primary unit where husband and wife form a cooperating and sharing unit. Thus, instead of the band as a whole, the basic unit of commensality is the nuclear family, although it can never reproduce itself and must be incorporated within a larger group.
5. *Forms of male solidarity*. In many hunting-gathering groups, men may have a special ritual status like among the Baruya studied by Godelier (1986), which led him to state that patriarchy predates all forms of division of labour. The men may form special cults like the totemic cult groups of the Australian Aborigines, though no such groups have been reported for women.

Thus, according to Morris (1982: 176), there are five basic levels of organisation 'relating to ownership of resources, residence, reproduction, commensality and male solidarity'. Where all five levels are well developed, the group may approximate to an agricultural society in its complexity, but there is not necessarily an absolute distinction between one form of subsistence and another.

Morris (1982) studied the Malapantarams of south India who are found in the forests south of Lake Periyar. Although classified purely as hunter-gatherers, they have had important trading links with neighbouring populations, earlier through silent barter and, in more recent times, through forest contractors. They form small groups that are constantly on the move in the forest, collecting valuable forest products. Although each band may consist of several nuclear families who live in rock shelters or in camps made from small leaf-shelters, the unit of consumption is always the nuclear family. Thus, while people may collect vegetables or even trade in groups, the products are always only for the family to consume. The Malapantarams show a degree of individualism that may not be the case for all foraging communities. Even when families do come together it is not for any environmental or economic purpose as these aggregations are not linked to any seasonal fluctuations of availability of resources as found among some other groups like the Bushmen. The Malapantarams have no concept of lineality, male fraternity or elaborate rituals or cults. There is a pervasive sexual egalitarianism among them, with men and women being equal in all respects including the division of labour. They have great preference for nomadic life and prefer to move around, usually within a radius of two miles on an average. And although they are usually confined within a territory for historical reasons, they have no claims to territory and feel free to move anywhere. They believe in hill spirits, but there are no linkages between specific spirits and specific families (like the kuldevta cults of the Himalayas).

In light of such a society focused primarily on the family, Morris (1982) raises the question as to whether it is valid to use the notion of a band or a 'local group' for the Malapantarams. They can be contrasted with the Andamanese who have well-established 'local groups' and engage in elaborate rituals of initiations that involve the group as a whole. The Malapantarams are more like the Paliyans and the Kadars, in being more individual and less group-oriented.

Through these examples we discover that hunting and food-gathering may be the first form of subsistence for humans. Yet in terms of social organisation, foragers show considerable variations, some of which are not necessarily related to the environment or technology. Although scholars like Steward (1955) and Meillasoux (1981) have emphasised the material base of society, yet ethnographic examples show enough variations to warrant the independent impact of local culture and history in shaping these societies. Thus, the individual family units compete with each other in barter and trade relations with the outside world, leading to an internal fragmentation and individualism, which overrides the group solidarity and cooperation characteristic of many foraging societies.

PASTORALISM

Pastoralism is defined as a way of life dependent upon the domestication of animals. It differs from animal farming in that for pastoral people, animals are a part of their society and not simply exploitable resources, with the animals leading a natural life rather than being held captive on farms. The human population adjusts its life to the needs of the animals rather than the other way around.

Pastoralism cannot be a self-sufficient mode of subsistence as humans need staple food from non-animal sources also. Therefore, pastoralists need to practise some form of cultivation or be in continued exchange relationships with those who are producers of food. The type of economy that combines food production with animal husbandry is known as a mixed economy. Those who are pure pastoralists are usually in permanent exchange relationships with adjoining populations of food-growers. In India, the Todas of the Nilgiri Hills (Walker 1986) had long-standing relationships with the Badaga cultivators who also inhabited the same region. They also had exchange relationships with forest dwellers such as the Irulas, Kurumbas and Kota, who practised different crafts. The various tribes of this region exchanged their skills and products with each other.

Pastoralism is a way of life dependent upon the domestication of animals. For pastoral people, animals are part of their society, leading a natural life rather than being held captive on farms.

To adjust to the needs of animals, pastoral people have to move from place to place in search of water and food. In some cases, where the movements are seasonal and take place between two fixed points, the practice is known as transhumance. When pastoralists move on pathways through designated territories, they are known as nomadic. However, pastoral movements can never be random, as shepherds need to know exactly what food and water will be available to them as they move. The life of animals is dependent on this crucial knowledge and cannot be left to chance.

Since water sources and pastures are vast resources, the access to them tends to be collective. The Jad Bhotiyas of Uttarakhand (Channa 2013) were granted access to higher altitude pastures, now near the Indo-Tibet border, beyond the Neilang Pass and beyond the Gangotri Glacier, by the Rajah of Tehri. During the British period, while Kumaon Garhwal came directly under colonial rule, Tehri Garhwal was ruled with the help of the local ruler, also recognised as the earthly incarnation of Badrinath (possibly the reason he was not removed by the British rulers). Thus, to the contemporary times, the local people consider the Rajah to be their sovereign, although now, slowly the impact of parliamentary democracy is being felt in the mountains too.

The Jads are transhumant and spend winters in a lower-altitude village called Dunda, near the religious centre of Uttarkashi. While the Jads move between two fixed locations, with an additional camp in the forests near Rishikesh, at a place known as Chorpani, the sheep along with their grazers have a different route and schedule for their movements. The Jad families do not follow the grazing route and live in properly constructed villages where some cultivation is also carried on, mostly by women and hired help. Earlier, the men were primarily engaged in cross-border trade with Tibet, with only a few men engaged in grazing activities. It is also customary for Jads to hire young men from other communities as shepherds. Even after the cross-border trade was clamped down, the men of the community did not go back to work in the village, choosing to engage in guiding tourists or trading in the local markets of Uttarkashi to keep themselves outside the purview of village life. Some members of the community are getting educated and moving to cities for work.

The sheep follow a cycle of grazing that is locally called *chaumasa* (literally, four months). The year is divided according to the movements of the sheep, and four seasons are recognised: *gunga* (spanning the Hindu lunar-calendar months of Paus, Magh and Phagun) roughly corresponding to winter; *pega* (the months of Chait, Baisakh and Jeth) roughly corresponding to spring and the beginnings of summer; *yerga* (Asadh, Sawan and Bhadon) roughly corresponding to summer and the rainy season; and *tonga* (the months of Asur, Kartik and Mansir or Marghsish) roughly corresponding to autumn and the beginning of winter.

In the yerga season, the sheep are taken to the highest pastures, where they spend four months from Asadh to Asur. Towards the end of this period, the grazers begin to climb down to the forests near their high-altitude village at Harsil. Here, the sheep are shorn of their wool, and while some wool and even sheep are traded, the bulk of the wool goes to the women in the village for processing. The sheep graze best in the high altitudes where there is no pollution and the grass grows green and fresh. They accumulate so much fat by the month of Bhadon that the shepherds have to keep them awake so that they do not get heart attacks. The wool that grows at this time is long and silky and fetches a high price. From Asur onwards, the sheep and their grazers keep going down, reaching the lower-altitude pastures near Dehradun and Rishikesh by Kartik, where they stay for four months till Chait. Then begins the upward climb, and they are back at the lower-altitude village by Jeth and then climb upwards till they reach the highest pastures, above the tree line at about 7,000 feet above sea level by Asadh, and then the entire cycle is repeated. The sheep are also sheared at the lower-altitude village, but the wool is of poorer quality than what is obtained after the winter pastures.

In winter, when due to heavy snow fall (about 6 feet of snow) the higher-altitude village is totally deserted with only one or two older men staying back, some families also go to the forests near Rishikesh, where they set up camp. This is a place to which the horses and dogs are brought from the village. The horses graze and can drink water from the streams and the puppies that are born here are often sold. The Bhotiya dogs, as they are known, are beautiful and fetch a high price. This is also a place for trading in various goods like shawls and sweaters as well as beautiful carpets, all made by the women. The Bhotiya women are adept at processing raw wool into skeins and knitting them. While earlier, the entire journey was done on foot and with loaded horses and male goats, in the present times, the Jads have started using trucks to bring their goods to the local markets near Rishikesh.

The livelihood and day-to-day life of the Jads is thus closely tied to their animals. They are also linked to other communities through their grazing fields and routes and waterways. They have a grazing route along a stream that takes them to Kinnaur over the Ranikanda meadows with its waterway. This is why the Jads have had relationships of marriage with the Kinnauries, but since Garhwal is believed to be more sacred than Kinnaur, the girls from Kinnaur would marry into Garhwal but not the other way around. Ever since Kinnaur became a part of the state of Himachal Pradesh, such marriage practices slowly died out as shepherds from Garhwal were not allowed to graze up in Himachal Pradesh. Earlier, they also shared lower-altitude pastures with shepherds from Kinnaur and Chamoli, and the Tolcha and Marcha tribes from Niti–Mana Valley. Gradually, the shepherds from Kinnaur stopped coming to the pastures near Dehradun after the creation of Himachal Pradesh in 1971. Shepherds from around the Niti and Mana areas have almost given up animal husbandry and turned nearly full-time to tourism after the creation of the Nanda Devi Biosphere Reserve in 1982.

The pastoral way of life is under threat due to diminishing pasture lands, as more and more land is being taken up for urban development. Modern technology no longer supports traditional ways of life. For example, the large number of Bhotiya communities that sustained themselves through cross-border trade had to redefine their livelihood pattern once this trade was stopped due to the changing political contours of the borders. The Jads as well as the Kinnauries of upper Himachal still do some animal husbandry, but it is increasingly not sustainable. Himalayan pastoralists have lost quite a bit of their prime grazing lands to the creation of nature reserves and sanctuaries like the Nanda Devi Biosphere and Askot Wildlife Sanctuary. The Jads told me that they have been banned from going to sacred Hindu areas like Tapovan near Gangotri due to objections from pilgrims. Since the government takes a hostile attitude towards pastoral people, they are also routinely harassed by forest officials when they pass through their traditional forest corridors as in the case of the Van Gujjars of the Rajaji National Park.

The other well-known pastoral groups in India are the Todas of the Nilgiri, the Bakkarwals of Jammu and Kashmir, and the Gaddis of Himachal. Some of these groups, like the Gaddis, are changing their grazing routes because of the lack of pastures, as even small mountain towns like Dharamshala and McLeodganj are expanding their boundaries. They have now started bringing their animals down to places where they did not go earlier, and this is causing problems for the local peasants. Mixed economy for pastoral communities is rare in India, unlike the Nilotic pastoralists of East Africa. Most pastoral communities in India have been living in close proximity to and in exchange relationships with cultivators.

Pastoral communities like the Raika and Rabari, the camel herders of Kutch and Rajasthan, are also feeling the pressure of diminishing resources. Earlier, when there was only one sowing season (during the monsoons) in this arid region, these pastoral communities were welcomed by the local farmers to graze their animals on the fallow fields, as the animal dung manured the fields and the land was loosened by their hooves, making ploughing easier in the next season. Thus, mutuality is now broken as new technologies of irrigation and chemical fertilisers allow for more than one crop a year, and there is no need for a symbiotic relationship with the pastoral people. Similar relationships of mutuality between the buffalo herders of central India and the cultivating communities are also breaking down. However, traditional pastoralists continue to survive, some of them because they produce certain niche and coveted goods such as the shawls, carpets and knitted goods (produced by the Bhotiyas). Saberwal (1999), who has detailed the ways of life of the Gaddis, points out how they manage to survive by negotiating with the authorities on the sly. The pastoralists make gifts of cash, milk, butter and woollen items to the officials, who choose to look the other way when they bring their animals to graze. They also participate in local vote-bank politics, where they extend support to the parties in power. To negotiate further, they either understate the number of their animals when they wish to get access to grazing or overstate when they wish to claim compensation for animal epidemics or accidental deaths. The Himalayan pastoralists are locally dominant because of their relatively higher economic status as compared to the agriculturalists, as animals are a high-value resource.

Pastoralists have property relations at two levels: the access to vital resources for their animals is always collective but the animals are owned by individual households, as they need to be cared for at a more personal level. Since animals are a source of wealth, pastoral people may be believed to have personal wealth. Therefore, some of them like the Jads described earlier prefer to live in settled villages and in permanent houses. The Todas also live in villages, and the buffaloes that they herd are taken to the rain shadow side of the mountaintop inhabited by them during the monsoon rains. Only a few persons accompany the animals, and the life in the hamlets goes on as usual. In this way, the Todas do not have to shift entire villages like the Jad Bhotiyas do. Some like the Gujjars and the Bakkarwals move around in family camps and do not settle in villages at all. In the latter type of communities, their entire lifestyle is adjusted to their animals as they do not have any settled village life like the Todas and Jads.

The Todas have their entire social and religious life focused on their buffaloes, which makes them different from the pastoralists who follow at least some form of religion like the Muslim Bakkarwals, the Muslim/Hindu Gujjars and the animist/Buddhist/Hindu Jad Bhotiyas. Yet, some form of ritual is always associated with animals and their life cycles. The Jads perform rituals associated with their movements and have a deity installed in their temporary camp at Chorpani. They also perform rituals for their village deities while leaving or going back to their villages. These people consider sheep to be the goddess Lakshmi and believe that their eyes shine like jewels at night, providing protection from evil spirits. Though the Jads sell their animals, they never slaughter them, and if a female animal dies, she is buried but not eaten. The Todas are pure vegetarian, and although they sell their male animals, they treat the female ones with respect and maintain a strict lineage of their sacred buffaloes. With the passing of time, the Todas have undergone many transformations. Walker (1986, 2004), who has studied them over many years, refutes many of the bizarre myths associated with the modern Todas, who, he argues, neither practise female infanticide nor fraternal polyandry as they did many decades back. Modern Toda settlements no longer have the famous Toda hut, of which only a few remnants are left. The contemporary Todas mostly practise agriculture and have moved over to other modern occupations; they live in houses that are made of bricks and mortar; and they rarely flaunt their traditional dress. The Toda buffaloes still survive and the ones believed to be sacred are still revered, though they have more ritual than economic value.

Pastoral people have long been seen as a threat by states as they are mobile and not permanently rooted in one place to be subjected to the authority of central rule. In the Middle East, there was a constant struggle in the colonial period to bring what were regarded as 'unruly' tribes under the control of the colonial administration. Even in the postcolonial era, the centralised states of Iran and Iraq have bombed and starved their pastoral borderland populations like the Kurds, in order to bring them under greater centralised control.

In India too, the pastoral nomads have not been seen in a positive light by the state. During the colonial period, some of them were even branded as 'criminal tribes'. Most pastoral nomadic people survived in the feudal era by being attached to some feudal lord, to whom they owed allegiance in return for protection and rights over common resources like grazing land and water. The Jad Bhotiyas, for example, consider the Rajah of Tehri Garhwal as their lord, and even today, they have his pictures on their walls, instead of those of any prominent national leader like Gandhi.

Pastoral people are problematic in a democracy and in a capitalist economy as their relationship to their animals and resources is not commodified. They rarely maximise their profits from the animals, yet they are able to have a sustained lifestyle. Their treatment of their animals as living beings is not compatible with the commodification and maximisation of profit through the exploitation of animals. Moreover, their traditional access to resources such as water and pastures limits the profit that the state can make through taxes, since these are vested in the community as a whole and not in individuals. The Jads pay taxes on their access to forests in the lowlands near Dehradun and Rishikesh but not for their higher-altitude pastures.

Since their mode of production is subsistence-oriented and not profit-oriented, it is not compatible with a cash economy. There have been efforts on the part of the state to bring them into the fold of the market economy, which forms the support base for the making of governments in a democracy. During a field visit in 2008, we discovered that the state is aggressively pushing commercial apple cropping in areas where it has never been cultivated. Traditional sheep farmers are being encouraged to take to apple farming as an alternative. One outcome of cash-cropping is that people become dependent on the market for staples as well as inessential goods.

More recently, the rhetoric of environment has been to project such ways of life as against the interests of the environment, to focus attention away from gross economics and to put the argument in a more modernist perspective. Thus, the state projects grazing by animals as responsible for the loss of cover and soil erosion and, therefore, one of the reasons for deforestation. Pastoralists like the Van Gujjars of Rajaji National Park, on the other hand, argue that grazing by animals is actually beneficial for forest regrowth. The issue of Muslim Gujjars remains contentious. Since these people have been grazing for centuries in these forests, the arguments put forward by the state seem to be politically motivated stance rather than based on scientific facts or rationale (Saberwal 1999). The state, for its own benefit of revenue, supports the commercial use of forests for timber and mono-cultivation of cash crops.

SHIFTING CULTIVATION

Shifting cultivation is the form of cultivation that has been practised for centuries, and is still prevalent in mountainous, and arid and semi-arid, terrains without enough irrigation facilities. It involves a rotational use of the soil, is rain-dependent and uses only natural fertilisers obtained through the burning of slashed vegetation. It is also known as slash-and-burn cultivation. It is particularly compatible with descent group, and tribal clan and community organisations, as the ones discussed earlier. The land for shifting cultivation is normally held by a community and is redistributed in every cultivation cycle by someone in authority, like a village chief, clan elder or shaman. Each household receives as much land as is required to feed its members. In India, it is practised in Odisha, the Northeast, Kerala, Karnataka and Andhra Pradesh. It is known by the names of *jhum*, *podu* and *bewar* in different parts of India.

> **Shifting cultivation is a centuries-old practice, still prevalent in mountainous, and arid and semi-arid terrains without enough irrigation facilities. It involves a rotational use of the soil. It is particularly compatible with descent group, and tribal clan and community organisations.**

In shifting cultivation, the land is cleared of its bushes and growth; these are left to dry and then set on fire, and the ash is later mixed with the top soil with the help of a hand-held hoe or digging stick. The important nitrogen compounds required for fertility are obtained from the ash. The seeds are lightly sown or simply broadcast. After harvesting one crop, the land is left fallow till the growth is sufficient for the next cycle. The fallow period varies according to the climatic conditions and population density. For the system to work efficiently, the fallow period must be sufficiently long for the land to revive fully. Since only the top soil is used for cultivation, and it is fertilised every season by the burning of dried and cut vegetation, this mode of cultivation does not require a very rich or fertile soil. Therefore, it is mostly practised where the soil is hardy and relatively less fertile, like on hilltops and mountainsides.

This mode of cultivation is also suitable for tropical rainforests where high humidity and warm climate lead to a quick regeneration of secondary growth. Under favourable conditions, the period of fallow may be only four to five years, but in more arid and less favourable conditions, the fallow period may stretch to 10 years or more, for the cultivation to be sustainable. Thus, the actual amount of land that is required to sustain this mode of cultivation is far more than the land under actual cultivation at any point of time. Shifting cultivation is hence known as extensive cultivation and supports only a thin population density. Only under exceptional climatic conditions, where regeneration is rapid, can it sustain a dense population. It is likely to break down if the population density gets high, and this is one of the reasons that it is not projected as sustainable for increasing populations, as it requires a low man to land ratio. For an optimum yield, on an average, the fallow period should vary between five and ten years. If the fallow period is less, the land becomes degraded by frequent firing.

Shifting cultivation is rain-dependent and the timely occurrence of rain is key to its success. Thus, under changing climatic conditions, it may become unsustainable as unpredictable rain patterns will play havoc with this system. Cooperation between men is required for the process of firing the field as controlled firing is a special skill and needs a large group of people to do it. Men do the felling and firing, but most other activities are done by women. The hoe or digging stick in most cultures is recognised as a woman's tool as it is hand-held and requires a lot of back-breaking effort. In some tribes, hoe cultivation is also accompanied by polygyny and the payment of bride wealth.

Men covet more wives to work on the fields, and the economic contribution of women is acknowledged by the transfer of wealth to a woman's lineage when she moves out of it at marriage.

Since land is rotated in every cultivation season and a large amount of land needs to be held fallow while a small amount is actually cultivated, most communities practising shifting cultivation have community ownership of land. The entire cultivable land and other resources like forests and water are held in common by a descent group or a village. Such common ownership is also conducive to the protection of large amounts of land, especially as much of it lies fallow at any point of time and there is always the danger of encroachment by neighbouring clans or tribes. The tribes of the Northeast such as the Nagas have had special social institutions, such as the men's houses, which provided a ready army of young men to protect the village whenever there was a raid by a neighbour. All the unmarried young men above a certain age (for example, 6–8 years) stayed together in a long house on the outskirts of the village, always alert to the dangers at the border.

In every cycle of cultivation, land is allotted to each household of the community by a religious or political leader who has the highest authority in that village or descent group. Each household has enough land to take care of its subsistence requirements. In several communities that practise shifting cultivation, there are some crops like bananas and coffee that are grown for cash. Such plantations or fruit trees are mostly owned by individuals or individual households. Shifting cultivation tends to emulate nature more than monocropping, and most shifting cultivators plant and harvest large varieties, often up to 60 species, from the same piece of land. This is done by multi-crop rotations and planting a variety of crops like tubers, legumes, shrubs, trees and grasses, as well as plants that ripen or bear fruit at different times of the year. For example, in Mizoram, where jhum or shifting cultivation is practised by a majority of people, the forests are selected and slashed in the months of December–January. The cut vegetation is left to dry and then set to fire in the months of February–March. In this region, the winter months are dry and cool, the temperature hovering around 9°C. The fields are sown in April–May, while the months of June–September are the wet months when the southwest monsoon winds bring rain to this region. The principal crops are paddy along with maize, cucumber, beans, ginger, mustard, sesame and cotton. But other fruits and vegetables are also grown, like cow peas, rice and French beans. Most requirements of a family, including oilseeds, staples, spices and vegetables, are grown by the household, and little is bought from the market. As reported by Sati and Rinawma (2014), each family sows up to 15–20 species in a year, on a plot sized 1–4 hectares.

Shifting cultivation is rain-fed and does not use any artificial fertilisers or pesticides. When fully cultivated, a shifting cultivation plot almost resembles natural vegetation, and often in a rainforest, outsiders cannot distinguish between the natural forest and its cultivated segments. A cultivated plot may contain big trees (that are kept standing when the shrubs and bushes are cut down), shrubs, bushes, legumes, tubers and a variety of plants that grow together and are often harvested at different times of the year. Although, some scholars and especially the state administration have been projecting shifting cultivation as the single reason for the degradation of forests, scientific research (Ramakrishnan 1992) indicates that shifting cultivation is far more sustainable than monocropping and commercial agriculture.

A detailed account of shifting cultivation was provided by Vidyarthi (1963) from his study of the Maler of Rajmahal Hills, a study that also provided the empirical basis for this theory of the nature–man–spirit complex. Vidyarthi's fieldwork was in the 1950s, and it is possible that many of the conditions, especially of the density of forests and wildlife, as described by him are no longer to be found. But his description shows how shifting cultivation can exist in diverse forms, with regional variations. The Malers, for example, have individually owned lands and cultivate their plots individually with help from kin and other villagers. The following is a description of *khallu* (shifting cultivation in the local language): Maler villages consist of about 10–30 huts made from locally collected bamboo, leaves and grass. These small villages are surrounded by three rings of forest. The first consists primarily of fruit trees of which palm trees predominate, although mangoes, bananas and tamarind are also found. The second ring comprises wild but useful trees such as bamboo groves, edible and useful plants, shrubs and tubers. The final ring is the wild and natural forest that extends for miles around these villages and has wildlife.

The trees, plants and shrubs, comprising about 50–200 varieties form an important source of food and medicines for the Maler. The reason the Maler do not wish to move away from their forest is that the forest is for them a safety zone, a reservoir they can fall back upon in case of crop failure or famine.

Shifting cultivation is practised by each family, which identifies some pieces of land that it can cultivate in any season, by checking on the existing vegetation. A piece of land, once cultivated, is usually left fallow to regrow and is referred to as *akola*. It may lie fallow for 6–8 years. A single piece of land may be cultivated twice or even thrice, but each time the yield is poorer than the first time. Once a household identifies a land for cultivation, a ritual sacrifice of a fowl, egg or even a goat is first made. If there is not enough akola (cultivable land) with a family, it may take akola on lease from others. The clearing of the forest involves the labour of all members of the household, who clear the forest with *tatro*s (sickles) and *maso*s (axes). Since this is a labour-intensive task, help is sought from other members of the family and villagers. If enough voluntary labour cannot be generated, then Santal and Pahariya labour is employed, with the payment made in cash and kind (for example, meals).

While clearing the vegetation, care is taken to not cut useful fruit-bearing trees like mango, mahua, *ber* and *karam*. Even when trees are cut, longish stumps are left for creepers to climb and also to provide wood for making hoes. Once dried, the cut branches and twigs are used as household fuel and also sold in the market for cash. The wood that is cut provides cash for the initial period of the cultivation cycle when the stored food from the last cultivation is running out. At this time, the household food supply is supplemented by hunting and gathering of vegetables and tubers from the forest. Once the field is dry, it is set on fire just before the onset of monsoon. After the firing and before the rains, luxuriant growth of grass takes place, which is also cut and burnt.

The sowing season begins in Asad (June and July) with the performance of rituals at the village as well as the family level. The Maler 'strongly believe that any kind of digging hurts the Mother earth (Ego Pacho) and annoys the forest God (Yamma Gossaiyan)' (Vidyarthi 1963: 37). To avert the wrath of the deities, the villagers collect money and purchase a pig that is ritually sacrificed on behalf of the entire village. The individual householders also make smaller sacrifices of fowl, egg and the occasional goat. The sacrifices by individual householders are made to ensure the safety and growth of their own crops—the Malers believe that only sowing is in the hands of humans, not the harvest. The richness of the harvest depends mainly on the benevolence of the *gossaiyans* (spirits).

For the sowing of seeds, both men and women engage in the digging of the soil with sticks, when holes are made in the ground and seeds of maize and beans are dibbled. After one month from this, the seeds of millet are broadcast, and finally at the end of the sowing season, the pulses are dibbled into the ground. The Malers are not able to preserve enough seeds for the next sowing season and have to buy them each time from the market. As a result, they become indebted to the *mahajans* (local moneylenders).

The protection of crops is a laborious and painstaking process, as the crops have to be defended from pests when they are growing and, once they are mature, from wild animals like bears and porcupines. The Maler make offerings to various deities and also engage in hard labour. A lot of effort is spent in weeding. Since a second crop on the same land gives rise to a heavy growth of weeds, the Maler prefer to clear fresh land, but it is not always feasible. To protect standing crops from animals and also from theft by other humans, they make a small hut in the field and live there for several months. According to Vidyarthi's (1963) estimate, up to 50–80 per cent of the standing crop is usually destroyed by wild animals.

Shifting to the field house is also not without its problems as once the husband shifts there, the wife may take on lovers (ibid.). If possible, the couple may shift but that is only if there is someone else to take care of the house. Finally, the harvest takes place and is marked by rituals and sacrifices.

The harvested grains are then brought to a clearing near the village for winnowing and threshing. The women clear a piece of land, level it with cow dung and then engage in these activities, while the men make arrangements for the harvest rituals known as Gangi or Khosre Pijje. Once the baskets full of the grain are brought to the hut of the householder, they are consumed only after ritual offerings are made to the *adda* gossaiyan (the spirit of the hut) and *atto* gossaiyan (the spirit of the hearth). The size and value of the animal being offered is proportional to the value of the yield. For higher yields, a pig or goat may be offered, otherwise a fowl or an egg. The mahajans also descend on the village at this time to claim their dues.

The Maler are happy with what they are left with and engage in merrymaking, dancing and drinking. Khallu remains at the centre of their lives. The first major ritual after harvesting is to make offerings to all those who have died that year. This festival, as Vidyarthi (1963) reports, is celebrated on a large scale, and is called Bhoj Pijje, Bandna or Pillai. Then the Maler also make offerings to all such spirits to whom they may have made vows in the course of that year. These vows are usually made to seek cures from illnesses or other forms of misfortune. This is also the time for negotiation and performance of marriages as food is at its maximum abundance at this time. This is also the time for repairing and replacing huts and equipment. Large hunts are also organised after making offerings to the god of the hunt (Raksi-Nadu). The meat is shared by everyone including the Maler's dogs. The women get busy grinding and storing grains, and also making maize and millet beer. Fruits are collected from the forest, and mahua is converted into beer. This is the time for abundance and enjoyment, which lasts till the next monsoon when the Malers are ready for another sowing season. As already mentioned, the forest provides stop-gap nourishment and acts as a safety valve for preventing hunger during the lean season.

Vidyarthi's detailed account covers not only the agricultural cycle but also the rituals and beliefs regarding nature that accompany this cycle of cultivation. The interweaving of economy and religion among the pre-industrial people has been noted by almost every anthropologist from Bronislaw Malinowski and E. E. Evans-Pritchard to more contemporary scholars like Mary Evelyn Tucker and John Allan Grim. As Vidyarthi (1963: 176) writes:

> As I went deep with the analysis of the Maler forest economy, the cycle of Khallu cultivation, and the various dimensions of the man to man interactions, the functions of the "spirits" (Gossaiyans) in regulating Nature-Man relationship and over all, moulding their culture, became

> clearer still. It appeared that by large the Maler represented a style of life in which maize, man and the "god" have definitely mutual role to play.

The most important contribution that Vidyarthi made was to indicate to policy planners that resettlement or displacement for a tribal people does not mean a spatial shift alone but displacement from a way of life, a 'life world' as it is now called (Grimm 2001: *xxxiii*). On examining the description provided by Vidyarthi, one is made aware of how the Maler were incorporated within a market economy, even as they pursued a 'traditional' subsistence pattern. The necessity of selling forest produce, and the compelling circumstances that led them to borrow heavily from the mahajans, indicate that tribes have never been 'isolated' and have always been in interaction with outsiders (Roy 1912). Where tribes differ from cash economies is that they are not able to produce a surplus to the extent that they can build up capital assets.

Prasad's (2004) description of bewar or shifting cultivation among the Baigas of central India indicates that the community, although identified as shifting cultivators by most scholars, actually had a mixed economy, which included hunting-gathering and trade in forest produce. She shows how the practice of bewar was possible only because it was supported by hunting and food-gathering, which was not a supplementary activity for the Baigas, but an intrinsic part of the rhythm of cultivation they followed.

Baigas cultivated each cleared field for three consecutive years, a practice that marks them off from others who cleared new fields more frequently. In the initial year, when the stalks ripened, the women collected tubers and mahua from the fields, while the men went hunting, for which they used bamboo bows, arrows and spears. In the first year, when there was a lot of preparation in the form of clearing and burning the field, hunting and food-gathering provided most of the food base. In the second year, when there was enough food left over from the first year to support them while they were preparing the fields, hunting and other activities were minimised. In the third year, when food supplies diminished, hunting and food-gathering were picked up again but on a reduced scale from the first year.

'Thus the three year cycle of survival was intrinsically dependent on the success of the crop of the first year' (Prasad 2004: 118). In case of crop failure, the entire system would be destabilised, with only hunting and food-gathering providing the subsistence base. If the Baigas were not practising hunting and gathering, the length of the fallow would be shortened and new fields would have to be cleared more frequently. Moreover, bewar was practised only in the mixed forests on the moderate slopes with thick undergrowth of grasses and bushes and several varieties of trees.

Another important aspect brought out by Prasad is the way in which the Baigas were linked to local peasants and artisans with whom they had regular trade in minor forest products like honey, lac sticks, silk cocoons, flowers, seeds and fuelwood. Both men and women engaged in gathering, but the men dealt in more lucrative goods like honey, cocoons and lac, while the women sold less valued products like flowers, seeds and fuelwood. This indicates that even if not very stark, there was a slight difference in the positions of men and women among the Baigas, especially in terms of their interaction with the outside economy.

The Baigas were in an interactive relationship with the Agarias, who repaired old sickles and axes for the local peasants in return for grain from these cultivators. The Agaria camped outside the peasant villages of the Baiga and Hindu castes. They were treated as untouchable lower castes by even the Baigas, who otherwise had to buy foodgrains and oil from these people at the time of famine, when their own food production failed. The Agaria were wandering nomads who were considered low in status even by the tribes but who nevertheless were part of the economic network. Thus, interaction with settled cultivators and wandering artisans connected the tribes to a wider economic network, and any myth about them being isolated or self-sufficient gets dispelled by such ethnographic evidence.

The Baigas had a sustainable economy in food production, and they also had an identity as 'kings of the jungle'. Local rulers often let the tribes have sufficient freedom in terms of access to the forest and freedom from paying excessive taxes as these tribes often served as a standby army for these rulers. However, things changed drastically under colonial rule. The British tried to bring most 'free' resources like land, water and forests under their own control. Land settlements in the early and mid-nineteenth century and the enactment of the forest laws in 1878, put restrictions on the Baiga's free access to all forest tracts, and they were restricted to the Baiga Chak and forest villages in the 1890s. Also from the late nineteenth century onwards, non-timber forest produce like lac assumed great importance for the growing European industries, and the colonial administration took away almost three-fourths of the forest from the Baigas.

The Baiga Chak consisted of 22,858 acres of land that was reserved for bewar cutting for the Baigas. The aim was to control the shifting cultivation of the Baigas and keep it regulated as they refused to take to plough cultivation. However, there are records of Baigas protesting the loss of land and the consequent insufficiency for maintaining a sustainable fallow period. The failure of bewar under these restricted conditions forced the Baigas to settle in the forest villages as labour providers for the colonial capitalist extraction of forest produce. As reported by Prasad (2004: 129), 'there were 454 forest villages in the Province by the turn of the century'. The people who were allowed to settle in these villages were, like the Baigas, knowledgeable about the forest, and they were solely responsible for extracting and exchanging forest produce.

By the late nineteenth century, some forest products assumed great commercial value for the growing industries in Europe and the local produce entered world markets. This induced the British to bring in their own commercial, technological and business entrepreneurs into the forest economy. The Baigas and Gonds then began to work directly for firms like Jardine and Skinner who set up their processing industries right next to the forests that provided the raw materials. There was thus a direct induction of the tribals into the world economic market. It is to be noted that although the British tried to introduce machine technology into the extraction products of value like lac, these methods failed. The time-tested processes used by the tribes proved to be most productive, though under controlled management by outside agents. By the 1930s and 1940s, labour became the main source of subsistence for the tribes living in the forest areas, and the near complete destruction of their original subsistence base had been achieved by the intrusion of colonial administration and market economy into their lives.

The tribals remained the poorest of the poor and did not benefit in any way from the rising commercial values of forest products, the profits being pocketed largely by firms and contractors. The Baigas were reduced to slave labour from being the 'kings' of the forest.

The postcolonial era has seen further pauperisation of tribes and further loss of their original subsistence base. The Indian government has taken an even less benign view of the tribes living in the forest, and most 'development' efforts have been directed towards pushing them out of the forests and their livelihood practices, forcing them into the 'mainstream' of the nation's life. Thus, just like in the case of pastoralism, shifting cultivation is also not seen as compatible with a market economy and a capitalist state. Yet the ethnographies of these people show that they have never been completely cut off from either. The state, however, perceives that common ownership of land and the inability to expand capital assets reduce the tax paid to the state. The subsistence-based self-sufficient economy is not conducive to the aggressive cash-based market activities that the state wishes to promote. In the Northeast, for example, the state, both central and local, has been pushing for settled cultivation to replace shifting cultivation. In Mizoram, the land under shifting cultivation has steadily reduced in favour of settled agriculture, from 68,114 hectares in 1997–98 to 28,562 hectares in 2010–11. Although this has marginally increased the forest cover, the quality of the environment has not substantially improved.

Politically, shifting cultivation has been associated with a segmentary or descent group-based political organisation, where the resource-holding clans are like equivalent segments that compete with each other. The tribe may not have any hierarchy but is composed of these horizontal rather than vertical divisions. As long as the segmentary nature of the tribe is maintained, there are internal mechanisms to balance the demography and resources of the descent groups so that they remain approximately equal (Evans-Pritchard 1940). Nowadays, with most tribes under external rule and integrated into larger democracies, the agency and independence of the clans are curtailed to some extent, for example, internecine warfare, though for administrative and ritual purposes the clan organisations may still function.

Under economic and political compulsions, the greatest loss is of the way of life or lifeworld of tribes, which was sustained by a certain mode of livelihood. As mentioned for pastoralism, it is not only an economy and technology, but also a world view associated with values of environmental sustainability. The value for nature as a lifeworld and not simply a commodity is an important aspect of tribal lifestyles. Community ownership of resources prevents internal fragmentation and the stratification of society, although it fails to generate revenue for the state. As in the case of the Maler, described earlier, even individual ownership does not produce radical stratification as there is hardly any capital accumulation. We shall return to some of these issues in Chapter 6.

PERMANENT CULTIVATION

This mode of cultivation gives rise to some important technological transformations from the earlier modes of livelihoods. First, it involves a permanent man–land relationship, where one individual and his/her household are associated with one piece of land over generations. This leads to an attachment to land as not seen in the modes of livelihood discussed earlier. Land becomes ritualised and sacred, as reflected in fertility cults and the deification of the earth as a mother goddess, which emerged with the advent of the agricultural revolution. The concept of private property has greater chances of developing in this mode, although for many centuries permanent cultivation arose and persisted in association with the feudal system, where the land notionally belongs to the lord of the manor (as in England) or to chiefs and lords—non-producers who lived off the labour of the tillers who were tenant farmers. The tribes that shifted to permanent cultivation often did so for ecological reasons, although in evolutionary terms, the transformation to permanent cultivation also sowed the seeds for the transformation of the political system to that of the state.

In many tribal societies, there is a mixture of shifting cultivation and settled cultivation, practised primarily according to the availability of water, condition of the soil and the needs of the society. In India, tribes were distinguished from Hindu peasants largely in terms of social organisation. While Hindus were stratified into castes and followed the *jajmani* system, tribes, even when they practised settled cultivation, did not have the same kind of political and social organisation as the caste Hindus. The tribes of central India, like the Gonds and the Santals, have been practising settled cultivation, but they have maintained their distinct political and social organisations.

Permanent cultivation has many varieties, ranging from dry grain cultivation (without irrigation) to wet cultivation (with permanent irrigation). The former is rain-dependent and is usually found in tribal areas where labour is organised on the basis of mutual cooperation rather than coercion by a centralised authority. Dry cultivation is less productive, supports a low-density population and produces a lower surplus. Wet cultivation requires elaborate systems of irrigation, and some tribes have managed to create some technological marvels for irrigation, like the Apatani of Arunachal Pradesh. Interestingly the Apatanis, who were first studied by Fürer-Haimendorf in the years 1945 and 1946, when he was acting as Special Officer of the Subansiri region for the government of Assam, have a mixed economy depending upon the nature of the land under cultivation. What had struck Fürer-Haimendorf at that time was their organised village structure and sedentary lifestyle based on elaborate wet-rice cultivation. In his work, *The Apa Tanis and Their Neighbours: A Primitive Civilisation of the Eastern Himalayas* (1962), he provides a comprehensive and accurate description of this mode of cultivation in a tribal region. Fürer-Haimendorf was impressed by the fact that the Apatanis were surrounded by shifting cultivating people like the Dafla, Miri and Abor, and had yet created and managed elaborate systems of irrigation based on the cutting of channels from the high-altitude streams that flooded their fields on a permanent basis. Terraces that were higher up and could not be flooded were used for sowing different varieties of rice. The Apatani, who lived in a valley (at less than 5,000 feet) embedded between mountains that rose to heights of 8,000 feet, occupied an area of about 20 square miles, in which they had seven closely packed villages, each within an hour's walk from each other. The villages had houses built on stilts from bamboos and thatched with rice stalks. The houses of the rich were near a wide street and the common meeting areas of the village, while those of the poor were huddled at the back of the village. As also described by Geertz (1963), rice terraces are highly labour-intensive and are owned by individuals. Thus, permanent cultivation is more often than not associated with permanently cultivated and individually owned plots of land. At the time of Fürer-Haimendorf's study, the rice terraces were very valuable and could be bought and sold only by exchanging with *mithans* (local variety of cattle),which were comparably valued. The value of mithans was not just in economic terms, but they had, and continue to have, high ritual and social value. Since the Apatanis had private property, they also had inheritance rules by which land and houses were more or less equally distributed between the sons of a man, that is, inheritance was patrilineal.

The rice fields were not the only kind of property individually owned; most families had their own bamboo groves, with some pine and fruit trees that were fenced with high enclosures and had padlocked doors. Bamboo was the primary house-building material and also used for making storage baskets. If a poor household did not have its own bamboo grove, they would have to walk a long distance to reach a wild forest of bamboos. Most houses had neatly maintained and properly fenced kitchen gardens in which vegetables, maize and tobacco were grown. There were patches of land on which a green leafy vegetable was grown, from which Apatanis made a black salt known as Apatani salt. And there were dry patches of land, also individually owned but much less valued, on which millets were grown. These were the patches that were rain fed and not irrigated. But most important were the wave after wave of rice fields, with their dams and terraces and channels of water supply that led Fürer-Haimendorf (1962: 15) to write that 'however far the eye reaches, there is not spot in this valley which does not show the traces of man's controlling hand'.

The villages had granaries, mostly situated on the outskirts, built on stilt-like houses in which rice was stored immediately after harvest. These were individually owned by the households. The second category of property, apart from the individually held houses, granaries, gardens, groves and irrigated fields, were the clan lands. These consisted of the public assembly grounds, burial grounds, pastures and forests where the clan members could hunt and trap animals and where useful trees were planted. Some of these lands, even the ones individually owned, were scattered and people would have different plots of land located in different areas. This also happened because land was continuously being bought and sold. Clan property, unlike individually owned property, was collectively accessed and jointly held. The common lands of the villages were only the wild forests that were located just above 1,500 feet of the mountain slopes.

Unlike the Shan people who practised wet-rice cultivation in the Burmese valley and developed a state system on the foundation of their mode of cultivation (Leach 1954), the Apatani did not develop a proper state because of their small size and limited land resources. However, the Apatani did have internal stratification into the rich and the poor, and they also practised the capture of slaves from nearby tribes as well as from the plains of Assam. These slaves were kept as members of the family, and many of them were able to set up their own households and gather some wealth so as to lead independent lives.

Both men and women need to work on the maintenance of irrigated terraces. As described by Geertz (1963), wet-rice cultivation can almost infinitely increase its level of production by intensifying the input of labour. In a process that he calls agricultural involution (as opposed to evolution), wet-rice cultivation tends to become more and more labour-intensive, thereby supporting a larger population, the needs of which again give rise to more labour inputs. Thus, increasing population and increasing labour requirements move along in an involuted spiral. However, if populations increase beyond a point, the level of subsistence falls and there may be poverty rather than prosperity in spite of the high input of labour. Such conditions of high population density do not appear to have happened among the Apatani, who led fairly contented lives. But there was the division of the rich and the poor, and there were mechanisms by which the rich became poor and vice versa. Illness depleted wealth for it required the sacrifice of mithans, their numbers for sacrifice increasing as per the scale of severity of the illness. If a man had too many sons, he would have to look for additional land to build them houses. Usually most families had additional plots of land that could be used as and when required. If a person was captured by the neighbouring Dafla, then a large number of mithans needed to be paid as ransom. Thus, the fortunes of individuals rose and fell just like in more complex, market-driven societies. Inequality was a way of life among the Apatani, and this indicates that irrigation usually paves the way for a more complex social organisation to develop.

The tools used for wet-rice cultivation by the Apatani were simple: an iron hoe and a flat wooden spatula for breaking the ground, mixing the earth and taking the earth out to be transported elsewhere. Weeding and planting of rice saplings was done mainly by women, as it is in almost all rice-producing economies. According to Wolf (1966), the peasantry emerges not with any particular technology, but when society is anchored to another in a politically subjugated manner. Thus, only when a community pays rent or tribute to a higher power holder, can it be described as peasant. Otherwise, it remains a folk (or tribal) society.

Fürer-Haimendorf described the Apatanis' system of wet cultivation nearly 70 years back. Yet, even today, most people in Arunachal Pradesh grow their own rice even if they are educated and well employed. During a visit to Itanagar, the state capital, in 2013, I was invited to dinner by a family where the head of the family was an engineer. When we sat down to dinner, the wife of the engineer told me that the rice I was served was produced by them with their own hands in their village. Most tribal individuals from the villages, even when they get educated and move to urban areas for work, do not give up on their traditional food-producing methods; they still cultivate rice and herd mithans. However, some changes have taken place, for instance, money is used as a mode of exchange today rather than mithan and pigs. But these animals are still raised as a source of wealth, prestige and food, and for ritual purposes. The traditional irrigation methods are still used in Arunachal Pradesh, and the complex systems of cutting channels and making dams persist. Some innovations like cemented channels instead of bamboo ones are being introduced, but they have their disadvantages as well as advantages. The way of life associated with a subsistence economy persists in tribal pockets all over India. In some regions, the changes are more than in others, but wherever there has been a change, it is more due to outside interventions rather than an inner motivation to change. This is not to say that the tribal people see no change as welcome. Education and jobs in urban areas have become priorities; yet, such changes have not always initiated changes in basic lifestyles in the villages. An assistant professor at University of Delhi told me how she still participates in rice cultivation when she visits her home in Arunachal Pradesh. Similar narratives exist in other parts of India as well. In Kinnaur, a young woman told me that her doctor husband was in the city and that she would join him only after all the work on their family's agricultural fields was done with.

The Badagas of Nilgiris can be taken as another example of a 'tribe' that has turned to cash-cropping and a changed lifestyle, where they now resemble advanced peasants rather than shifting cultivators. The Badagas are classified as a tribe primarily because of their well-known symbiotic relationship—taken as a primary example of such 'symbiosis' in anthropological literature—with other tribes of this region such as the Todas, Kotas and Kurumbas. Their closest ties are with the Kota villagers (Hockings 1999: 31) who provide music at Badaga weddings and funerals, and 'who regularly furnished the Badagas with pottery, carpentry, thatching, and most leather and metal items'. In return, the Kotas are provided with a portion of the harvest of the Badagas. While the Kotas, Irulas and Kurumbas were treated as lower than the Badagas, the pastoral Todas were considered the Badagas' equal [see Walker (1986) for the complex relationship between the two]. However, since the mid-twentieth century, the population of the Badagas has increased exponentially, and they have also modernised much more than their neighbouring tribes. They are no longer into the barter relationships of the past.

The Badagas have adopted several European crops including tea cultivation and are now using machines to make terraces as well as using all other trappings of modern agriculture like chemical fertilisers and lorry transport. They are now maintaining standards appropriate for participating in world markets. Interestingly, before they began to practise shifting cultivation on the slopes of the Nilgiri Hills, they migrated from the north of the Mysore state, where during the medieval times they were settled cultivators. Their migration was driven by the destruction of the Vijayanagar Empire by Muslim invasions in 1565 AD. Thus, we have another example of a people who changed over from settled cultivation to shifting cultivation under historical circumstances and then transitioned to modern farming with changing times. Such examples clearly indicate that livelihood patterns are not fixed but are dynamic and adaptive to changing circumstances.

URBAN AND INDUSTRIAL SOCIETIES

Not everyone who belongs to a tribe is still a part of the paleotechnic economy—industrialisation has profoundly affected tribes, especially with the spread of such activities in their own regions, for example, coal mining in the Santhal Parganas (in present-day Jharkhand) since the nineteenth century and the establishment of the Tata industrial hub in Jamshedpur. Such developments have forced tribes out of their traditional subsistence economy to enter paid employment, often as low-level menial workers in factories. Slowly, some of them have become educated, but the harsh impact of mining and deforestation, and the forcible takeover of tribal lands, especially in central and southern India, has come to a head. Tribal protests and extreme left insurgencies have marked these regions, which have now been dubbed as the 'Red Corridor'. Many of the tribal agitations have met with harsh state retaliation, which is discussed in detail in Chapter 6.

Most tribal areas are rich in minerals that are coveted by the developing, industrial capitalist economy, which is now global in its expansion. Regions such as Chhattisgarh, Jharkhand, and the tribal belts of West Bengal, Odisha and Andhra Pradesh have all seen the impact of industrialisation and mining (Padel and Das 2010).

The transformation to an urban and industrialised economy involves not merely a change in livelihood, but rather a change in world view. Changing lifestyles and participation in the urban economy, getting formal education, getting jobs and moving to the city have not resulted in overnight transformations of world views. In Kinnaur and in Garhwal, my field experiences have shown that even if people go to megacities like New Delhi and Mumbai for work, their lives in their villages remain relatively unaffected. Since most young tribals are first-generation participants in the urban economy, they have parents and family that are still carrying on traditional occupations. In many places, women keep the family gardens and livelihoods going, while the men shift to the city. When changes have occurred over several generations, then there are chances of a reversal to the old ways as a part of identity politics.

In the tribal villages, the old ways are slowly transforming. Dress patterns are changing as are some food habits. Most of the staple daily food remains the same, but cola drinks and chips are add-ons, especially for the young. One can see large dish antennas over the roofs of many houses and mobile phones are ubiquitous, although the signals are usually poor. Gas cylinders are seen being lugged over mountainsides, although most household fuel is still collected from forests. Some tribal villages may look more prosperous, like the Angami Naga villages that are part of the city of Kohima. But there too the essential aspects of the village—close community life, consensual decision-making and marking of boundaries against outsiders—continue to prevail.

It is those tribes that live in close proximity to non-tribes, like the Bhils in the villages of Udaipur, that are the worst off. They are made to live like second-grade citizens, while the upper-caste Hindus dominate their lives. Occupationally, these tribes are mostly reduced to doing wage labour or petty servile work. A few manage to get education but face stiff resistance from the high-caste Hindus, like Brahmins and Rajputs, who do not want the tribes to compete with them. However, these caste groups also depend on the tribes for some essential services as well as the performance of rituals.

A key outcome of urbanisation and diversification of occupations has been the internal stratification of tribes. While those dependent on permanent cultivation like the Apatanis and the Khasis have always been internally stratified, those tribes that had only community-held resources are now building up individual property through alternative non-traditional occupations.

SUMMARY

In this chapter, we examined the various modes of livelihood practised by tribes, many of which also illustrate how tribes have adapted to various ecological zones over centuries of human evolution. Many of these modes of adaptation, such as cultivation and even pastoralism, may not be exclusive to tribes but are also followed by others, for instance, peasants. According to Wolf (1966), the difference between a peasant society and a folk (or tribe) group is that the former is part of a larger urban state or society to which it pays rent. A tribe is recognised by its independent status, both politically and economically. It is supposed to have evolved independently, but in real terms, most tribes have been parts of kingdoms and states, for example, the Bhils of Rajasthan have traditionally been under the patronage of royal houses and feudal lords. The isolation of tribes is a myth, although they have often kept themselves from accepting the hierarchy of the societies in whose proximity they have lived for decades or centuries. In India, tribes have been identified as those communities that do not subscribe to the Hindu caste system, though there are exceptions. For instance, in Kinnaur, communities identified as tribes self-identify as Rajputs, a Hindu upper caste, but they do not believe in Brahmins and do not rely upon them to perform rituals, nor do they follow any of the norms or rituals of caste Hindus.

What sets tribes apart is mostly their self-identification and a desire to not be merged with the mainstream. Those identified as tribes by the administration engage in a variety of livelihood practices. The following practices are closely identified with tribes:

1. They are mostly subsistence economies, and even when they are linked to a market economy, most daily requirements including medicines and herbs are locally produced or collected.
2. They have a special relationship with nature and their habitat, including the non-humans, trees, rivers and animals, which is based upon the principle of unity of the living world.
3. There is no separation of the field of economy or subsistence from that of the social and the ritual world.
4. There is rarely a production of surplus directed towards the creation and reproduction of stratification. In other words, most tribes are largely egalitarian, and even if inequality of some sort exists, it rarely crystallises into actual class differentiation. However, when tribes urbanise and modernise, such stratification tends to emerge.

5. Most subsistence resources such as water, pastures and forests are accessed by membership to the community and are not individually owned. It is rare or impossible for a tribal person in her/his habitat to be blocked from the essential life-giving resources.
6. Tribes have a technology based on a direct relationship between the producer and the product so that a people have a sense of creation and ownership over what they make, produce or procure. Cooperation and sharing are cherished values that make survival possible even where there is an overall scarcity of resources.
7. The influx of markets and the destruction of their habitats as well as the introduction of market-based values such as commodification of resources are posing threats to the tribal economies and ways of life.
8. Even with urbanisation, formal education and cash economies, many tribes still retain most of their values and still cherish their traditional lifeworlds.

REFERENCES

Bird-David, Nurit. 1999. '"Animism" Revisited: Personhood, Environment, and Relational Epistemology', *Current Anthropology*, 40 (1): 567–92.

Chang, Cynthia. 1982. 'Nomads without Cattle: East African Foragers in Historical Perspective', in Eleanor Leacock and Richard Lee (eds), *Politics and History in Band Societies*, pp. 269–82. Cambridge: Cambridge University Press.

Channa, Subhadra Mitra. 2013. *The Inner and Outer Selves: Cosmology, Gender, and Ecology at the Himalayan Borders*. New Delhi: Oxford University Press.

Evans-Pritchard, E. E. 1940. *The Nuer: A Description of the Modes of Livelihood and Political Institutions of a Nilotic People*. Oxford: Clarendon Press.

Fürer-Haimendorf, Christoph von. 1962. *The Apa Tanis and Their Neighbours: A Primitive Civilisation of the Eastern Himalayas*. London: Routledge and Kegan Paul.

Gardner, Peter M. 1988. 'Pressures for Tamil Propriety in Paliyan Social Organization', in Tim Ingold, David Riches and James Woodburn (eds), *Hunters and Gatherers: History, Evolution and Social Change*, pp. 91–107. Oxford: Berg.

Geertz, Clifford. 1963. *Agricultural Involution: The Processes of Ecological Change in Indonesia*. California: University of California Press.

Godelier, Maurice. 1986. *The Making of Great Men: Male Domination and Power among the New Guinea Baruya*. Cambridge: Cambridge University Press.

Goodale, Jane C. 1971. *Tiwi Wives*. Seattle: University of Washington Press.

Grimm, John A. (ed.). 2001. 'Introduction', in *Indigenous Traditions and Ecology*, pp. *xxxiii–lvii*. Harvard: Harvard University Press.

Hockings, Paul. 1999. *Kindreds of the Earth: Badaga Household Structure and Demography*. New Delhi: Sage Publications.

Leach, E. R. 1954. *Political Systems of Highland Burma: A Study of Kachin Social Structure*. London: G. Bell and Sons.

Lee, Richard B. 1976. '!Kung Spatial Organisation: An Ecological and Historical Perspective', in Richard B. Lee and I. Devore (eds), *Kalahari Hunter-Gatherers: Studies of the !Kung San and Their Neighbours*, pp. 73–98. Cambridge, MA: Harvard University Press.

Lee, Richard B., and I. Devore (eds). 1968. *Man the Hunter*. Chicago: Aldine.

Meillassoux, C. 1981. *Maidens, Meal and Money: Capitalism and the Domestic Community*. Cambridge: Cambridge University Press.

Morris, Brian. 1982. 'The Family, Group Structuring and Trade among South-Indian Hunter-gatherers', in Eleanor Leacock and Richard Lee (eds), *Politics and History in Band Societies*, pp. 171–88. Cambridge: Cambridge University Press.

Morrison, Kathleen. 2006. 'Environmental History, the Spice Trade, and the State in South India', in Gunnar Cederlof and K. Sivaramakrishna (eds), *Ecological Nationalisms: Nature, Livelihoods and Identities in South Asia*, pp. 43–64. Ranikhet: Permanent Black.

Padel, Felix and Samarendra Das. 2010. *Out of This Earth: East India Adivasis and the Aluminium Cartel*. New Delhi: Orient BlackSwan.

Prasad, Archana. 2004. 'Reinterpreting Tribal Livelihood Systems: Underdevelopment and the Local Political Economy in Central India, 1800–1940', in B. B. Chaudhuri and Arun Bandopadhyay (eds), *Tribes, Forest and Social Formation in Indian History*, pp. 109–42. New Delhi: Manohar Publications.

Radhakrishna, Meena. 2012. 'Thought for Food: Starvation among Forest-dependent Communities', in Dev Nathan and Virginius Xaxa (eds), *Social Exclusion and Adverse Inclusion: Development and Deprivation of Adivasis in India*, pp. 145–55. New Delhi: Oxford University Press.

Ramakrishnan, P. S. 1992. *Shifting Agriculture and Sustainable Development: An Interdisciplinary Study from North-Eastern India*. Carnforth, UK: Parthenon Publishing Group.

Roy, S. C. 1912. *The Mundas and Their Country*. Calcutta: Kuntaline Press.

Saberwal, Vasant K. 1999. *Pastoral Politics: Shepherds, Bureaucrats, and Conservation in the Western Himalayas*. New Delhi: Oxford University Press.

Sahlins, Marshall. 1972. *Stone Age Economics*. Chicago: Aldine.

Sati, Vishwambhar Prasad and P. Rinawma. 2014. 'Practice of Shifting Cultivation and its Implication in Mizoram, North-East India: A Review of Existing Research', *Nature and Environment*, 19 (2): 179–87.

Singh, Neera M. 2004. 'Women and Community Forests in Orissa: Rights and Management', in Sumi Krishna (ed.), *Livelihood and Gender: Equity in Community Resource Management*, pp. 306–24. New Delhi: Sage Publications.

Steward, Julian. 1955. *Theory of Culture Change: The Methodology of Multilinear Evolution.* Chicago: University of Illinois Press.

———. 2008. 'The Great Basin Shoshone Indians: An Example of Family Level of Socio-cultural Integration', in Michael R. Dove and Carol Carpenter (eds), *Environmental Anthropology: A Historical Reader*, pp. 168–80. Malden, MA: Blackwell Publishing. (Condensed from the original essay, 'Basin-Plateau Aboriginal Sociopolitical Groups', 1938, *Bureau of American Ethnology Bulletin*, 120: 1–316.)

Vidyarthi, L. P. 1963. *The Maler: A Study in Nature-Man-Spirit Complex of a Hill Tribe.* Calcutta: Bookland.

Walker, Anthony. 1986. *The Todas of South India: A New Look.* Delhi: Hindustan Publishing House.

———. 2004. 'The Truth about the Todas', *Frontline*, 21 (5): 18–23.

Wiessner, Polly. 1982. 'Risk, Reciprocity and Social Influences on !Kung San Economics', in E. Leacock and R. B. Lee (eds), *Politics and History in Band Societies*, pp. 61–84. Cambridge, MA: Cambridge University Press.

Woodburn, James. 1968. 'An Introduction to Hadza Ecology', in Richard B. Lee and I. Devore (eds), *Man the Hunter*, pp. 41–56. Chicago: Aldine.

———. 1988. 'African Hunter-Gatherer Social Organization: Is It Best Understood as a Product of Encapsulation?', in Tim Ingold, David Riches and James Woodburn (eds), *Hunters and Gatherers: History, Evolution and Social Change*, pp. 31–64. Oxford: Berg.

Wolf, Eric. 1966. *Peasants.* Englewood Cliffs: Prentice Hall.

SUGGESTED READINGS

Black-Michaud, Jacob. 1986. *Sheep and Land: The Economics of Power in a Tribal Society.* Cambridge: Cambridge University Press.

Brower, Barbara Anne. 1991. *Sherpa of Khumbu: People, Livestock, and Landscape.* New Delhi: Oxford University Press.

Cohen, Yehudi A. (ed.). 1968. *Man in Adaptation: The Cultural Present.* Chicago: Aldine.

Coon, Charleton S. 1976. *The Hunting Peoples.* Harmondsworth: Pelican Books.

Croll, Elisabeth and David Parkin (eds). 1992. *Bush Base: Forest Farm-culture, Environment and Development.* London: Routledge.

Ninan, K. N. 1992. 'Economics of Shifting Cultivation in India', *Economic and Political Weekly*, 27 (13): A2–A6.

Sharma, Vijay Pal, Ilse Kohler-Rollofson and John Morton. 2003. 'Pastoralism in India: A Scoping Study', Centre for Management in Agriculture, Indian Institute of Management Ahmedabad and League for Pastoral People and Natural Resources Institute, University of Greenwich, UK.

Skaria, Ajay. 1999. *Hybrid Histories: Forests, Frontiers and Wildness in Western India.* New Delhi: Oxford University Press.

4

RELIGION AND WORLD VIEW

HIGHLIGHTS

- Classical views on tribal religions
- Contemporary views of religion and cosmology
- Conversions and the politics of religion
- Revivalist movements and identity politics

INTRODUCTION

Religion has always been viewed as primary to the existence of the Homo sapiens and an institution that is specific to only humans. Religion goes beyond sensory perceptions as well as the basic needs of food, shelter and sex. By its very definition, religion involves beliefs and thoughts about the otherworldly as well as what Rudolph Otto (1923) has called the numinous, the extrasensory, as opposed to the sensory realities of the phenomenological world. It involves that aspect of the brain that is capable of abstract thought and the capacity to imagine and move beyond the obvious. Anthropologists from Durkheim onwards have put forward various ways of defining and studying religion. There have been theories that explain the origins of religion, while others explain its functions as well as dysfunctions for society; some have called it an illusion and some have recognised it as real in an ontological way. Anthropologists have been particularly interested in the symbolic aspects of religion and how these symbols are interwoven with the overall social and cultural context in which they arise.

Since anthropology is a subject rooted in colonial history and circumstances, the early phase of the discipline was theorised mostly by White Europeans, who only regarded their own religion, namely, Christianity as the true religion and all others as irrational beliefs or superstitions. These early anthropologists also speculated that those regarded as 'primitive' and/or tribal had forms of practices and beliefs that indicated their incapacity for higher abstract thinking, which forms the metaphysical foundation of the higher or universal religions. Tribal religions were seen as more instrumental and less philosophical. However, as anthropologists came into contact with real societies, they were convinced that the beliefs and practices of tribes were of value and had functions. In contemporary times, there is a growing understanding that religion may be linked to ontological realities and is not merely a set of speculations or imagined states. This chapter will examine various theories about tribal religions, which are contextualised within the development of anthropological theory.

The institutions of family, marriage and kinship, and those of religion and magic have been regarded as universal human institutions, almost from the beginnings of the discipline. These aspects of human society were the first to form the subject matter of study of the earliest scholars of human society and culture. From evolutionary theory to the most contemporary perspectives, religion remains at the core of anthropological thinking.

ANIMISM, TOTEMISM AND MAGIC

Edward B. Tylor (1871), known as the father of social anthropology, devoted himself to the study of the origin and evolution of religion, taking as his basic premise the postulate of 'psychic unity of mankind'. He assumed that the so-called primitives, the humans at the dawn of civilisation, would have the same thought process as modern-day humans, being of the same species; but they would have lacked the technological expertise of civilised humans (by which he meant nineteenth-century Europeans). Tylor postulated the existence of eternal questions to which humans sought answers, since they were sentient beings with the capacity for reflexive thinking. The eternal

Tylor postulated the existence of eternal questions to which humans sought answers, questions about life and death, dreams and awakening, nature of the world and the mystic realities of natural phenomenon. He termed this belief in spirit or soul 'Animism'.

questions about life and death, about dreams and awakening, about the nature of this world and the mystic realities of the natural phenomenon would have led him to the belief in a non-sensory or spirit body, which evolved into a full-fledged belief in spirit or soul—what Tylor termed 'Animism'.

The early humans reasoned that the life-force or anima resided in something unseen and unknowable, and it left the physical body when a person died. Its temporary sojourns outside the body led to a state of sleep, where one could feel that one was doing many things, while the body lay inert and unmoving. One could speculate that the early humans believed that it is the soul or spirit whose adventures or experiences are recalled by us as dreams. In death, the spirit departs the body, and different cultures believe in varying destinations for the departed soul. While belief in ghosts, ancestral spirits, heaven and hell, the abode of the dead and rebirth, and suchlike, vary from society to society, every society has at its core the belief in a dual body—one material and another non-material. From this primary faith in the existence of the soul, humans built further notions and beliefs like heaven and hell, rebirth and ancestor worship. Since beings other than humans also seemed animate or had life in them, they too went through the cycles of birth, growth and death; the concept of soul or anima was extended to the non-human world of animals, plants and also entire landscapes like mountains and forests (Evans-Pritchard 1965).

In India there are tribes, like the Bhotiyas of Uttarkashi, who believe that the trees of the forest are *devta*s (gods). The Nagas believe that stones have life, and there are tribes in the Northeast and elsewhere who think that the same soul can exist in both an animal and a human, so that a human can change into animal form and vice versa. Forests and streams are believed to be alive and animate and seen as life-giving and sustaining. Animals are related to humans in terms of kinship and so on.

Vitebsky (1993: 52) has described the concept of consciousness among the Soras (Saoras) of Odisha: 'Consciousness is essentially fluid and in one sense it takes on form and identity by filling a bounded space . . . it is clear that a person's boundary is important, at least when it is conceptualised in terms of the person's body.' He further writes,

'In living animals, humans and even plants, soul animates the body. It is contained in the blood and is said to be like the shadow or photograph of the body, in other words, it takes the same form and occupies the same space as the body' (ibid.). The Soras believe that the soul occupies the centre of the body, like the liver. Their belief is similar to that of the Bhotiyas who believe that the life-force or *neeng* is located in the navel (Channa 2013).

Frazer (1922), a classical evolutionist, had graded entire societies into three stages of beliefs and practices, namely, magic, religion and science. According to him, the more primitive people were incapable of higher spirituality as found in religious doctrines and were instead pragmatic self-seekers, who tried to apply the same means–end practices as we find in modern science, though without the benefit of scientific knowledge. They too followed laws of nature like science, primarily identified as laws of sympathetic magic. Basically, these laws were based on influence through association, that is, through either the law of similarity or the law of contact.

Although tribal people across the world have animistic beliefs, such beliefs are also found in universal religions like Hinduism, Buddhism and even Christianity. Even if these beliefs are not part of the core doctrines of the religion, they constitute an essential aspect of the folk or day-to-day beliefs of the people. Buddhism, for example, in its most esoteric form does not believe in god and is recognised as a non-theistic religion. Yet Buddhists, in Burma, for instance, believe in a range of spirits and superhuman beings, of both benevolent and malevolent nature (Spiro 1967). These beings are made offerings and worshipped on an almost daily basis. The local Buddhist pantheon incorporates a large number of Hindu deities as well as many regional spirits, and it is complemented by beliefs in witchcraft and sorcery. Similarly, Hinduism too has many animistic beliefs.

Totemism has been regarded by many Western scholars as a primary religion of humankind, and many speculative theories of human origins are rooted in totemic practices and beliefs, the most recognised being Freud's work *Totem and Taboo* (1913). Durkheim (1995 [1912]) studied the Australian Aborigines and their totemistic practices, making a transition from an evolutionist to a functionalist perspective. In India, well-formed totemistic clans of the kind described for the Australian

Aborigines have not been reported. Many central Indian tribes like the Munda and the Oraon did have clans or kinship lineages named after birds and animals, but under Hindu influence, these social formations were often converted into *gotra*. Roy (1912) had reported that the *killi* (clan-like kinship groups) of the Munda were often associated with animals and birds like snakes, tortoises and sparrows, and in each case there was a myth to explain why the particular Munda group was grateful or obliged to that species, which was given as the reason for their protecting and not killing that species. However, even at the time of Roy's writing, many such killi were claiming to be Hindu gotras by changing their names. Roy was writing at a time when concepts such as totemism were yet to develop, and evolutionary theory was predominant. Tribal attempts to convert their totemic clans to gotras may be seen as a movement towards Hinduisation. The difference between clan and gotra is that the latter are always ancestral humans and not plants, animals and other beings of nature. The Hindus treat gotras as exogamous units just like clans, but there are no rituals specific to the gotra as there are for the totemic clans, and the gotras are not subjected to taboos of the kinds found in totemism either.

Durkheim was the first to put forward the theory that religious beliefs and rituals are functional in maintaining social solidarity. He was the precursor of the theory of cultural relativism, which rejected the theory of stages of evolution and the consequent labelling of some communities as 'primitive'. The functionalist perspective focused on the role of each institution in maintaining what it termed as 'social equilibrium'. The functionalist school rejected the theory of stage-by-stage evolution by deeming such stages as speculative and not based on any rational criteria. It also considered the search for origins as fruitless as it was near impossible to get to the origin of human life, the sequences of which are yet to be established properly. More importantly, as Paul Radin argued in his book, *Primitive Man as Philosopher* (1927),

Durkheim's theory that religious beliefs and rituals are functional in maintaining social solidarity was the precursor of the theory of cultural relativism, which rejected the labelling of certain communities as 'primitive'.

human beings everywhere and at all times are not of one kind, but rather there are all kinds of people in all societies—agnostics, atheists, conservatives, spiritual and ritualistic. Thus, there is no essential difference between the people in one society and another. Radin was responding to the evolutionist's proposition that the so-called primitives were incapable of higher, esoteric forms of religion and that they believed more in pragmatic and instrumental rituals and practices. In the evolutionist perspective, philosophical and metaphysical spiritualism were characteristic of only 'higher' civilisations.

On the ground, many people, not necessarily just the tribal, believe in ideas such as magic, witchcraft and sorcery. Take, for example, the Catholic practice of keeping the relics of saints in their churches. These relics, which are often body parts like a bone or the blood of a saint, are supposed to carry the spiritual essence of sainthood, by the simple rule of association or contact. Because once they were a part of the saint, they still carry the spiritual power of the saint. The practice of wearing amulets or eating prasad (Hindu food offerings to god) follows the same principle. An ordinary sweet becomes sanctified when it is offered or kept in close proximity to the idol of a deity. The sacred properties of the deity are transferred to this sweet, and it is transformed from ordinary food to a prasad and thus becomes holy.

Many people with conservative beliefs do not like being photographed. In villages in the upper Himalayas, old people often indicated to me that they did not wish to have their photographs taken. A photograph is a likeness, and a likeness means that I would have power over the person whose photograph I have taken. A photograph, in other words, could function as a voodoo doll. Therefore, some of the principles described by Frazer (1922) or even by Tylor (1871), such as those of animism, naturism, mana and sympathetic magic, seem to be relevant in explaining many beliefs and practices of most people, and are not just confined to tribes. They seem to be more universal than understood. Weekly forecasts about horoscopes appear in the most modern of newspapers; people wear stones that they believe would influence their lives, a typical example of what Frazer called the magic of contagion. People believe in lucky pens or shirts, avoid unlucky numbers and engage in a host of practices that are nowhere near the rational scientific mindset that Frazer had attributed to the so-called civilised societies. As we examine religious practices and beliefs, the difference between the tribal and the non-tribal becomes more and more blurred, as do the lines dividing what were known as different modes of thought, namely, magical, religious and scientific.

In the colonial period in India, when the first Census was carried out, tribes were identified as tribes on the basis of their 'animistic' beliefs rather than any other criteria. Later, they were identified in terms of having a 'tribal religion', which meant that they were not followers of any of the major religions like Hinduism, Christianity or Islam. However, a look at the list of Scheduled Tribes reveals that many of them were and are still classified as Hindus. There are some who are Muslim and many have converted to Christianity. In fact, the region where there is the densest population of tribes, the northeastern states of Mizoram and Nagaland, we also find the maximum tribes following Christianity. During the colonial period, many tribes were persuaded to identify themselves as Hindus by the nationalist Hindu politicians, and many of them, especially those from central India, like the Bhils, Gonds and Oraons, did so at first. However, as pointed out by Maharatna (2005: 10), 'The motivation for refuting the British stance (namely that tribal people were essentially outside the Hindu caste system) was more nationalist and political than scientific or academic.' After Independence, many of the same people reverted to calling themselves 'tribes' and not Hindus, and the distinction between tribe and caste in peninsular India remains blurred as ever (we have discussed this aspect in Chapter 1).

Differentiating tribes from Hindus has always been problematic, especially as many of them, like the Bhotiyas of Uttarakhand and the Girasias of western India, insist on their self-identification as upper-caste Hindus, even as they are regarded as 'tribes' according to official records. Yet, tribes continue to be recognised as having animistic beliefs (Channa 2013), for example, the Dongria Konds of Odisha worship the Niyamgiri mountain as a god. The difference between Indian tribes and Hindus, who too believe in the sacred nature of mountains (Kailash), rivers (Ganga, Yamuna and Narmada), trees and animals, is slight, which is at the root of the persisting confusion regarding classification.

FUNCTIONALISM AND SYMBOLISM

The functionalist school dominated anthropological theory for a long period and continues to be used sporadically by scholars. Functionalism became a dominant mode of thinking after Durkheim explained the contribution of totemic rituals to the maintenance of social solidarity and social identity. The British school was led by A. R. Radcliffe-Brown who explained rituals and customs, such as taboos, as contributing to the maintenance of what he defined as social structure, the structure of social relationships. He understood relationships in terms of their abstract rules and norms and not in terms of their content. In this way, the British school was known as the structural-functional school as Radcliffe-Brown was followed by Evans-Pritchard, with this functional explanation of witchcraft among the Azande, and an entire generation of scholars trained in this school, including Indian ones like Srinivas. The functionalist school regarded society as analogous to an organism, where each organ of the living body contributed to the functioning of the whole. For the body to survive, it must remain in equilibrium; in other words, they treated change as extraneous to the system. If not disturbed, a society would remain static. This was another theoretical justification for treating tribal societies as ahistorical and static in time and space. The organic analogy also led to the conceptualisation of societies as bounded and enclosed. Malinowski, on the other hand, explained function in terms of the contribution made to the needs of individuals, which he identified as primary, secondary and tertiary needs. He referred to the basic needs of food, shelter and sex as primary; technology and communication were at the second level; and aesthetics and spirituality at the third. But all three aspects are equally necessary for humans to have a healthy social life.

The functionalist school regarded society as a living body, where each organ contributed to its functioning. Malinowski, however, explained function in terms of the basic human needs necessary for a healthy social life.

Let us consider two examples to illustrate these diverse views of functionalism. Radcliffe-Brown had explained the existence of taboos as contributing to the strengthening of relationships essential for the survival of society. For example, before a child is born, the various persons who will have potential relationships with the child are subjected to taboos. This often depended upon the structural closeness of the persons with the unborn baby. The father is usually the one subjected to most taboos and rituals, for although he is not physically pregnant, he has often the most important structural placement with respect to the child. The child in a patrilineal society is responsible for continuing the father's social identity. Fatherhood is made to feel significant to the potential father by the observance of taboos as is common among most tribes but even among non-tribals. Therefore, the explanation of Radcliffe-Brown focuses upon the structural relationship as central to the explanation of function. Malinowski, on the other hand, explained how such taboos and rituals alleviated anxiety or instilled a positive mindset. Among the seafaring community of the Trobrianders, for example, there are many rituals and taboos that pertain to the making of canoes, to fishing and to sea voyages. The more difficult or uncertain a task, the greater the significance of such practices. For example, if a person is going deep-sea fishing, he will perform rituals and observe taboos that will give him solace that he has done enough to compensate for the potential danger and uncertainty of the situation. While fishing in the backwaters, on the other hand, he may not perform any ritual at all. In the same way, Malinowski explained the function of rituals in regulating horticultural activities. One of his most well-known works using this functional method was that of horticultural activities among the Trobriand Islanders and the functional role of magic and other rituals in regulating such activities (Malinowski 1935).

The most important work on an Indian tribe using the structural-functional perspective was that of Radcliffe-Brown (1922) on the Andaman Islanders, also regarded as a classic work of its kind. Radcliffe-Brown has provided an elaborate description of the beliefs and rituals of the Andamanese. The major deities of the Andamanese are the sky god and the wind goddess, who are also husband and wife. The deities have human traits, for example, the female goddess is fickle and temperamental, being as she is the southwest monsoon wind. The northeast monsoon wind, who is her husband, is more predictable and steadier in his behaviour. In this way, the key institution of marriage, that is, the basic unit of all social structure is also the fundamental principle of the creation and existence myths of the Andaman Islanders. In his description of the initiation rituals of the Andamanese, Radcliffe-Brown indicates how these rituals help the young imbibe those values, ethics and principles that would make them well-adjusted adult members of their own society. For example, the foods that are taboo during these rituals are the ones that are the most precious in that part of the world in terms of their food value and the difficulty in procuring them. Through these taboos, the young initiates learn the value of these foods and develop a sense of responsibility towards their use and maintenance. The major contribution of the functional approach was that it rescued tribes from the ignominy of being labelled irrational and childlike by showing the usefulness of all customs and rituals. However, none of these scholars ever said that the tribal people were aware of the functions of their behaviour and gave the entire credit of understanding to the observer/ analyst. In this way, the (mostly) Western scholars did not contribute to actually raising the position of tribes and treated them as being ignorant and backward.

The most obvious flaw of the functionalist approach was that it assumed equilibrium to be the most essential aspect of society. As pointed out by the postcolonial critique of anthropology, such equilibrium was only wishful thinking on the part of the colonial administrators, the image of which anthropologists helped keep up. At the time when Radcliffe-Brown studied the Andamanese, they were already heavily depopulated by the impact of maladies like measles and venereal diseases brought to them by the Europeans. Postcolonial scholars have critiqued functionalists for always emphasising stability and coherence, even when the societies they were studying were ravaged by the impact of colonisation. In referring to the study done on the !Kung bushmen by Richard Lee, Pratt (1986: 49) writes:

> What picture of !Kung would one draw if instead of defining them as survivors of the stone age and a delicate and complex adaptation to the Kalahari desert, one looked at them as survivors of capitalist expansion and a delicate and complex adaptation to three centuries of violence and intimidation.

In the same vein, there has been criticism of the Eurocentric analysis of the indigenous people, where the anthropologist, usually a White male, expected them to interact with the scholar as another White man. Rosaldo (1986: 91) has criticised Evans-Pritchard's interpretation of a Nuer man he met in the field, who was sceptical of Evans-Pritchard's queries about his name and lineage. To Evans-Pritchard, the refusal to answer was an indication of abnormal behaviour, but to Rosaldo, there was a failure on Evans-Pritchard's part to put the reaction in its context. The question was asked just two days after the British government forces had raided camps of the Nuer and taken many of them prisoner. The Nuer were under constant threat from White men, and to look upon another White man with suspicion was only natural under the circumstance. Rosaldo also quotes Evans-Pritchard as he narrates how he resorted to actual participant fieldwork and observation from the door of his tent, when he failed to elicit data by simple interviews. The rich ethnography that Evans-Pritchard later produced was by his constant observation of the Nuer as they went about their daily routine. But Rosaldo comments on the 'lack of accountability to, the political context of his fieldwork' (1986: 91) by the British scholar.

Moving away from the functionalist explanations, the real value of rituals often lay in their innovative dimensions to deal with suffering and marginalisation, or to make the voices of the oppressed felt. Later scholars have demonstrated how some rituals were actually improvised or scaled up as a reaction to colonial oppression. History has played an important role in the transformations of tribal religion, and hence it is important to understand religious practices in terms of their situatedness in real historical conditions. While the functionalist school underlined the context and relative value of rituals, it ended up giving them an ahistorical, timeless character. Much of the recent work on tribal religions has seriously paid attention to historical and spatial contexts. Tribal beliefs and practices are no longer viewed as superstition and tribal world

Recent work on tribal religions has paid attention to historical and spatial contexts. Tribal beliefs and practices are no longer viewed as superstition; tribal world views are considered on a par with those of any other so-called universal religion.

views are seen as relevant cosmologies that are on a par with those of any other so-called universal religion.

In India, the work of Vidyarthi (1963) best exemplifies the application of structural-functional theory to the study of religion among tribes. Vidyarthi is known for his formulation of the nature–man–spirit complex of the Maler and for pointing to the harmonious integration of rituals with the social and economic systems of the hill tribe (see Chapter 3 for more details on Vidyarthi's work).

Several other works on Indian tribes have woven their ethnographies around the concept of religion and have examined the symbolic aspects of rituals and practices. Ghosh (2006) has described the symbolisms of space and time among the Oraon. Writing about the symbolic significance of the most important festival of the Oraon, namely, the Karma celebrated on the eleventh day after the new moon in the month of Bhadon, he argues that the main significance of this festival is to awaken the dormant fields. The fields that are pale yellow in colour when the ceremonies are performed turn into lush green after the performance and become fertile. Ghosh's explanation lies in the symbolic realm and not in the instrumental realm as in the case of the classical functionalists. Descriptions of such rituals to enhance the fertility and productivity of land abound in the literature on Indian tribes, especially the ones that practise agriculture.

Most agricultural tribes of central India show a great affinity with Hinduism, as the Hindu peasants and even local royalty often participate in the tribal festivals. A myth among the Oraons shows their ideological closeness to Hinduism. In the heartland of the Oraon territory is the village of Anjan. This village is supposed to be the birthplace of the mother of the Hindu deity Hanuman, who is the son of Vayu or the wind god. Anjani Devi, Hanuman's mother, is supposed by the locals to be a tribal woman. It is believed that Lord Rama himself visited the village to meet Anjani, after winning the war against Lanka. The tribals in the village shouted, 'O Ram! O Ram!'—this became 'Oraon', giving them their name (Ghosh 2006: 204). Such myths illustrate the process of tribe–caste continuum and also point to the close interaction between Hindu and tribal peasants.

Channa (2005) has also shown how Hindu deities and symbols get mixed up with tribal ones, producing a kind of hybrid mythology that not only shows the linkages between tribals and Hindus, but also their differences as the myths are always rewoven within the tribal symbolic system. The acceptance of Hindu deities and some beliefs among the Bhotiyas is also related to the historical shift in their location from being in close economic and social relationships with Tibetans to coming closer to the Hindu populations of the Indian mainland, mostly in terms of trade and commerce and also through participation in national institutions like schools, colleges and workplaces. But, quite often, the Hindu deities are relocated within the tribal symbolic systems, for example, the Pandavas are incorporated within their cosmology as kuldevta or clan deities. These kuldevta are seen as living social beings part of the day-to-day life of these people, and there is no concept of deities enshrined in temples. In the entire tribal belt of the upper Himalayas, the people interact with their gods as if they were living beings and they do not have any temples with icons in them. At most, they have a concept of 'descent', whereby the deities are believed to descend onto a material object like a palanquin or a drum or into the body of a human medium. For the pastoral people, their animals too are seen as sacred, as is the environment that often gets represented as a sacred landscape.

Walker (1986) has given an elaborate account of the religious symbolism of the Todas and the ritual role played by buffaloes, which are the most sacred objects of the Todas and reside in the sacred dairies that serve as temples. The Todas believe that their supreme goddess created humans and buffaloes together, and they maintain a strict genealogy of the sacred buffaloes (those directly created by their goddess). These sacred dairies and sacred buffaloes are the collective responsibility of the tribe as a whole, and each Toda clan has to make available a dairyman–priest who performs all the rituals in the sacred dairies for one year. All adult Toda men have to take on this service at least once in their lifetime.

Each tribe organises its ritual life and sacred symbols around the most important basis of its livelihood. Thus, the agricultural Oraon focus upon agricultural activities, the shifting cultivators like the Maler, upon the various stages of their cultivation, and the hunter-gatherers upon the forest spirits and the water hole spirits.

Wolf (2005: 6) describes the ritual life of the Kota, a tribe providing ritual music to all its neighbours including the Hindu Tamils, as revolving around their music and the playing of this music. In his symbolic analysis of the two most important rituals of the Kota, namely, the god ceremony comprising the ceremonial complex of the *dur* (god) and the death ceremony that comprises a cremation and a secondary mortuary ceremony. Wolf argues that the god ceremony draws in people from different locations and acts as a centripetal force, while the funeral disperses people at first (centrifugal) but then again draws them together. For a people whose lives depend on their music, these ceremonial complexes involve the most significant musical compositions. Thus, the two ceremonies that involve the greatest investment in time, money and energy of the Kota also incorporate their most significant music.

The Kotas are firm believers in the amalgamation of music and the sacred, and they consider their own music to be especially pleasing to the gods. Even the local Tamil deities and those of adjoining groups, like the Todas and the Badagas, prefer Kota music. Thus, the Kotas have provided music to all adjoining groups for their special occasions, both life cycle rituals and specific ceremonies involving their gods.

Many tribes that practise shamanism have specialist ritual drummers who play an important role in bringing on the trance. The role of the rhythmic music to create an atmosphere conducive to people going into altered states of consciousness has been recognised as well as recorded by many anthropological studies of shamanistic rituals. However, all 'tribal' rituals and beliefs are as rational or as commonsensical as that of other peoples. The tendency to treat tribes as exotic and as 'different' is, therefore, unwarranted, even though it continues to persist.

THE EXOTICISATION OF TRIBAL RITUALS

The evolutionary perspective had incorporated the deep-seated prejudice about tribal rituals and beliefs being 'primitive' and superstitious rather than coeval with universal religions. Although functionalists redeemed the situation by pointing to the function of the tribal beliefs and practices, these were rarely raised above the level of misplaced rationality. Tribes were specifically targeted for practising exotic rituals, as this was seen as a marker of their savage state. Even the caste Hindus supported the European evolutionary ideas as 'they meshed well with South Asian elites' hierarchical attitudes towards people living in forests' (Schendel 2011: 21). At times, such European influence turned around the earlier symbiotic relationship of castes and tribes into a hierarchical and exclusionary one, as in the case of the Konds of Odisha. Padel (2011) has elaborately discussed the so-called (by the British) barbaric practices of human sacrifice and female infanticide by the Konds of Odisha. He located these practices in the context of British colonisation and the Eurocentric views of those who described these rituals. The Konds did not just think of human sacrifice as a ritual but as a core of their sovereign identity. The Kond cosmology is centred around their villages. They believe that their village is the centre of its world. They have their own version of how the earth was created, and how it was inhabited by the first beings. They worship the earth goddess who is responsible for the welfare of their village and community. Human sacrifice is made to appease the earth deity. The Konds are fiercely independent about their identity and dislike any kind of interference.

This kind of village sovereignty and identity is found in the Himalayas as well, where the village deity is like a local sovereign, ruling over his/her subjects. The Kond ritual of human sacrifice is directed towards appeasing this deity who always thirsts for human blood.

The relationship that the Konds have with the persons to be sacrificed is not one of violence or cruelty as it is made to appear. The Konds were certainly not bloodthirsty or inhuman people. The *meriah* or the persons to be sacrificed were bought by the village headman, often procured when they were children, and they lived in the Kond village, forming a part of the household of the village chief. They lived a normal life, doing agricultural and other work. The human sacrifice in one village took place only once in about three years and people from surrounding villages would take away some of the body parts to bury in their own villages, so that they did not have to perform the sacrifice that year. Those who never performed human sacrifice avoided any such body part to be brought to their village as they feared that the earth goddess will demand blood sacrifice if she gets a taste of human blood. This indicates that the Konds did not enjoy the sacrifice and did it only as a compulsion and also as sparingly as possible.

According to Padel (2011: 119), the primary reason Konds sacrifice humans is to replenish the fertility of the earth. Frazer, in his classic work, *The Golden Bough* (1922), first described the Kond human sacrifice as one of the most significant and elaborate instances of human sacrifice found in any society. He calls it a fertility ritual. In most religions, it is recognised that fertility and death are related, as the decaying bodies of the dead replenish the fertility of the earth. According to at least one myth of the Konds, the creator goddess Nirantali was once cutting vegetables and she cut her hand. When her blood fell on the earth, it became excessively fertile and vegetation began to grow in abundance. The goddess wanted to sacrifice herself to increase the fertility of the earth, but the Konds did not want her to do so, and they got a person from outside of the Kond villages for the sacrifice. Even later, the meriah who were bought for sacrifice were never Konds but mostly Dom or other people who were either captured or bought by paying money.

An important aspect of the Kond sacrifice was its patronisation by the local Hindu *rajahs*, who were associated with Konds through this sacrifice. The historical relationship of equality and mutual respect that existed between the tribes and the local rulers is exemplified in this royal patronage and participation in the sacrifice. When the British requested the local rajahs to help them stop the sacrifice, they were reluctant, as they were exercising their symbolic association with the Kond chiefs by their support for their ritual. Also, the practice of human sacrifice was not limited to the tribes, as some Hindu kings also practised it. In the forts of Rajasthan, there are places earmarked for blood sacrifice to the goddess Kali or Durga (according to the locals, human sacrifice also took place there). The Boad kings, who were the ones who considered the Konds as their allies, were also reputed to practise human sacrifice to the goddess Durga. Blood sacrifice is made to the goddess Kali even today at Kalighat in Kolkata, as also to goddesses at many other Hindu shrines.

The dharma of the Hindu king is to uphold existing customs and not make new ones. Respect for other people's traditions has always been a part of the larger Hindu philosophy. When local Hindu chiefs asked Kond chiefs to give up human sacrifice, they made it clear that the order was coming from the British rulers and not from them. Padel mentions how the Hindu rulers of Odisha made a fusion of their own religious practices, such as the establishment of a tribal deity as Lord Jagannath, to negotiate power with the tribal chiefs. 'But the fact that Hindus who lived in the Kond hills readily identified Tari Penu with the goddess Durga when talking to British officials, alerts us to the meaning that the Kond custom held for them' (Padel 2011: 129). Human sacrifice was also a part of the political negotiation of power between the tribal and the Hindu chiefs. Padel further comments that the so-called barbarism of the ritual was described as such by the British to show that the tribes they wished to subdue were already violent and had savage, inhuman customs. He notes that no British person had actually ever seen a human sacrifice and that the British built up much of their gory descriptions through their imagination.

There are several aspects of the sacrifice that must be noted to show that it was as painful for the Konds to take a human life as would be expected from any person with normal human feelings. The first was the distancing of the meriah, as he/she was always bought from outside Kond society (Padel 2011: 133). Also, the sacrificing priest absolved himself of the sin of killing his victim by saying that it was the victim's parents who sold him, that they have been paid and that the sacrifice is made for the sake of the earth goddess, thus establishing himself as only a mediator. The meriah sometimes lived for many years in the Kond villages, and sometimes their child was sacrificed instead of them. While they were treated as equal on a day-to-day basis, just before the sacrifice, they attained the status of a god and were venerated and offered worship. After the sacrifice, the village observed mourning for the death of a human being, and there would be a general feeling of sadness. Padel (2011) also observed that the British had recorded that none of the meriah they had rescued wanted to be freed and that all of them wished to go back to the village from where they were rescued. They were acutely unhappy in British custody and many of them died while in custody.

Padel manages to demonstrate that the violence that the British unleashed and the number of lives that they took far exceeded the violence that was attributed to human sacrifice. The main purpose of the British propaganda of the savagery of human sacrifice was to reinforce the stereotype of tribes as uncivilised and to use this as an excuse to subjugate and annex their sovereignty. 'To be tribe meant to be subordinated to a superior power with a civilizing mission' (Schendel 2011: 21).

As highlighted in other contexts of colonisation, it is also likely that the calamities brought upon tribes because of colonial invasion—the rampant spread of diseases, loss of life and failure of crops due to drought—would have increased the fear among them about the invading outsiders and led them to appease their goddesses and seek succour through more sacrifices. Thus, the British presence among the Konds might have triggered more defensive rituals including blood sacrifices.

THE RELIGIOUS EXPERIENCE

Contemporary anthropologists look upon tribal religious practices and beliefs as neither stages of evolution nor specifically goal-oriented pragmatic practices. The religious experience is recognised as a universal human experience that happens in response to an extra-human reality beyond the capacity of ordinary human capacities to fathom. Tribes or indigenous people are no different when it comes to experiencing what Otto (1923) has called as the numinous, the otherworldly. The major experiential difference between the indigenous people and others is in the nature of their lifeworlds. Most tribal people even today live in close proximity to nature and have a cosmology that sets them apart from the urban populations.

Indigenous people experience the otherworldly just like the others. The major experiential difference is in the nature of their lifeworlds: most tribal people live in close proximity to nature and have a cosmology that sets them apart from urban populations.

The tribal people of the upper Himalayas whom I have studied expressed this relationship with nature in a succinct way. A woman informant told me that the devtas are alive on the mountains and have become stone idols in the plains. For the indigenous people, their devtas are alive and part of their existing society. In the same region, when I asked about the difference between the human and the superhuman, I was told by a local man that the devtas are exactly like humans, in that they have emotions and relationships—they marry, they quarrel, they also have internal hierarchies. The only significant difference is that the superhuman are not bound by time–space coordinates. They remain the same age and they can be wherever they wish to be, any time. They can even be in many places at the same time. The indigenous people worship or view the superhuman mostly in natural forms like the landscape, and they rarely make human-like replicas of them. These beings are known by their 'presence' and are not installed as idols in temples. They converse and interact with the living as well as the non-living, in exactly the same manner as humans do with each other.

In his impressive analysis of shamanism, personhood and cosmology among the Sora (or Saora), a tribe of Odisha, Vitebsky (1993) interprets what many anthropologists would have dismissed as 'unreal'—the dialogues that occur regularly between the dead and the living, through the medium of shamans. The nature of these dialogues is reflective of a continued relationship between the dead and the alive. For the Sora, there is nothing called death, in the sense of an annihilation or transition to another realm; death for the Sora is simply a 'a phase of a person's total conscious existence' (ibid.: 9). The dialogues reflect not a divide but rather an ongoing relationship where both the dead and the living shape each other through a process where speakers 'persuade, cajole, tease, remind, deceive, plead with each other' (ibid.: 5).

The Sora are not alone in their relationship with the dead. Among the Tangkhul Nagas spread in the Senapati and Ukhrul districts of Manipur and in the adjacent territory of the Kachin state in Mynamar (Burma), there is no final separation of the living and the dead—ancestors continue to live in close proximity to the living and have to be sent off to the Land of the Dead ceremoniously. The Naga scholar

Khongreiwo (2014: 80) has described how the Nagas used to see the dead—including the animals that had been sacrificed in various rituals during the year—on a specified day, moving away from the village through the exit gate. It was a moving sight as people could see and recognise people they knew as they moved in a slow procession carrying torches. The scholar writes, 'My paternal grandfather and grandmother (who died in their mid-nineties in 2007 and 2009 respectively) used to narrate such marvelous sights they themselves had experienced before they converted to Christianity in 1942' (ibid.). The Tangkhuls believed that marriages were possible in the Land of the Dead, and many estranged lovers died in the hope that they would be reunited and live in blissful happiness in the next world.

While not raising any issues about ontology or rationality, Vitebsky (1993) raises the issue of personhood. Unlike Western and other similar cultures, where the person is a bounded entity with boundaries that define the self and the other, the Sora are made out of relationships to the extent that they hardly exist as persons outside of these. 'Instead of being a bounded entity, the person can also be interpreted in this light as having a core, or forms of concentration, which at its outer edges diffuses into other persons' (ibid.: 9). Relationships are not interrupted but simply take on a different character after death. Like in most tribes, the Soras consider the relationship with the dead as an important determinant of health and healing. Since the dead (*sonum*) have a closeness to the living (as ancestors or ones with shared experiences), they tend to revisit their experiences of illness and death with those who are close to them.

The Soras have two kinds of shamans: the funerary ones and the healing ones, the former having a more exalted position than the latter, as the former are the ones who really carry on the divination, while the latter perform healing rites. The Sora shamans, like the Native American shamans, undertake a journey into the other world where they converse with the inhabitants of that world. In case of the Soras, the shamans are usually women who have a husband and children in the other world, with whom they have a relationship like with any normal family member. These shamans are the funerary shamans who undertake these journeys and continue their dialogues over a period of time that extends beyond their lifespan. In other words, death only implies a new location, but there is a continuity of both consciousness and relationships.

The healers on the other hand have a more restricted role, which is defined by the immediate task at hand. While the funerary shamans are diviners, the healers only provide remedies. The most important causative factor for most illnesses is the disturbance of relationships, both with the living and with the dead. Women are mostly affected as they are placed in a contradictory position between their father's and their husband's families. They have close emotional ties with their natal families but have to produce children for their husbands' lineages, which may go against the interests of their fathers and brothers. In his classic work on the Ndembu, Turner (2009 [1969]) has described how women are afflicted because of the contradictions that exist in their social positions, roles and responsibilities. The matrilineal Ndembu are virilocal, and a woman has to move to her husband's village after marriage. Her affliction is mostly in the form of miscarriages and the failure to conceive, which is attributed to the curse put on her by a female relative, usually the mother or the grandmother, who is unhappy if the woman is paying too much attention to her husband. As a woman remains part of her own matrilineage, her loyalty is expected be towards her mother's people and not so much towards her husband. The elaborate ritual Isoma restores the balance between her various relationships and ensures that she does not neglect her matrilineal kin even as her fertility is restored and she is able to live happily with her husband. 'The Isoma (or Tubwiza) ritual belongs to a class (muchidi) of rituals, recognized as such by Ndembu, known as "women's rituals" or "rituals of procreation"' (ibid.: 11).

Although the methods to deal with such tensions are cultural and situational, the tensions and emotions involved are near-universal. Tensions between husband and wife, between mother-in-law and son-in-law, of men torn between loyalty to parents and towards wife, of women torn between husband and father, are common human social experiences, and even though the means of resolving these tensions across societies may seem incongruous, the reasons for these tensions are often understood universally. The most important aspect of the Vitebsky's (1993) analysis is that it truly reflects the changes in anthropological perspectives in terms of both theory and the attitude towards the tribal or indigenous. Unlike classical anthropologists, his analysis does not raise questions raised or seek answers as if one were trying to explain something that did not actually exist or that was unreal but needed to be explained any way. His interpretations are rooted in commonalities of human experiences and, to some degree, in the same sense as Tylor (1871), in common questions to which all humans seek answers. Many scholars like Vitebsky have also linked tribal practices to actual psychoanalytic theory, demonstrating the efficacy of the healing rituals from a psychological perspective [see, for instance, Kakar (1982)]. Doubts regarding indigenous knowledge have also been rested—with increasing evidence of the wisdom of the indigenous people with respect to the environment and ecological relationships, there is a greater acceptance of tribal cosmologies and sacred beliefs that now merge with the contemporary trends of deep ecology and spiritual ecology.

SHAMANISM AND HEALING

Most tribes are marked by the presence of shamans and healers as most of them believe that illness is caused by spiritual rather than physiological causes. Although earlier such beliefs were dismissed as superstition, the value of psychological healing is now recognised by medical science and modern-day psychologists. Medical practice recognises many illnesses as psychosomatic, and the rigid mind–body duality introduced by nineteenth-century European rationality has been deconstructed to the extent that much of what is physiological is seen as linked to the mind. Advancements in medical science have led to scepticism about conservative medical practices, and modern physicians are not averse to turning towards what are known as alternative medical practices.

Shamans are viewed as mediators between the spiritual and the material worlds, and they are required for primarily two kinds of rituals: first, the oracular or predictive ones and, second, the healing practices. In other words, at the first level, the shamanistic healer is required to diagnose the cause of illness that mostly takes the form of determining which spirit or supernatural being has been offended and why. The second part concerns the actual healing rituals that are directed towards appeasing the offended spirit. The shaman's body is only a medium for the descending spirit, and in some cultures, the shaman can also venture into the spirit world in his non-material or spirit body. Many shamans acquire the status involuntarily as they are forced by the spirits to allow them to possess their bodies. In my experience of shamanism among the Bhotiyas (Channa 2013), I found that most of them had been visited by the spirit who was to possess them in a dream. Shamans or mediums are rarely people of high social status and are rarely treated as such by their fellow tribesmen. Among the Jads (ibid.), they were mostly men who had been afflicted by tuberculosis and were also older, less active members of the community. One woman became a medium after giving birth to seven daughters and then a son, but she was a wealthy woman having inherited her father's property as she did not have a brother. Pastoral people like the Jads, however, relied more on outside healers than on the members of their own village. The ones from their own community were used only for predictions and almost never for the actual healing, for which they relied more on the local Buddhist lama or the Hindu priest.

Shamans act as mediators between the spiritual and material worlds, taking on predictive as well as healing roles. So, they diagnose the cause of illness (determine which spirit is offended and why), and recommend ways to appease the offended spirit.

The Jads have a number of deities (devtas) including those they call their kuldevta, the village devta and some deities of the Hindu pantheon, most notably, the Pandavas, who are only worshipped in the mountains of Garhwal (Sax 1991) and nowhere else in the Hindu mainland. Each devta has his or her own medium, who remains so for life. As discussed elsewhere (Channa 2005), the incorporation of the Pandavas into the Jads' pantheon of devtas is a comparatively recent phenomenon and is linked to the historical conditions of their relatively recent closeness to their Garhwali Hindu neighbours and the loss of their erstwhile trade with the Tibetans across the Indo-China border. There have been other changes in their ritual practices that symbolise their attempts to move closer to a Hindu identity.

In most tribal societies in India, there are two kinds of shamans. The first kind includes the *bhagat*s of the Oraon, the *ojha*s of the Santals and the *bhopa*s of tribes in Rajasthan—these are full-time specialists who act as medicine-men and also as mediums for the deities, the two roles often being combined. The second kind, as found among the Jad Bhotiyas of Uttarakhand, are simply mediums for the gods, and they are otherwise perfectly ordinary men and women. In all tribes, even the full-time specialist is not accorded too much power or deference as most tribes do not believe that people should be set aside for specialisations, including being medicine-men or diviners.

One of the most detailed descriptions of the working of a sacred specialist in a tribe is that by Bodding (1986: 11) for the Santals. The sacred specialist or ojha among the Santals can give medicines and also drive away evil spirits causing illness. He can perform several tasks, for instance, he can consult the oracle and carry on divination by leaves or oil. Such divination is important in both assessing the cause of the disease and finding out about its cure. For example, if the divination tells that the illness is caused by the wrath of a deity or the invasion of the body by an evil spirit, then at the next level, it will be necessary to find out the manner of dealing with this problem. Rice often forms an important part of divination, as by throwing rice and counting, the diviner can find answers to many things. The Santal ojha can make the disease gather at one point of the body and then suck it out by biting or sucking. Santals believe in *bonga*s or powerful spirits that can cause harm. The ojha is specially qualified to drive out such bongas, and in addition to all this, the ojha can administer actual medicine.

Many other tribes also have similar processes or rituals of divination and of finding cures. Most often, as among the Bhotiyas, the divination takes place in two stages: one for finding the cause of the illness and the second for finding a cure. For example, if it is found that the illness is caused by the evil eye or by the breaking of a taboo or by the wrath of a deity, the manner of dealing with each case would have to be found through divination, especially if the displeasure of a deity is involved. The throwing of rice and catching a few grains in the hand and then counting to find out causes and cures is a common practice among hill tribes.

Many of the medicine-men have a wide range of knowledge about the human body and also of herbal medicines. The Santal ojha have the proficiency to be able to recognise 23 kinds of pulse by just putting their finger on the wrist of the patient.

The causes of diseases are classified into four broad categories by the ojhas of the Santals: (i) natural causes, (ii) human beings, (iii) bongas and (iv) ancestors. The first category refers to causes like bad food, infections and epidemics (*disamduk*); the second refers to the practice of witchcraft; the third to spirits that can cause harm; and the fourth to ancestors who cause illness on being displeased because, for instance, their rituals were not performed properly or they had been disrespected. Thus, the tribal world view encompasses all the dimensions of life. Kinship and religion are intrinsically tied together since ancestors and elders can cause misfortune if displeased. Social relationships are important, and any breach in them can make people angry and make them practise witchcraft on a person they are displeased with. The world of the supernatural hence encompasses all of one's surroundings, the physical as well as the social environment.

The myth of tribal isolation now stands dispelled, and in South Asia, most tribes show a close interaction with and influence from the local Hindu pantheon as well as the Hindu state, especially in the Hindu heartland. Tribes have only notionally been isolated or independent. In many parts of India, they have lived in close cooperation and interaction with the local rulers and have had a two-way interaction with them. They have often been given equal status, and their deities have received offerings and patronage from the local royal families like in the case of the Konds described earlier. In Kinnaur, during the séance held in the temple of the village deity of the Kinnaurie, which I attended in the year 2008, local political leaders had taken part. I was also told that this is a regular feature of most of the important rituals. Similar situations are found across India.

In many parts of India, tribes have lived in close cooperation and interaction with local rulers. They have often been given equal status, and their deities have received offerings and patronage from the local royal families.

CONVERSIONS AND THE POLITICS OF RELIGION

In the preceding section, we discussed the spiritual, cosmological and experiential dimensions of tribal beliefs and practices. At the same time, religion is also a social institution with its concomitant political and economic dimensions. In India, Hindu kings have lived in harmony with tribes and shared the latter's cosmologies to a large extent, as we have seen in the case of the Kond tribes of Odisha. Hinduism, being a primordial religion without any concept of conversion, has interacted with indigenous beliefs through the complementary processes of universalisation and parochialisation (Marriott 1955). The former refers to the incorporation of tribal deities and beliefs into Hindu society, such as the homology created between local deities and universal Hindu deities. The local deity Jagannath is now worshipped as Krishna, an incarnation of the Hindu deity Vishnu. Many tribal local deities have been transformed into major Hindu gods like Mahadev and Vishnu. In the opposite direction, many Hindu deities have been localised and become a part of tribal local cults, in the process of parochialisation. Channa (2005) has shown how the Pandavas, in the sacred Hindu epic *Mahabharata*, became local kuldevtas or lineage gods of the Bhotiyas of Uttarakhand. Moreover, the Bhotiyas are also trying to elevate their village god into a Hindu deity (Channa 2010). In spite of the local Hindu or Muslim rulers extending a protective and even cooperative hand towards the tribes, at certain periods in time, especially during the colonial period and the rise of a capitalist economy, tribes have been subject to large-scale exploitation by the local Hindu and Muslim traders and power holders.

As Hinduism has no concept of conversion, it has interacted with indigenous beliefs through the complementary processes of universalisation (incorporation of tribal deities and beliefs into Hindu society) and parochialisation (localisation of Hindu deities into local tribal cults).

Major transformations in tribal world views took place with the entry of missionaries into tribal regions. After some initial resistance, large-scale conversions were witnessed in the tribal belts of central and northeastern India. Some tribal regions like Nagaland and Mizoram have witnessed almost complete conversion, while other northeast regions like Manipur, Arunachal Pradesh and Meghalaya have undergone large-scale conversion and yet many people in these places still adhere to their original beliefs and practices.

Missionaries have used many tactics for conversion, and many times, they have cleverly played on the original beliefs of the local people to lure them into conversion. The exploitation of tribal people and their marginalisation by caste Hindus is one factor that favoured conversion, but this was not the only reason. As Padel (2011: 11) has pointed out, although missionaries arrived in tribal areas during the colonial period, mostly around the end of the nineteenth century, conversions picked up only after the British left because then Christianity was no longer associated with the oppression of the colonial rulers. On the other hand, the newly formed Indian nation was least sympathetic towards the tribal way of life. Exploitation of tribals increased with the inroads made by Hindu moneylenders, the spread of outsiders into tribal territories and the consequent dispossession of tribes of their land and resources. For example, the Terai region of the Himalayan foothills was once the domain of the Tharus, a proud tribal people, who have been reduced to serfdom, a poor and exploited minority, after the influx of refugees from Punjab after the 1947 partition of the Punjab region. The refugees cleared the land for agriculture and are now prospering on the land previously held by the Tharus. The Tharus have been impoverished and pushed to the brink of survival.

There is a significant prejudice among upper-caste Hindu populations about tribes, whereby they consider tribes as uncivilised and ignorant. Tribal practices of meat eating (even beef) and liquor brewing and drinking are looked down upon by upper-caste Hindus. In the present day, the marginalisation of tribes is increasing as the state is now encroaching on their territories in the name of development, by making dams, mines and industries.

The Christian church could make an impression on tribes by enticing them with the hope of deliverance from marginalisation by providing them with an identity that they mistakenly believed would give them a higher status in the eyes of the upper-caste, urban people. As described by Munda (2013) with respect to the tribals of

Jharkhand, the missionaries sometimes did not directly promote or carry out conversions, but began their work by helping the tribals fight their battles. They would help them fight legal cases against the usurpation of their lands. They made great inroads into the lives of the tribes by providing them with high-quality education, building hospitals and setting up self-help community centres. They also used other kinds of tactics, especially as they derived some power by being associated with Western culture, which in a situation of colonisation symbolised dominant power. The tribal people believed that the gods of the White people had greater power, which they transmitted to their people. I encountered an old man in the hills who told me sheepishly that he had just converted to Christianity. I asked him the reason as to why in his old age he had gone over to another religion. His narrative went like this:

> I was in the army and there I ate some bad things, wrong kind of meat [probably beef], and incurred the wrath of my kuldevtas. They were so angry that I could do nothing to control them. I would be sitting in my room and a large black man would come in through the window threatening me. Everywhere I was pursued by these demons. I went to all the local *guni* [shamans], but no one was able to help me. Then I went to the Issa Masih [Jesus Christ] person, and he assured me that his god was very powerful and would definitely remove these demons from my life. He told me that if I swore allegiance to his god and did as I was told, the threats would be removed. This is exactly what happened. Ever since I have adopted Issa Masih as my god, all my problems are over. Issa Masih is very powerful and he has subdued my lineage gods. Now they have become *shant* [calm].

This narrative brings us to another important dimension of indigenous beliefs. What is the nature of religion among tribes and other people with ancient cosmologies? I have discussed elsewhere (Channa 2013) that the notion of a bounded religion with a specific doctrine is a later development and is linked to complex civilisations. For most people, especially those who have cosmologies that have evolved indigenously, there is no separate sphere of religion or metaphysics. Such people have a different perception of ontology where the sacred is part of their environment, and there can be no being or phenomenon that is sacred for some people and not for others. The entire universe has its logic, and there are beings with varying degrees of power and ability. The indigenous people also recognise that individuals may differ as to which sacred being or phenomenon they choose to owe allegiance to, but there is no dichotomy between one religion and another in terms of what more complex societies recognise as ideological differences. The sacred is sacred no matter who worships what. Thus, religion is the same as cosmology—existence and the distribution of power in the universe are realities not beliefs. Tribal people almost never say 'we believe in this or that'; they describe gods and the sacred as ontological realities. These sacred beings exist independently of people's beliefs. They exist; they are of a particular kind and they are real. Whether one has faith in one or the other or whether one wishes to follow one or the other is a completely different matter than their existence. Belief is a matter of choice; existence is not.

Indigenous people recognise that individuals differ as to which sacred being or phenomenon they choose to owe allegiance to. The sacred is sacred no matter who worships what. Thus, religion is the same as cosmology.

Thus, all the phenomenon in the realm of religion are not set apart from the rest of society but situated as an integral aspect of it. Take, for example, the villages of the upper Himalayas, where all activities—social, political and economic—are guided by the village deity, who is the sovereign. In Kinnaur, I came across a village whose inhabitants had not harvested their crops (although it was well past harvest time) because their village goddess was on a trip to visit her husband. I was told that the goddess was camping at a spot near the village for several days and was unable to return as her journey was hampered by bad weather. Only after her return could the villagers harvest their grains with her permission. The abodes of deities are referred to as their houses and not as temples, as they contain no idols. The deity lives inside just like a human being but is invisible. It is only when deities come out of their abodes and interact with people that they put on their *vesh* (dress) and become visible.

Such an ontology would be disrupted when a tribe accepts another religion, especially one like Christianity with a given doctrine.

However, it is not evident whether in such situations, the transformation is complete or there are remnants of cosmologies persisting. Quite often, the new religion builds upon the old and finds strength in the homologies between the new and the existing beliefs. Khongreiwo (2014: 67) writes, 'The attributes of the God of the pre-Christian Tanghkul Nagas (known as Ameoa, Kasa Akhava or Varivara) were/are almost wholly identical with the attributes of the Christian God.' Yet, the beings that were most often taken cognisance of and interacted with were the closer and active spirits, ancestors and other beings who were important for day-to-day life rather than some esoteric, distant, benign god. These were spirits and beings with human attributes that could be pleased, cajoled and interacted with.

I have been told by people from tribal regions that their acceptance of Christianity was made easy by the similarities between Christianity and primordial religions. One of the major criteria by which the tribal religions differed from Hinduism and were closer to Christianity was the absence of concepts of inequality as exhibited by the caste system. The egalitarian tribes could understand the concepts of equality preached by Christians, and they were hopeful that after conversion they would be equal to their fellow Christians and not be treated as lowly as they had been by caste Hindus.

Feminist scholars among tribals have a different opinion about Christianity, which they believe transformed relatively more gender-equal beliefs among tribals into a patriarchal religion. God appears as the father in Judeo-Christian theology, while in most non-Western religions and world views, the sacred is not always masculine. Indigenous communities also sometimes have deities of unspecified gender. Hinduism, with its strong tradition of female or mother goddess worship, has also influenced them. The Naga tribes, for instance, have traditionally had female deities or even androgynous ones. According to Hümtsoe-Nienu et al. (2012), the traditionally holistic concept of divine being (as both female and male) of many tribes of the Northeast was transformed into a male god under Christian influence. The Mizo, for example, had two names, one masculine (Pathian) and the other feminine (Khuanu) for referring to their supreme being, but under Christian influence, they retained only the former. Similar occurrences of changeover from an androgynous concept to a masculine one have taken place among the Tikhir, the Kyong, the Chakhesang, the Angami and the Zeme Naga, and others. The Todas of Nilgiri believe in a female goddess of creation, although the ritual status of women among them is very low. The Girasia (Unnithan-Kumar 1997) have a major male deity—Mountain God (Bhairu)—who symbolises conquest and territory and two female deities, the clan mother and the pox goddess, the former marking out lineages for the purpose of marriage and the latter a protective deity, especially from deadly diseases. The division of labour between the deities of the Girasia indicates the cultural conceptualisation of sexual division of labour, with the masculine associated with war and territory and the feminine with sociability and nurturing. Even after conversion, many such beliefs of the indigenous people as well as many of their customs and rituals have persisted. This persistence is also closely linked to the resurgence of tribal and ethnic identities through which contemporary tribes are questioning their marginal status with respect to the dominant religions and the Indian state.

IDENTITY AND RELIGION

Since many tribes, especially those from the northeast region, have resisted what they felt was their forced incorporation within the Indian nation, there is a political motivation to mass conversion, which served, in their eyes, two purposes. One was the rejection of the dominant religion of the Indian state, namely, Hinduism, and the second was their incorporation within a larger global community of Christians. The early leaders from this region, such as the Naga leader Phizo, had looked towards the West for support and held a belief that they could draw support from a global Christian brotherhood. Another important aspect of the benefits of conversion is the creation of a common identity that would facilitate the creation of a political community. As is well known, the concept of tribe is used to give a blanket cover to a multitude of identities. Even within this larger category, more specific ones like Naga and Khasi actually cover many internal divisions. The Nagas, for example, cover almost 50 small and large identities. Christianity and its association with a Western culture serve to give commonality to a multitude of fracturing differences.

Thus, while each of these identities is still operative, some common ground is gained with a common religion.

Conversion and colonisation served to divest tribes of some of their core cultural identities, such as human sacrifice in the case of Konds, and headhunting among the tribes of the Northeast. As Padel (2011) has shown, these practices were exoticised and showcased as indicators of savagery, giving both the colonisers and the missionaries the moral justification for the havoc they caused. Naga villages, for example, had the institution of *longshim* (longhouses), where the youth of the village would sleep and gather to act as a standing army to defend the village against headhunters from neighbouring tribes. Longshims were also institutions of cultural transmission where the youth learned the culture, including songs and dances, specific to their tribes. With the banning of headhunting and Christian influence, longshims began to disappear, taking with them the age-old cultural elements of the tribes. When young people started going to schools and colleges, they were no longer interested in their traditional institutions. As more people became Christian, they lost interest in the music and art of their tribes, turning instead towards Western music and art. For instance, the Khasi choir of Shillong has now acquired great fame. Naga scholar Vashum (2014: 150) has written about how many young Nagas resist playing traditional musical instruments in church and prefer to strum guitars or play the piano. However, over the years, as the colonial influence is waning and the tribes are also becoming politically conscious of their identity, as they are coming into closer contact with the outside world, there are tendencies towards reviving their 'traditions' or at least an effort to move away from external influences to more introspective cultural revival.

TRIBAL THEOLOGY AND INDIGENOUS CHRISTIANITY

Although, initially, missionaries had the attitude that they were introducing the concept of god among people who had no sacred teachings or no higher spiritual cognition, later, as the tribal people themselves became educated and were able to develop a critical view of their own, there have been efforts on the side of the Christian preachers to pay heed to local sentiments and also dissociate religion from culture. The native priests and church functionaries are re-examining religious practices to identify and differentiate the truly religious elements from those introduced by Western missionaries in the name of 'civilisation'. Thus, Vashum (2014: 150) comments that 'the view that anything that comes from the West is Christian and anything that concerns with tribal culture and tradition is unchristian is a serious concern one needs to address'. To this end, the term 'tribal theology' was coined by some Tangkhul tribal Christians.

Vashum, a functionary of the church, directly relates tribal theology to the 'chicken neck' (a long strip of land that connects the northeast of India to the rest of the country), which, according to him, 'symbolizes the profound isolation, neglect and exploitation the people of this region suffer at the hands of the Central Government' (ibid.: 138). His statement is representative of the sentiments of many tribals from this region and as well as other parts of India. In response to the political and social isolation of tribals, and to assert their identity, some tribal Christian leaders such as Nirmal Minz, Renthy Keitzar, Thanzauva and Longchar coined the term 'tribal theology' in the late 1980s and early 1990s to interpret religion from a tribal perspective. At the core of this interpretation lies the interaction between the gospel and the realities of socio-economic conditions of the tribes and their struggles to be free of their exploitation.

Several important tribal study centres in the northeast and other parts of India are also engaged in seriously linking religion with tribal traditions and in upholding the goodness of tribal values. One may say that they are attempting to undo some of the damage done by the early missionaries, but they are also staging a protest against the treatment they have received from the state in an independent country. The core aspects of tribal theology lie in its emphasis on the harmony that exists between tribal lifeworlds and nature. These aspects have been taken up in cultural ecology and by those schools of thought that are critical of consumerist and capitalist economies on which the onus of the present environmental degradation rests.

Tribal theology is a way for tribes to reaffirm their faith in themselves and enable them to regain their self-esteem. Politically, this is a way to assert and also demand a place in the sun.

From the point of view of tribes, tribal theology is a way to reaffirm their faith in themselves and a way to enable them to regain their self-esteem. Politically, this is a way to assert and also demand a place in the sun, not by imitating the ways of the non-tribes but as themselves. This is a clear rejection of the earlier acceptance of superiority of outsiders, including that of Western missionaries. While some are reinterpreting Christianity, others are reinventing their traditional ways, like the revival of Sarna (a religious system) among the Oraon and Munda tribes of central India and of Sona Mahi, the traditional religion of the people of Manipur.

RELIGION AND DIVISIVENESS

The conversion or non-conversion of tribes to a universal religion like Christianity has created an internal hierarchy, which was relatively absent in tribal societies. Conversion among tribes has not been total, and only the people of Nagaland and Mizoram are largely Christians and also the most Westernised. The people of other regions have been mixed in their response to proselytisation, with some like those in Arunachal being largely unconverted.

In places like Jharkhand, where only a part of the population converted, there exists a hierarchy based on education and access to jobs. The converted tribals have mostly received good education in the missionary-run schools and hold better jobs, while the non-converted remain agriculturalists or pursue traditional occupations. As Munda (2013) mentions, a majority of white-collar jobs are held by tribals educated in missionary institutions, and such opportunities are extended to mostly those who are converted. These people have developed a sense of superiority over their brethren who follow the traditional forms of religion and ways of life. The converted tribals often tend to look upon the unconverted as 'primitive' in the same way as the missionaries did.

In recent times, the aggressive Hindutva political movement is targeting tribals by urging them to acknowledge their Hindu identity. Many politically conscious tribals are resisting these efforts, which are directed at breaking down their autonomy and identity. Contemporary tribals do not wish to have their identity submerged within any larger, universalistic identity. Even the Christians among them are asserting their separate existence by asserting a tribal theology.

SUMMARY

Religion has been one aspect of human society that has attracted the most attention from anthropologists, and it is this one institution that has been used both academically and politically to unite and divide human cultures and societies. The approach to the study of tribal religion has followed the larger developments in theory within the discipline of anthropology. Thus, the early anthropological interpretations of the religion of the so-called tribes were overshadowed by the power hierarchies of colonial rule and the adjunct processes of proselytisation carried out by Christian missionaries in their zeal to redeem the world. Both colonising powers and the Christian church justified their actions in the name of civilising the savages. Thus, tribal religious practices were always constructed as exotic, barbaric and illogical.

The functionalist school turned away from what it believed was cultural ethnocentrism and moved towards cultural relativism. It looked for the functions of all religious practices and made attempts to contextualise these to the living conditions of each tribe. However, the major criticism of this approach has been that it was positivist and that it looked for explanations in the logic provided by the analyst, while ignoring the interpretations of the practitioners. All the classical approaches assumed that tribal religions were not really spiritual or mystical but simply pragmatic processes that served some social end. More contemporary perspectives have criticised this Eurocentric approach to the study of tribal religions, of treating them as certain aspects of native life of which the people themselves had no true awareness.

Works like that of Radin (1927) have paved way to deconstruct the myth of tribal exoticism and to show that there was actually very little difference between tribes and the rest of the so-called urban civilised people. One can easily show that elements of beliefs and practices such as magic, witchcraft and animism are found in all cultures in some form or the other. On the other hand, tribal people also have theological doctrines such as belief in the existence of a higher god and forms of spirituality, just like those following universal religions. Religion is a reality shaped by experiences that are universal to all humans. Contemporary anthropological approaches to the study of religion tend to contextualise the lifeworlds of tribes, describing their cosmologies and world views, trying to see the relevance of these practices not in functional terms but as a way of understanding the world from a different perspective.

With political decolonisation, the privileging of Western knowledge and epistemology is being seriously questioned, as is the treatment of non-Western cosmologies with scepticism. The relevance of the non-Western, especially nature-centric world views, is now being seen as both relevant and logical. The entry of native anthropologists has enriched anthropological perspectives, and in this chapter we have tried to incorporate some of these perspectives.

Religion also needs to be understood as a social institution, and here the intersection of religion with economy and politics becomes very relevant. In the modern world, religion has become one of the important tools of identity politics. The tribes of India have been using religion, and especially the transition to other religions, as a significant means for attaining political identity and negotiating power-sharing. The assumption of a common religion, especially Christianity, has paved way for the creation of collective tribal identities such as those of the Nagas and the Mizos of the Northeast. The association of Christianity with the West has led to the acquisition of a global identity and attempts at gaining global support. While the latter has not really materialised, for many tribals, the assumption of a Christian identity has led to increased self-esteem and feelings of equality with the non-tribals. In some tribal areas, conversion has also led to internal stratification as well as conflicts between the converted and the non-converted sections of the tribes. Proselytisation has brought about important changes in the culture and ways of life of many tribal people. Missionaries have also made significant inroads into the field of education, and missionary institutions provide quality education to the people, thus enabling them to attain a social status closer to that of the powerful elite.

Tribes today are asserting their identity in a manner that defines them as they are, and does not require that they get 'civilised'. The transformations are to be on their own terms and not dictated by others. Thus, there are efforts to revive what they deem as their traditions and authentic religions. Even if they convert, the notion of tribal theology interprets Christianity in the context of their life situations, especially the marginalisation and oppression that they have faced and are still facing. Thus, they now view conversion not as an imitation or imposition by a higher power (colonisation) but rather as a protest against the imposition of the Indian state that is also viewed as representing Hinduism.

The relationship of tribals with Hinduism is now changing from a mutually respectful interaction, as was the case of the central Indian rulers with the tribal chiefs of Rajasthan, Odisha and Bastar, to one of suspicion and resentment. At other places, the tribes may be asserting their own deities as part of the Hindu pantheon in their claims for equality (Channa 2005, 2010). Contemporary tribes are resentful of submergence and are asserting their rights to their own ways of life and philosophy. Environmental disasters propagated by an industrial civilisation are turning attention to tribal cosmologies, with their emphasis on living in harmony with nature. Thus, tribal philosophy is now often looked upon as indigenous wisdom. Such a change of attitude from the outside is also bringing about a change in how tribes view their own culture and religion and is promoting a renewed confidence in their age-old philosophical traditions.

REFERENCES

Bodding, P. O. 1986. *Studies in Santal Medicine and Connected Folklore*. Calcutta: Asiatic Society.

Channa, Subhadra Mitra. 2005. 'The Descent of the Pandavas: Ritual and Cosmology of the Jads of Garhwal', *The European Bulletin of Himalayan Research*, 28 (Spring): 67–97.

———. 2010. 'A Ritual Transfer: From the High to the Low in Hindu-Tibetan Himalayan Communities', in Gita Dharampal-Frick, Robert Langer and Nils Holger (eds), *Ritual Dynamics and the Science of Ritual, Vol. 5: Transfer and Spaces*, pp. 43–64. Wiesbaden: Harrassowitz Verlag.

———. 2013. *The Inner and Outer Selves*. New Delhi: Oxford University Press.

Durkheim, Émile. 1995 [1912]. *The Elementary Forms of Religious Life*, trans. Karen E. Fields. New York: The Free Press.

Evans-Pritchard, E. E. 1965. *Theories of Primitive Religion*. Oxford: Oxford University Press.

Frazer, James George. 1922. *The Golden Bough: A Study in Magic and Religion*. New York: MacMillan.

Freud, Sigmund. 1913. *Totem and Taboo*. Boston, MA: Beacon Press.

Ghosh, Abhik. 2006. *The World of the Oraon: Their Symbols in Time and Space.* Jharkhand: Manohar Publishers and Distributors.

Hümtsoe-Nienü, Eyingbeni, Paul Pimomo and Venusa Tunyi. 2012. *Nagas: Essays Responsible For Change.* Dimapur: Heritage Publishing House.

Kakar, Sudhir. 1982. *Shamans, Mystics and Doctors.* Chicago: Chicago University Press.

Khongreiwo, Rammathoi. 2014. 'Landscapes, Memories and Pre-Christian Tangkhul Naga Eschatology', in R. Vashum (ed.), *Encountering Modernity: Situating the Tanghkul Nagas in Perspective*, pp. 64–88. New Delhi and Chicago: Chicken Neck.

Maharatna, Anup. 2005. *Demographic Perspectives on Indian Tribes.* New Delhi: Oxford University Press.

Malinowski, Bronislaw. 1935. *Coral Gardens and Their Magic.* London: George Allen and Unwin.

Marriott, McKim. 1955. 'Little Communities in an Indigenous Civilization', in Alan Beals and McKim Marriott (eds), *Village India: Studies in the Little Community*, pp. 181–218. Chicago: University of Chicago Press.

Munda, Meenakshi. 2013. 'An Anthropological Study of Religion of Oraons in Tribal Jharkhand', unpublished PhD dissertation, University of Delhi.

Otto, Rudolph. 1923. *The Idea of the Holy*, trans. John W. Harvey. Oxford: Oxford University Press.

Padel, Felix. 2011. *Sacrificing People: Invasions of a Tribal Landscape.* Hyderabad: Orient BlackSwan.

Pratt, Mary Louise. 1986. 'Fieldwork in Common Places', in J. Clifford and G. Marcus (eds), *Writing Cultures: The Poetics and Poetry of Ethnography*, pp. 27–50. Berkeley: University of California Press.

Radcliffe-Brown, A. R. 1922. *The Andaman Islanders: A Study in Social Anthropology.* Cambridge: Cambridge University Press.

Radin, Paul. 1927. *Primitive Man as Philosopher.* New York and London: D. Appleton and Co.

Rosaldo, Renato. 1986. 'From the Door of His Tent: The Fieldworker and the Inquisitor', in J. Clifford and G. Marcus (eds), *Writing Cultures: The Poetics and Poetry of Ethnography*, pp. 77–98. Berkeley: University of California Press.

Roy, S. C. 1912. *The Mundas and Their Country.* Calcutta: Kuntaline Press.

Sax, William. 1991. *Mountain Goddess: Gender and Politics in a Central Himalayan Pilgrimage.* New York: Oxford University Press.

Schendel, Willem van. 2011. 'The Dangers of Belonging: Tribes, Indigenous Peoples and Homelands in South Asia', in Daniel J. Rycroft and Sangeeta Dasgupta (eds), *The Politics of Belonging in India: Becoming Adivasi*, pp. 19–43. London and New York: Routledge.

Spiro, Melford E. 1967. *Burmese Supernaturalism: A Study in the Explanation and Resolution of Suffering.* Englewood Cliffs, NJ: Prentice Hall.

Turner, Victor. 2009 [1969]. *The Ritual Process: Structure and Anti-structure*. Ithaca, New York: Cornell University Press.

Tylor, Edward B. 1871. *Primitive Culture* (Vols 1 and 2). London: John Murray.

Unnithan-Kumar, Maya. 1997. *Identity, Gender and Poverty: New Perspectives on Caste and Tribe in Rajasthan*. Oxford: Berghahn Books.

Vashum, Yangkahau. 2014. 'Introducing Tribal (Tangkhul) Theology: A Case for Contextual Theology', in R. Vashum (ed.), *Encountering Modernity: Situating the Tanghkul Nagas in Perspective*, pp. 137–53. New Delhi and Chicago: Chicken Neck.

Vidyarthi, L. P. 1963. *The Maler: A Study in Nature-Man-Spirit Complex of a Hill Tribe*. Calcutta: Bookland.

Vitebsky, Piers. 1993. *Dialogues with the Dead: The Discussion of Mortality among the Sora of Eastern India*. Cambridge: Cambridge University Press.

Walker, Anthony. 1986. *The Todas of South India: A New Look*. Delhi: Hindustan Publishing House.

Wolf, Richard K. 2005. *The Black Cow's Footprints: Time, Space and Music in the Lives of the Kota of South India*. New Delhi: Permanent Black.

SUGGESTED READINGS

Bird-David, Nurit. 1999. '"Animism" Revisited: Personhood, Environment, and Relational Epistemology', *Current Anthropology*, 40 (1): 567–92.

Galey, Jean Claude. 1985. *Space, Routes, Mediations*. Paris: Editions of the School of Social Sciences.

Ngakang, Tuisem. 2014. 'Loss and Revitalization in Traditional Art: The State of Tangkhul Naga Music', in R. Vashum (ed.), *Encountering Modernity: Situating the Tanghkul Nagas in Perspective*, pp. 170–90. New Delhi and Chicago: Chicken Neck.

5

CONCEPTS OF JUSTICE AND LEGAL MECHANISMS OF TRIBAL SOCIETIES

HIGHLIGHTS

- Concepts of justice and law
- A history of anthropological approaches to the study of the law of tribal societies
- Some ethnographic examples of legal mechanisms among Indian tribes

INTRODUCTION

Western philosophers such as Hobbes (1973 [1651]) and Rousseau (1970 [1762]) have posited that the 'primitive' people, meaning the past of humankind as well as those not influenced by Western civilisation, lived or were living in a state of 'nature'. In other words, they did not have well-formed and established institutions for maintaining law and social order as found among the Europeans of the seventeenth to nineteenth centuries—the age of Renaissance and Enlightenment as well as of colonial expansion and conquest. While Hobbes was of the opinion that the primitives lived in anarchy, without a civil code to regulate them, Rousseau romanticised their freedom and lack of shackles.

As scholars like Lewis Henry Morgan, and later fieldwork-based anthropologists like Malinowski and his successors, came into direct contact with the people termed 'primitives', they realised that far from being anarchical or even living as simple 'children of nature', the people designated today as tribal, indigenous or aboriginal had well-regulated social systems and followed rules and regulation that were based upon philosophical and ethical premises drawn from their own life conditions and ecological relationships. They had a highly developed sense of justice and moral values and lived more orderly lives than their civilised counterparts in the West. Yet outside of the scholarly world, popular opinion still stereotypes tribes as the bearer of exotic customs and as not having proper civil codes. This illusion is also created because in tribal societies, most functions such as those of law and maintenance of social order are carried out by basic institutions like family and religion. Not many tribes have formal institutions for dispensing justice like courts or a set of exclusive legislative functionaries, yet they do have councils and sometimes informal judicial bodies that may be temporarily set up to deal with specific situations.

CONCEPTS OF JUSTICE

Although inextricably linked, concepts of justice and law vary slightly in that the former is drawn from the philosophical and metaphysical world view of a society and the latter refers to the practical application of these principles in terms of institutional mechanisms. The concept of justice is directly influenced by how the cosmological order is conceived and by the fundamental ways of life of the people. In describing the justice system of the Canadian aboriginal people, the *Report of the Aboriginal Justice Inquiry of Manitoba* (Aboriginal Justice Implementation Commission 1999) mentioned how the value system of the aborigines differed markedly from that of Western people whose judicial system the former were forced to follow because of colonisation.

Concepts of justice are derived from certain fundamental premises about the nature of the world and the position of humans within this world. The most important of these is the concept of personhood. 'Who am I?', 'What am I?'. While basic questions such as these exist across cultures, there is a distinct dichotomy between the concepts of personhood of the Western world and of the non-Western world. While the Western perspective regards a person as an individual circumscribed from others as a distinct entity, most other people across the globe view a person as interconnected with others, both human and non-human. Strathern (1999) and Marriott (1991), in their works on New Guinea and the Indian caste system, respectively, point out that non-Western people are more 'dividual' than individual. People who are dividual understand themselves and are understood by others as part of an interconnected set of relationships rather than as stand-alone beings. In this sense, people are not judged as individuals or as even equal and separate beings but in terms of their embeddedness within a set of relationships that is inclusive of rank, gender and other social markers. Hence, as pointed out in the *Report of the Aboriginal Justice*, mentioned earlier, the administration of justice among tribes is centred on relationships and the punishment is evaluated against the effect it is going to have on the people who are connected with the crime.

Important to concepts of justice is the concept of personhood. While the Western world regards a person as an individual, distinct entity, the non-Western world views a person as interconnected with others, both human and non-human.

Among the clear distinctions between Western formal legal organisations and those of many non-Western cultures, the most fundamental one is the lack of clear dichotomies or the dialectical perspective that predominates Euro-American thought. In the Western legal system, there is a clear dichotomy between the 'guilty' and the 'not guilty', but in many cultures such black and white distinctions are absent. Every action is evaluated in a context and is examined from many angles and perspectives. A second distinction is the reliance on one source of authority. Most tribal societies, while not being individualistic, respect the integrity of the individual and are largely egalitarian in principle such that everyone's opinion is taken into consideration while deciding upon a case. Since there is no specialised legal institution like a court, justice is seen as a collective domain with the elderly and the wise (as considered by community) playing an active role in decision-making. Also, with the absence of hierarchy, everyone is free to give an opinion and is also heard. If a person has greater authority in terms of decision-making or is heard with greater respect, it is purely because of the person's own qualities and not because he or she has any official position or rank. However, there is a great diversity among tribes, and some may have a council of elders, like the Naga Hoho or the village council of the Khasis. Yet, common people are rarely excluded totally out of the judicial process.

WRONGS AND THEIR REMEDIES

In most tribes, only matters that disturb community life and are disruptive of the social order are seen as worthy of sanctions. Personal traits or concerns, such as one's religious or sexual preferences, are ignored and left to the individual unless they are socially disruptive. The predominant values are respect for all beings, human as well as non-human, lack of criticism and avoidance of confrontation.

Radcliffe-Brown (1922) makes a distinction between crime and sin, arguing that a crime is an action committed against society, while a sin is an action committed against supernatural entities. However, in most tribal societies, even actions committed against superhuman beings may be evaluated as wrongdoings that affect the individual concerned and not the entire community. Most such minor aberrations fall in the domain of medical anthropology as they cause personal physical discomforts to the individual concerned and not the entire community, and they need to be treated accordingly. A crime is mostly evaluated in terms of the disruption of social life and not in terms of universalistic criteria as in the Western legal system.

> **While crime is an action committed against society, sin is an action committed against supernatural entities. However, in most tribal societies, even actions committed against superhuman beings are evaluated as wrongdoings that affect the individual and not the entire community.**

Let us, for instance, see how a crime like murder is evaluated differently in the two systems. In the Western system, a murder is seen as a crime against the state and the punishment is given to the individual irrespective of the effect it will have on his/her social circle or that of the victim. Even if the punishment causes misery to other individuals or is socially disruptive, the law, as they say, will take its own course. In a tribal society, the sanctions are in accordance with the effect they would have on the affected persons. The aim of punishment is not to treat the crime as act isolated from its context, but rather as something that has caused distress to some people—the aim is to remedy the distress and, most importantly, restore social harmony. The foremost concern is to make the family of the victim feel compensated for the crime and be satisfied that justice has been done. Thus, justice is not an abstract objective process like in modern societies following the Western system of jurisprudence, but is directed towards social harmony and restoration of social balance.

Blood-feuding is a common aspect of many tribal societies. It derives from the principle of equivalence as, in a clan system, a person is substitutable by another person of the same clan who is in a structurally similar position, like a classificatory brother. Equivalence directs responsibility to the entire group, unlike the Western principle of individual responsibility. By this principle, retribution for one life may be obtained by taking another life from the group of the perpetrator of the crime. Such actions may trigger a chain reaction that sometimes continues over generations. But at the same time, a murder can be compensated in other ways, like paying a fine or even giving over a person in marriage to the other group. As far as possible, the elders and the community try to bring matters to an end rather than perpetuating a state of imbalance.

Blood-feuding derives from the principle of equivalence. In a clan system, a person is substitutable by another person of the same clan who is in a structurally similar position.

In tribal or indigenous societies, all lives including those of non-humans is held as precious. In societies practising totemism, the life of a totemic animal is treated like a human life as totemic animals are considered to be ancestors. The killing of a totemic animal is as serious as, or even more serious than, the taking of a human life. Desecration of sacred sites or parts of a sacred landscape is viewed as a serious crime. The most stringent punishment is reserved for a crime that affects the entire community. It may also be meted out to those who are repeat offenders and whose actions are causing disruption of the social life of the community. Since the taking of a human life is rarely, if ever, resorted to in any tribal community, the most stringent punishment for this is excommunication. A tribal person is, as already mentioned, incomplete as an individual. Each person is complete only in relation to the community and by being part of the social life of the community; hence such banishment is equivalent to death. For lesser offences, the sanctions are mostly at the level of the community and involve shaming, ridicule and avoidance as standards measures. The offences are usually those that go against the values of the tribe, such as sharing; cooperation and generosity; and being honest, upright and morally responsible. Causing conflict or being habitually quarrelsome can be seen as a serious offence that calls for sanctions. When I asked the Bhotiya tribal women (Channa 2013) about the most desirable traits of a woman, they said she is one who does not gossip or spread rumours about others. A woman who is often the cause of quarrels is seen as undesirable and is subjected to sanctions of avoidance and ridicule, and may even be shamed in front of everyone for her undesirable behaviour.

Taking someone else's things without asking (called 'theft' in more urban societies) is not often seen as a serious offence in tribal societies. This is because in subsistence economies that are yet not fully integrated into capitalist market economies, material things have less value. At the same time, there is more emphasis on sharing than on hoarding, and having too many things of value may be seen as being selfish and unsocial. Within this framework, the person *taking* may be viewed as more justified than the person *having*. It is the latter who would be considered selfish and greedy and more unsocial than the former.

LAWS AND THEIR IMPLEMENTATION

Most aborigines, including those in South Asia (including India), believe that a person is composed of a body, mind and spirit, and that these are integrated not only with each other but also with those of others. Thus, the human spirit is in harmony with those of other beings, both natural and supernatural. Tribal laws are those rules of conduct that take into account the philosophies regarding the living world and the general cosmology. Thus, 'laws' are not placed in any particular or separate domain but are pervasive of all aspects of life. Most studies of

Tribal laws are those rules of conduct that take into account the philosophies regarding the living world and the general cosmology. Thus, 'laws' are not placed in any particular or separate domain, but are pervasive of all aspects of life.

tribal law are actually ethnographies that encompass all aspects of life such as family, kinship, economy, power and religion. Tribal laws are mostly referred to as customary laws that take into account the entire body of customs and rules of behaviour of a tribe. The custodian of these rules is the entire community, and there is almost never any specialist.

These rules are internalised as part of the process of socialisation that takes place within the family or in tribal institutions such as the men's and girls' houses of the Nagas, the *dhumkuria* of the Santals and the *ghotuls* of the Mundas. These institutions are residential houses for the youth where they learn the ways as well as the skills of their respective tribes. These youth dormitories are equivalent to the schools of modern society except that they do not bind young people in any artificial bondage of discipline but rather let them enjoy their youth and also get socialised into responsible members of their community. The works of anthropologists such as Radcliffe-Brown (1922) and Turner (1970) have also demonstrated the educative role of initiation rituals of young children. These rituals are performed when children transition into adulthood, and they have elaborate symbolic aspects that instill the core values of the community as also educate the children into the rules and norms of the community and absorb the expectations that they are obliged to fulfill as adults and adjusted members of the tribal community.

Tribal customary laws are thus not written and strictly enforced coded commands—they are simply generalised norms of conduct that are naturally followed by most members of the community. Minor aberrations that do not affect community life are tolerated. Most tribal people respect individual decision-making and are not prone to unnecessary confrontations with their community members. Only those infringements that are seen as serious threats to social life are considered worthy of sanctions. Most sanctions, as mentioned, are consensual and involve soft measures like boycott, avoidance, ridicule and, at the most, shaming of the person concerned.

Tribal customary laws include inheritance and property rules, marriage rules and norms, taboos and restrictions, food patterns and norms of eating, house plans and village settlements, and norms for dealing with the supernatural and the natural worlds. They also involve norms of day-to-day interactions, patterns of sharing and distribution of resources such as food and subsistence goods, gift giving, showing respect, and ways of shaming and ridicule—in short, they cover the entire gamut of behaviour that one is expected to encounter in daily life. Unlike popular conceptions, tribal laws are not rigid but rather are often manipulated, adjusted, contested and transformed according to the situation and context. The important requirement is that the basic structure of social relations such as gender norms, rules of kinship and marriage, religious values and symbolic dimensions of social life should not be disturbed in the process of such adjustments.

THE AGENTS DISPENSING JUSTICE

Tribes have been erroneously regarded as egalitarian, with complete gender equality. In the smallest of the bands, the situation may approximate to equality, but there is still deference towards elders, respect for the wise, and admiration for the young and able. Case studies of band societies indicate that these societies have the most equal relations possible, although age remains a key factor for gaining respect and prestige, as most knowledge is acquired with age and experience. There may be specialists, that is, people with specific abilities, like the person who is able to locate water by tapping on the ground or the person who has better knowledge about herbs or about hunting than others. However, there is no power of coercion and no power to punish others. Such matters are mostly left to the supernatural. If the community is small enough to have face-to-face interactions, then most decisions are made on a consensual basis. Someone is thrown out of the community only as the last resort, and this is the maximum possible punishment. In tribal societies where there is little recognition of hierarchy, those getting possessed are not treated as shamans or even as special people. They are simply seen as vehicles of the supernatural, but they do not have any right of recognition on their own. In some communities, especially those practising agriculture, there may be specialist shamans who evoke a little more consideration in that they receive gifts for their services. For example, in some tribes, those taking part in a séance are treated to a sumptuous meal for their efforts.

Where descent groups exist and control resources, like among the Toda, lineage-elders command a lot of prestige and power of persuasion. What they lack, however, is the power of possession. Elders manage resources on behalf of the community as a whole and hold a position of responsibility. The power that they have is in the form of having a voice in community matters. This power is enhanced or reduced depending upon the reputation of the person. Although such positions are traditional in essence, yet the individual always plays an important role. All elders must be respected, but a particular person may command more respect than others because of personal qualities. Such individuals can emerge as tribal leaders.

The Nagas have an institution known as *ang*, which is the equivalent of a chiefship. The person occupying this status is both a lineage leader and a village head as most Naga villages are clan-based. The patriarchy of the Nagas was based in their practice of headhunting—the single most prestigious activity that conferred both ritual and social status. Since this could only be performed by the men, the women could never get to acquire real power. Even after headhunting was banned during the colonial period, the patriarchal nature of society did not change, for Christianity, adopted on a large scale by the Naga, supported the submissive status of women even more emphatically. Yet, Naga women have played an important role in society and continue to be involved in the public sphere. The Naga Hoho or council of elders, however, comprises only men.

The Khasis have tribal councils that are headed by men, even though Khasi society is matrilineal. Traditionally, the headman managed all the land in the village, but after the British came to the Khasi and Garo Hills, they needed to buy land, and thus slowly the practice of landowning was established. In the present times, land and property in this region are mostly individually owned and passed down the female line of inheritance.

In most tribal societies, in the absence of any secular authority, it is the supernatural agent that provides the greatest source of controlling power. While in many tribes, the supernatural exists in the otherworldly realm, in the mountain realm of the Himalayas, tribal (even some non-tribal) villages are ruled by sovereign supernatural deities, which behave like they were the actual rulers. Ethnographers of this region have made special note of these supernatural sovereigns (Channa 2010; Galey 1994; Sax 2002), who are regarded by the people as living with and in constant interaction with the people they rule over. In a visit to the tribal belt of Kinnaur, I found that these rulers are in command even in the present day. They live in palaces that are called abodes and not temples, and they have their treasury, their attendants and their media, whose jobs are to take care of the treasury, to look after the royal residence and to act as the communication channel between the sovereign deity and his/her people, respectively. The customary laws here are directly translated as the wishes of the deity, and no significant action can take place without the deity's explicit consent.

Any couple that wishes to get married has to take the consent of the deity. Any important activity, like travel, house-building, and even sowing and harvesting of crops can be done only with the deity's acquiescence. In the summer of 2008, when I visited the village of Chitkul, the presiding deity, a goddess, had gone visiting her husband, the god Badrinath, residing in Uttarakhand. Although it was way past the harvest time, the villagers were waiting patiently for the deity to return and give permission to them to harvest the crops. Thus, a high degree of social control is achieved by the superhuman beings, as Spiro (1966) would call them, in the absence of any human authority. None of these regions have any system of tribal authority like a council of elders or a chief—they are totally ruled and controlled by their village gods. This is not to say that the rule is tyrannical or that the deities cannot be cajoled or manipulated, but at the same time, in the perception of the local people, the deities are the supreme authority and uphold the customary laws of the community. Since the deities are living and ever-present, there is never any need to codify and write down the laws. The deities are, like in all other tribal societies, in the realm of the known and understood, but they are not to be translated into any institutional framework.

One immediate outcome of the lack of codification and scripting of laws is that the laws remain situational, flexible and contextual. As with the living deity, customary laws are manageable and considerate. Unlike in Western societies, justice in tribal societies is not blindfolded, but has her eyes wide open. She listens, she is humane and she responds to situational exigencies, taking the opinion of ordinary people into account. She is not harsh or unrelenting.

Unlike in Western societies, justice in tribal societies is not blindfolded but has her eyes wide open. She listens, is humane and responds to situational exigencies, taking the opinion of ordinary people into account. She is not harsh or unrelenting.

THEORETICAL APPROACHES TO THE STUDY OF CUSTOMARY LAWS

The pioneering work in studying the legal systems of non-Western people was done by Maine (1861), who, unlike Bentham (1948 [1789]), did not believe that there should be only one legal system for all of humanity if society was to be understood as civilised. The individual-centred, objective rationality of the Benthamites was not supported by Maine, who strongly believed that there was a close link between culture and law and that every cultural system and historical period needed its own legal principles that were compatible with the rest of its values. Maine's scholarship focused on ancient civilisations such as Greece and India. Like most of his contemporaries, Maine was an evolutionist, and he put forward a thesis of societies evolving from status to contract. In his work, *Ancient Law* (1861), he analysed various historical societies to indicate that earlier societies put emphasis on social aspects of relationships and laws were formulated keeping relationships in mind, while modern societies focused on the individuals who enter into contractual relationships with each other. Thus, earlier laws were subjective and flexible, while more evolved legal systems are rule-bound, more rigid and codified. It was on Maine's insistence that the Indian legal system was formulated with deference to local traditions and culture, even as most of the basic rules were adapted from the Western legal system. For the sake of administrative simplicity, the British decided not to interfere too much with the customary laws of the fringe people of the continent and let tribal areas live according to their own culture. The British, however, did interfere where there was a crisis of power, that is, where local chiefs and tribal leadership had a greater role to play. Two such examples are the suppression of human sacrifice among the Konds and of headhunting among the Nagas.

Following the evolutionists, there were many functionalist studies of customary laws of tribes, the most prominent ones being those of Hoebel (1954), Pospisil (1958) and Malinowski (1926). Predictably, Malinowski criticised Maine for his speculative theory and advocated the use of fieldwork to directly collect data on the living customs of communities. All functionalists foregrounded the rationality of tribal customary laws and demonstrated their relevance in the context of tribal lives. They were interested in demonstrating that tribes had functioning, stable societies and that there were sanctions and methods of social control that were effective in these societies, even if the methods were not coercive and were most often not institutionalised in separate domains. Both Bohannan (1957) and Gluckmann (1955), who have done significant work on the maintenance of law and order among tribes, advocated the use of local, native terms, as not all ideas are directly translatable and terms often lose their actual meanings in translations. Quite often, terms such as the already mentioned 'guilty' and 'not guilty' are rarely found in non-Western societies, where the concept of guilt is rarely a clear-cut either/or situation. There is considerable wisdom in this suggestion. The *Report of the Aboriginal Justice Inquiry of Manitoba* (1999) shows how the use of interpreters to try the tribal accused often led to great confusion, with the accused frequently admitting to incriminating actions or saying they were guilty, when they had in fact misunderstood what was being asked of them. The over-representation of tribal persons in prisons in Canada, Australia and New Zealand, where the indigenous populations are subject to an alien system of law with which they are not familiar, indicates that the law is often misused to unjustly convict the aborigines, who are unfamiliar with the terms and processes of the Western-style courts.

By the 1970s, the theoretical emphasis shifted to describing the judicial process rather than simply identifying the rules, as scholars like Gluckmann (1955) found that tribal law was best understood in its application, given that its rules were not coded and fixed, and the real effectivity of social control lay in how the rules were interpreted and applied. As already mentioned, tribal law is embedded in social relationships. Therefore, it is best understood as the unfolding of social relationships through contestations and the manner in which norms are evoked and refuted in the process.

In his study of the judicial process among the Barotse, a people he calls the Lozi, Gluckmann described the working of their local courts, called *kuta* in the local language. He found that although the structure of the court, with its judges and its basic principles of judgement, was similar to that of the judiciary in other parts of the world, the tribal Lozi, in the process of dispensing justice, were informed by their society and their value systems. The Lozi have what Gluckmann terms as 'multiplex relationships', and they have a society that is comparatively 'simple' in that there are not too many separate roles for individual men and women, most of whom occupy several roles, with their kinship ties acting as the key provider of most social resources like property, occupation, and political and religious power. Each individual resides in a village through a kinship bond, yet the village is also a political unit integrated with the larger Barotse nation through the king.

The Lozi have a king and a nation that is composed of many villages. The king receives tribute but lives like any other ordinary person because his kingship involves distributing most of his earnings to his followers and dependents. The village headman is both kin and a political leader to all the residents of the village, and the king is the religious and political head who holds the nation together. The good fortune of the nation is dependent upon the benevolence of the king's ancestors, who are the spiritual heads.

Thus, when a person appears in court, he or she does not appear only in the context of a particular complaint but is always viewed in terms of the entire gamut of his/her social personhood. The key aim of the court is to cause the least disruption of existing social relationships and to foster new ones. In this context, Gluckmann notes that the greatest care is taken if the persons concerned are linked by kinship ties and the breaking of kin relations is perceived as disastrous. In such a case, the judges focus more on the relationship than on the case in particular. If the persons concerned are linked as husband and wife, then the nature of the complaint can be of more central concern as the marital relationship is not a fundamental kinship relationship. In case the parties are strangers, then the law will take its own course in a more objective manner and the judges are likely to give a judgement only on the merits of the case, unfettered by concerns of relationship. The Lozi do not like to see any irreparable damage to existing relationships and also desire the continuity of relationships for the future. Thus, while the judges have to ensure that individual wrongdoings do not go unnoticed or unpunished, they also have to ensure that this is accomplished in a manner that does not disturb social cohesion. All disputes need to be amicably settled so that in future the parties concerned can coexist amicably. The closer the relationship between the parties, the more it influences the judgement.

Like in all other judicial systems, the concept of the 'reasonable person' plays a key role among the Lozi, but this is implicitly linked to the concept of the moral person. Thus, although technically law is rule-bound rather than a moral concept, the Lozi judges are reluctant to support a person who may be legally right but morally wrong. They are not likely to uphold the law against justice, where justice belongs to an overall moral universe of right and wrong. Thus, Gluckmann successfully demonstrates the actual working of the legal system of a tribal people and demonstrates how the concept of justice that is deeply embedded in the social dimension intersects with the rational and technical aspects of legality. The internal variations of the processes of application are made clear by the ethnography of the cases. Gluckmann (1955) along with Pospisil (1958) advocated for a notion of universal legalism, trying to show that there are fundamental similarities in all legal systems in spite of cultural differences. Bohannan (1957), on the other hand, based on his fieldwork among the Tiv of Nigeria, was in favour of legal relativism, that is, analysing each legal system in its own context. To some extent, the differences in opinion could have been informed by the very different nature of the societies Gluckmann and Bohannan studied. The Barotse were a nation and had formal courts of law, while the Tiv were decentralised, with little formal institutionalisation.

A major contribution of anthropologists working among tribes and recording their customary laws was that they managed to put in written form much that earlier existed only as oral traditions. Some of these works, like that of Schapera (1938), of recording the customary laws of the Tsawana, are still used by law courts there. A more recent work on customary law is by Nader (1990) among the Zapotec of Mexico.

The extended case method has been used by anthropologists to study the judicial process in particular. Its proponent van Velson (1967) suggested that the real process can only be understood if it is followed over the entire period of its execution, and its ramifications and relations are examined holistically. Each stage of the case needs to be seen as an unfolding of the successive stages of the relationship. Other Africanists, like Turner (1953), also used the extended case method or situational analysis, where the inductive method was used to first collect the data or the cases, and then generalisations were drawn from them. Others like Clifford Geertz were of the opinion that by using the case study method, the anthropologist was confining herself to the exotic and the extraordinary while ignoring ordinary and routine cases. Geertz (1983) also extended his interpretative approach to the field of law to argue that while most data that enters law courts (formal or informal) are taken to be objective facts, in reality they are only subjective interpretations put forward by people, who filter the information according to their perceptions derived from their own meaning systems. He pointed out that even the concept of justice has no universal referent but is understood by each culture according to its own cosmology and religious values. The Islamic concept of justice, for example, is based on truth, while the Indian system of dharma emphasises duty and the Malayo-Polynesian *adat* system revolves around the notion of socially accepted behaviour prescribed by cultural etiquettes.

A major contribution of anthropologists working among tribes and recording their customary laws was that they managed to put in written form much that earlier existed only as oral traditions.

Contemporary studies mostly examine customary laws in terms of their meaning and the relationship and intersection of law with other social variables like the state, gender and internal stratification. These works also see customary laws in terms of their rationality and relevance in the context of global situations of environmental degradation, encroachment of the capitalist system and the destruction of social life and culture.

In his frequently cited work on customary law, Malinowski (1926) had designated tribal laws as rigid and as eliciting conformity and compulsory reciprocity. He defined 'civil law' as controlling and defining all dimensions of tribal life and referred to it as a 'body of binding obligations', enforced by rules of reciprocity involving complementary rights and duties. However, in later times, including in the works of Gluckmann and others, tribal customary laws were seen as more flexible, adjustable and contextual. In fact, they were seen as less rigid than the codified Western legal systems. Geertz defended the concept of relativism that had been earlier endorsed by Bohannan.

In contemporary studies, these aspects of interpretation and differential impact have been foregrounded, especially from a gendered perspective, whereby the notion of the customary has been challenged by arguing that it is often constructed by those in power to serve their interests. The immutability of custom and its very construction have been interrogated by recent scholars like Bond (2011: 472), who writes:

> Although conceptually distinct from culture, customary law is a legal expression of cultural norms and values. Like culture, customary law is dynamic and changes based on social, economic, and legal developments. It is internally contested, and powerful elites often determine the dominant cultural interpretation and provide what is seen as a definitive interpretation of customary law.

Thus, feminists in particular have been critical of the blind acceptance of customary law as the genuine and true representative of the identity of a tribe by arguing that these laws are often used to dominate and discriminate against women and the weaker sections of the tribe. Those in power try to project these laws as part of the tribal identity, but in this process, they manage to subjugate some sections without the possibility of redress. Naga women, for example, are highly critical

Feminists have been critical of blindly accepting customary law as the true identity of a tribe. Those in power project these laws as part of the tribal identity, in the process subjugating some sections without the possibility of redress.

of the state's position on letting the Naga people follow their customary laws, which they feel are highly patriarchal. They often mention that as women they would be better off under the Indian nation's civil laws that greatly favour women. In her work on the customary laws of the Rongmei, Panmei (2016) has mentioned that in contemporary times, many tribal people prefer to go to civil courts as they feel that their tribal councils will not provide them with justice.

It is clear that customary law is a variable and flexible dimension of tribal life that is as varied as the tribes are, because being intrinsically interwoven with tribal culture, it exhibits as much variation as tribes and their cultures do. The next section will illustrate some of these variabilities.

ETHNOGRAPHIC EXAMPLES FROM INDIAN TRIBES

The tribes of Meghalaya have held a unique position in that they are among the few tribes in India that still have a system of active matrilineal inheritance. In studies of the Pnars of Meghalaya, Nongbri (2016) and Nongkynrih (2002) have described these inheritance patterns in details.

The concept of private property was introduced by the British in the North Eastern Hill Region, and it also brought about changes in the patterns of inheritance. In the period before the introduction of a capitalist economy, the possession of material things was limited to a few household goods and personal belongings, but with the introduction of markets and capitalism, things changed to include the concept of market-acquired goods as well as the sale and purchase of land. By the early part of the twentieth century, one could distinguish between two types of property in Pnar society: *kaiongrim* or ancestral property, and *kayutran* or self-acquired property. The ancestral property was inalienable (that is, it could not be bought or sold), and it passed down from mother to daughter. The youngest daughter or *kawasdiah* inherited the parental house. If there was other landed property, it was distributed among all the daughters along with the personal belongings of the mother. If the youngest daughter died, her share was inherited by the sister just above her in age. If there was only one daughter, she became the sole heir to her parents' property and all belongings. Theoretically, the sons had no right to the ancestral property, and in the absence of a daughter, the system of adoption *karap yung* was resorted to, preferably of a relative with the same clan name. The adopted girl would then inherit all the ancestral property of the family. Another option was for a son to inherit the property but only for the duration of his lifetime. When he passed away, the ancestral property reverted to the nearest female maternal kin. However, in the present times, parents prefer to give their son all the property in the absence of a daughter rather than to another relative.

In the monetary economy, it is possible for a man to acquire property and wealth of his own. The self-acquired property, kayutran, can be disposed of to whomever the owner chooses through the tradition of *pynkam* or oral will. However, if a man dies without having willed his property, the same will pass on to his mother or, in her absence, to his sister. If he has no female relatives, his property will pass on to his children, mostly his daughters. The wife may get half the property of her deceased husband if she promises not to remarry again. The youngest daughter is the custodian of the household rituals and is the social representative of her clan. Yet, while women hold social and religious power in Pnar society as well as in other communities in Meghalaya, political power lies in the hands of men. The woman has unquestioned power as a mother when she controls every aspect of the household economy.

In most households, every adult member of the family engages in some productive work to meet the needs of the family. Although the bulk of the villagers are still engaged in agricultural activities, at least one or more member of the family is likely to be engaged in an occupation for cash income. Both daughters and sons of the house hand over part of their earnings to the mother or, in the absence of the mother, to the youngest sister. She looks after all expenses related to household affairs. However, according to Pakentyne (2018), the practice of who keeps the yields from the fields or the earnings of the family members, and who actually manages the same, is more complicated than the ideological norms for these practices. Day-to-day affairs of the household are managed according to the personalities and interpersonal relations of the family members. Men who earn independent incomes may take care of their personal expenses like putting in fuel for their cars or buying gifts for their wife and children. All customary laws provide broad outlines but are not rigid in their implementation. As long as no serious disruption of relationships takes place, adjustments take place within the gamut of formal rules.

The Nagas of the Northeast provide a contrast to the Khasi and Garo communities of Meghalaya, in being strictly patrilineal. Das (1993) has given a comprehensive account of the Zounou-Keyhonou Nagas. They are known as the Southern Angami in official parlance—a designation that is not acceptable to them, as they have their own name with which they identify. Das studied the village Viswema that is under the supervision of the circle officer of the region whose office is located in the village of Jakhama. The tribal court, known as the *dobhashi* court, is attached to this circle office. The smallest functioning unit of this society is the patrilineal family known as *misokeswe*, that is, a property-owning group where husband and wife jointly own both moveable and immovable property. Misokeswe basically refers to the hearth. The general pattern among the Zounou-Keyhonou is for the sons to separate from the household after marriage till the youngest son is left to take over the property and the house of the parents. Although the elder sons also inherit, the largest portion usually goes to the youngest son. Authority is, however, vested in the eldest son, who takes over from the father after his death. Thus, the youngest gets largest share of property but the eldest is the social inheritor of the father's status. This family is part of the larger lineage that has rights over assets like land and forests. People generally consider the presence of three married women in the same family to be inauspicious and also socially burdensome, which is why sons tend to separate sooner or later, after they get married. Although daughters do not inherit the lineage property, they retain the right to maintenance throughout their lives. Sometimes, a widowed daughter may come back to her parental family with her children.

Since property passes in the male line, a couple usually resorts to adoption in case there is no male heir. No man is allowed to marry a second time, even if they do not have any children. But in case the couple has a daughter, they often adopt the daughter's son (if there is one) as their own son. The person who performs the funerary ritual of a person also retains the right to inherit from that person, so that even if a non-agnate does this duty, he can be adopted into the lineage.

The Zounou-Keyhonou practise clan exogamy for their patriclans, but they also do not marry their mother's agnates like MB (mother's brother), MZ (mother's sister), MBD (mother's brother's daughter), MZS (mother's sister's son), MBS (mother's brother's son) and MZD (mother's sister's daughter). Interestingly, there are no rigid rules for endogamy, but it is only a preferential rule that they mostly marry in their own village. According to tribal custom, the proposal for marriage must come from the household of the man who seeks the bride. It is considered socially appropriate for families of equal status to enter into a marital arrangement. In the recent times, when internal stratification is more common because of the market economy, families of rich young men and women may even seek equal-status partners in other villages, overriding the earlier preference for village endogamy. Although after marriage a woman moves to her husband's house and her sexual, economic and reproductive rights are transferred to her husband's lineage, she never truly becomes a member of her affinal lineage and remains for life a member of her father's lineage, entitled to both property and maintenance.

Each clan has its own land, and it is this land that is the core reference of identity for the Zounou-Keyhonou. The villages are for day-to-day administration, with the village headman, the village priests and the village-level council of elders playing key roles. In terms of laws, there are certain infringements that are taken as very serious—these include murder, incest and the violation of the sanctity of the *thenu* gates. In case of murder, the victim's family has the right to take the murderer's life. In case they do not, the murderer is banished outside the village and his property given to the family of the victim. At the second level are laws or rules pertaining to divorce, marriage, inheritance, disputes over property, theft, assault and trespass. While the village headman or *gaonbura* holds a formal position, there are informal arbitrators called *sechomi* who help in the arbitration, like calling witnesses, acting as the mediator between the plaintiff and the defendant, and performing other duties related to disputes and their settlements. The sechomi are chosen according to age and wisdom, and their office is neither hereditary nor formal. However, the final authority is that of the village headman, whose authority is seen as next only to god. Anything that cannot be resolved at the level of the clan or lineage is placed before him and his decision is regarded as final.

In line with what has been already discussed, the main role of the sechomi is to restore order and ensure that no dispute goes out of control or that tribal cohesion is not affected. They are also representative of public opinion as well as of the moral and ethical values of society.

In her study of the Zeliangrong of Manipur, Panmei (2016) has described the changes in the social organisation of the Rongmei, who earlier had exogamous moieties, namely, Pamei and Newmei. These moieties, over a long period of time, split into exogamous clans, sub-clans and lineages, giving rise to the possibility of moiety endogamy. At present, the Pamei have the component clans of Kamei, Malangmei, Singongmei, Daimei, Phaomei and Kamson. On the other hand, the Newmei split into the clans Gonmei, Gondamei, Panmei, Thaimei, Maringmei, Riamei and Gonthangmei. These clans have further split into sub-clans and lineages, making the system far more complicated than before. Sometimes, the clans have split to allow for marriages to take place, in order to keep the rule of clan exogamy undisturbed. The Rongmei are patrilineal and patrilocal, and they follow rules of marriage that enforce monogamy, but both sororate and levirate are almost obligatory. These practices ensure the unity of the lineage group and the security of the children.

The Rongmei have always had a village council known as *pei*, even before the Village Authority Act of 1956 made village councils mandatory. The pei represents every clan in the village by one male representative. The villages also have a hereditary chief along with the elected or chosen head according to the act of 1956. The latter is known as the chairman and is chosen by the village elders in consensus, along with the approval of the government officials.

There are rules of social conduct that are unwritten yet enforced by public opinion, and also collective enforcement by shaming, humiliation and non-violent coercion. Divorce for various reasons is permissible among the Rongmei. If a man wishes to marry again and bring in a new wife, the existing property is divided equally between the husband and wife, and the children are given the choice to go and live with either parent. However, the biological or social father retains the sole right to receive bride price for his daughters, irrespective of where they may be staying. Both men and women may seek divorce on grounds of infidelity of the spouse. A wife may sometimes return her bride price if she feels very unhappy in her marriage, and thus seek freedom from the marriage. Although women do not have access to immovable property, they can take away some moveable items at the time of separation but not their husbands' ritual objects, clothes and livestock. However, divorce is not taken lightly and every effort is made by the community to restore peace between the couple. Sometimes, the restitution of conjugal rights takes place after divorce and the couple starts living together again.

If a girl gets pregnant before marriage and the paternity of the child is known, then the man is often made to marry the girl and apologise to her male relatives, like father and brother. He also has to take full responsibility of the birth of the child, in case he is unable to marry the mother. After birth, such a child becomes a member of its father's lineage, even if the parents are not married. However, the case of a child whose father is not known is considered as both unfortunate and inauspicious. A woman carrying such a child may be forced out of the village and allowed to return only after the birth of the child. Such a child can get social recognition only if it is adopted into the mother's brother's clan; otherwise it may have to lead a life of social ostracisation and may never be able to marry on growing up. In case a couple is childless, it can adopt a child to make it their legal heir. Sometimes, very poor parents may give their child up for adoption. In all cases, it depends upon the person who adopts, whether or not he or she wishes to give his or her property to the adopted child. A widow too can adopt a child if she wishes to.

Rape is considered a serious offence among the Rongmei, and the rapist is exiled from the village for a period of three years and his property stoned. No one touches such property as it is believed to bring ill luck. In case a married woman is impregnated by another man, it is entirely up to her husband to decide how she will be treated. If he wishes, her bride price can be returned and her head shaved, so that she is humiliated; on the other hand, he can be kind and accept the baby, and their married life will continue as normal. Thus, we see that customary laws are flexible and can be interpreted by the people according to their own liking. If the relationship between husband and wife is strong then it can overcome many hurdles.

Like most other Naga societies, the Rongmei are patrilineal and follow the rules of primogeniture, so the firstborn is the last to get married and is the one left to look after his old parents. He gets the ancestral house, though the parents may decide to give it to another son if they like. The property is nearly equally divided among all the sons. In case one of the brothers dies, then his property is also equally divided among the other brothers. Adopted sons have same rights as the others. In case the adopted child has his own property, then he inherits it in addition to the property inherited from his adopted father. In case the adopted child dies, then his adoptive father gets his property.

Although women do not inherit land and immovable property from their fathers, they do have some kind of property rights. These are mostly accessible to her after marriage. A married woman has rights over property paid as her bride price and over goods that she has received as marriage gifts from relatives and others. She has full rights over self-acquired property as well as any wealth given to her for the maintenance of her minor children by her husband's family. In case a woman has no brothers, she may inherit from her father or more likely from her widowed mother. A widow has rights to one-third of her husband's property, while the rest goes to his male agnates. However, if a woman remarries, then she has to forfeit her rights to her first husband's property. Such property includes land, forests, domestic animals, irrigation canals, houses and jewellery.

The preceding discussion was on the rules pertaining to individual ownership of property. However, the Rongmei, like most other tribal societies, have community ownership of property as well. At the village level, these include public places (including buildings) like schools, post offices, roads, community halls, playgrounds, forests, lakes and churches, which are for everyone's use but are not possessed by anyone in particular. All members of the village have user rights over these but not rights of possession.

At a higher level of ownership are clan property, comprising mostly land, forests, meadows, grazing land and large resources like water bodies. Every member of a clan has to ask for permission from the clan elders to take land for cultivation, which is redistributed every cultivation cycle. Other resources like forests, streams and grazing land can be used by any member of the clan. Since most tribes of the Northeast including the Rongmei practise shifting cultivation, it is necessary for the land to be owned by the community as a large amount of land has to be kept fallow and cultivable plots are distributed each cycle to individual households according to their need. Such community ownership also ensures that each member of the clan is provided with basic subsistence requirements.

The common resources are for everyone's needs but cannot be exploited or wasted. Thus, water sources are used with caution, and bamboo, forest produce, timber, grass for thatching and grazing, and water for self-use and for animals has to be used with caution and with respect towards other members of the community. There is a sense of community ownership that comes with collective responsibility. A notion of ethics and morality is intrinsically interwoven with customary laws in tribal society, especially with respect to common resources necessary for the survival of the tribe as a whole. In case of selling land or forests, permission needs to be taken from the household elder or the clan elder, whichever may be the case. Buying and selling of land and forest resource is very rare and seldom occurs.

CRIME

The concept of crime and sanctions against them are well defined in Rongmei customary laws. Theft is understood as taking things without permission from the owner, but buying of stolen goods is also a crime and blaming someone for theft unjustly too is wrong and a punishable offence. A thief if caught has to pay seven times the price of the stolen goods to the owner; a person knowingly buying stolen goods has to pay twice the value of the goods; and a person who unjustly blames another to be a thief has to pay half the value of the goods to the blamed person. In each case, as we see, the restitution is directed to the affected person and not to the community.

Cheating and not keeping a promise is also seen as a grave offence and the person, who is found cheating—like not paying back money owned, or selling something twice over to different people, or trying to mislead or make a fool out of others—can be subject to physical punishment, though never too serious. In case of a monetary offence, the offender can be asked to pay a fine. Behavioural offences like use of force, abusing and threatening are also viewed seriously and punished adequately. Such matters may be brought up before the village elders, for taking appropriate measures or fixing the quantum of sanction, like the amount of fine to be paid. It is also considered a serious offence to cause loss of livelihood to someone by an act of mischief like setting fire to someone's jhum cultivation field before time, thus causing loss to the person. In a jhum cycle, after the cutting of the vegetation, the time for setting fire is carefully calculated, and if the fire is set before the vegetation is completely dry, the entire cycle of cultivation is disrupted, leading to loss of crop yield. In such a case, the offender is asked to clean half of the field of the affected person in the next cultivation cycle.

Since domestic animals like cattle and pigs are common in this region, disputes also arise over them. If a person's animal is unjustly killed by another, then the killer has to pay twice the value of the animal. If a person's animal is causing harm to another person's fields and no remedy is undertaken even after repeated complaints, then the affected person has the right to kill that animal. If two animals get into a fight and one dies, then the owners of both the animals will share the one remaining one equally, for instance, it may be sold and the money divided.

If someone borrows a good and spoils it, then he/she has to replace it. The accepted procedure for all misunderstandings and cases of doubt of guilt regarding any offence is for people to take oaths. Oath taking is taken very seriously among tribal people and is a major deterrent for aberrant behaviour. However, among the Rongmei, as among all other tribal communities, the major aim of customary laws is not to punish but to maintain social harmony. Thus, as far as possible, there are efforts towards negotiations for reconciliation between the aggrieved parties. Third-party mediation without bias is seen as an accepted mode of settlement of disputes. Mediators include village elders, clan elders, people of good reputation and ultimately the village council. In fact, even if a dispute has been resolved by mediation by anyone, the actual resolution always takes place in front of the village council, and usually takes the form of drinking and eating together.

Even the case of what is considered a criminal offence in the global justice system, for instance, murder, the offence is treated not in abstraction but contextualised in terms of its subjective content. Thus, not all murders are treated as equal but are classified according to the intention that led to the crime. Accidental causation or some kind of justified homicide is hence treated differently than crimes committed because of jealousy, greed, anger or hatred. In case of a crime driven by bad intention, the culprit and his family are excommunicated from the village for seven years. The house of the culprit is stoned and sealed and declared as a place of ill omen. The children of the culprit's family and of the victim's family cannot marry for 10 generations.

In case of an unintended crime, the banishment is also for seven years, but the culprit is allowed to take his possessions out of his house before leaving the village. After seven years, he and his family can come back to the village if the family of the victim allows it. In case the family of the victim expresses doubt over the intentionality of the action, then the person can only return after taking an oath. In case he refuses to take an oath, he may not be allowed to return. If a child under 10 years of age commits a serious crime like killing someone, the child is also sent out of the village with his guardians. If a man kills his friend accidently, he is supposed take care of the funeral and also take care of the family of the victim.

In case a victim does not die but survives an attack, like that by poisoning, then the person who has accidently administered the poison will be asked to take an oath. If the person attacked dies, the culprit will be excommunicated for seven years.

In case of murder, there can be retribution or the matter can be settled in the house of the victim, where there is a one-to-one negotiation between the victim's household and that of the culprit.

In such a situation, the matter is dealt with as between two affected families and is settled according to the negotiations between them. At times, there can be a reciprocal killing also. However, once the matter is brought before the pei, it goes out of the hands of the parties concerned. The pei is always inclined to settle the matter so that there is least disruption of the village social life. Most matters are settled with the imposition of fines and a village feast where old enmities are buried and harmony restored.

SUMMARY

In this chapter, we have examined the concepts of justice and the maintenance of law and order in tribal societies. All tribes, small or big and with a variety of livelihood patterns, have definite systems of maintaining social order. These systems are also synchronised with their modes of livelihood, habitat and ways of life. Unlike Western societies, where all crimes are measured against uniform laws and treated as equivalent if they are of the same type, tribal societies situate each crime within its context of social relationships and treat it according to merits measured against tribal values and sense of morality. Each case has its own perspective of right and wrong, course of action to be taken or not taken, and there are no fixed punishments, although broad guidelines exist. The most important aspect of tribal justice is that individuals are treated as persons, as having emotions and relationships. The process of justice tries to bring the affected persons back to a state of normalcy by redressing the wrongs that have been done against them. Instead of having clear-cut dichotomies such as guilty–non-guilty, tribes have a flexible system of judgement and dispensation of justice. For example, if someone has harmed someone's agricultural field, instead of simply punishing the guilty, the effort is to make him compensate the victim by putting in his labour and effort to put things right.

Unlike Western societies, where all crimes are measured against uniform laws, tribal societies situate each crime within the context of its social relationships. Each case has its own perspective of right and wrong; there are no fixed punishments, only broad guidelines.

Justice is not limited to humans but extends to non-humans, animals, natural objects as well as sacred beings, all of which are encompassed within the ambit of the justice system. The cosmos is a web of life with its own principles that need to be respected. Humans do not have primacy and are not the centre of the universe. They are embedded in relationships with all other beings, and the merits and demerits of actions are judged with respect to these relationships and the overall equilibrium of things. The aim of all retributive and restitutive action is to restore the balance of these relationships. As we have seen, customary laws both define and maintain relationships and the distribution of power in society. These laws are thus both flexible and subject to change as the nature of power and relationships change. We have seen how the influx of a market economy changes the nature of inheritance patterns as persons can acquire wealth that is not necessarily bound by customary laws. With changes in occupation and nature of the economy, there are changes in gender relations, intra-family relationships, village authority systems, marriage patterns, etc. Contemporary tribes consider their customary laws as symbols of their identity, and the state has also conceded that at the level of civil society, tribes can continue with their customary laws. But tribes are also under stress in the present times. Poverty, marginalisation, dispossession of their lands and destruction of their habitats are taking a toll on many tribes, leading them to frustration and despair. As Brant (1990) has analysed, aborigines often tend to shift the blame—in psychological terms, 'project' the tension and frustration—onto an external agency like a witch or a demon. As has been documented, there has been a rise in witchcraft accusations and the persecution of witches in many tribal areas in India, especially among tribes that are facing a lot of suffering (Mishra 2003). The accused are usually the most vulnerable members of society, poor and single women, widows and the elderly. Thus, customary laws are sometimes distorted in times of stress, as such projections in an indirect way serve to maintain overall harmony by transferring the stress on to 'victims'.

Tribal people are aware of the laws of the land, and as Panmei (2016) has shown in her field study of the Rongmei tribe, at times, if certain individuals are not satisfied with the verdict of the village council, they take recourse to the legal system of the Indian state. Tribal people do take matters to the police or to law courts. But such incidences are rare as of now. Even though women in patrilineal systems and men in matrilineal systems are not happy with their traditions, there have not been strong voices of protest. The question of identity and the need for a political platform have led to continued adherence to tribal customary laws.

REFERENCES

Aboriginal Justice Implementation Commission. 1999. *Report of the Aboriginal Justice Inquiry of Manitoba.* Winnipeg: Aboriginal Justice Implementation Commission.

Bentham, Jeremy. 1948 [1789]. *An Introduction to the Principles of Moral and Legislation.* New York: Hafner Publications.

Bohannan, Paul. 1957. *Justice and Law among the Tiv.* London: Oxford University Press.

Bond, Johanna E. 2011. 'Women's Rights, Customary Law and the Promise of the Protocol on the Rights of Women in Africa', in Jean Marie Fenrich, Paulo Galizzi and Tracy Higgins (eds), *The Future of African Customary Law,* pp. 467–93. Cambridge: Cambridge University Press.

Brant, Clare. 1990. 'Native Ethics and Rules of Behaviour', *Canadian Journal of Psychiatry,* 35 (6): 534–35.

Channa, Subhadra Mitra. 2010. 'A Ritual Transfer: From the High to the Low in Hindu-Tibetan Communities', in Gita Dharampal-Frick, Robert Langer and Nils Holger (eds), *Transfer and Spaces,* pp. 43–65. Wiesbaden: Harrassowitz.

———. 2013. *The Inner and Outer Selves.* New Delhi: Oxford University Press.

Galey, Jean-Claude. 1994. 'Hindu Kingship in its Ritual Realm: The Garhwali Configuration', in M. P. Joshi, Allen C. Forger and Charles W. Brown (eds), *The Himalayas: Past and Present,* pp. 173–237. Almora: Shree Almora Books Depot.

Geertz, Clifford. 1983. 'Local Knowledge: Fact and Law in Comparative Perspective', in *Local Knowledge: Further Essays in Interpretative Anthropology,* pp. 167–234. New York: Basic Books.

Gluckmann, Max. 1955. *The Judicial Process among the Bartose of Northern Rhodesia.* Manchester: Manchester University Press.

Hobbes, Thomas. 1973 [1651]. *Leviathan.* London: J. M. Dent and Saw.

Hoebel, Adamson E. 1954. *Law of the Primitive Man: A Study in Comparative Legal Dynamics.* Cambridge, MA: Harvard University Press.

Maine, Henry. 1861. *Ancient Law, its Connection with the Early History of Society, and Its Relation to Modern Ideas*. London: John Murray.

Malinowski, Bronislaw. 1926. *Crime and Custom in Savage Society*. London: Routledge and Kegan Paul.

Marriott, McKim. 1991. 'On "Constructing an Indian Ethnosociology"', *Contributions to Indian Sociology*, 25 (2): 295–308.

Mishra, Archana. 2003. *Casting the Evil Eye: Witch Trials in Tribal India*. New Delhi: Roli Books.

Nader, Laura. 1990. *Harmony and Ideology: Justice and Control in a Zapotec Mountain Village*. Stanford: Stanford University Press.

Nongbri, Tiplut. 2016. 'Khasi Women and Matriliny: Transformations in Gender Relations', in Nandini Sundar (ed.), *The Scheduled Tribes and Their India: Politics, Identities Policies and Work*, pp. 85–108. New Delhi: Oxford University Press.

Nongkynrih, A. K. 2002. *Khasi Society of Meghalaya: A Sociological Understanding*. New Delhi: Indus Publishing Company.

Pakentyne, Valentina. 2018. 'Matrilineality and Power Dynamics among the Pnars of Meghalaya', unpublished PhD thesis, University of Delhi.

Panmei, Mary. 2016. 'Customary Law and Gender Relations among the Rongmei Tribe of Manipur', unpublished PhD thesis, University of Delhi.

Pospisil, Leopold. 1958. *Kapauku Papuans and Their Law*. New Haven: Yale University Publications in Anthropology, No. 54.

Radcliffe-Brown, A. R. 1922. *The Andaman Islanders: A Study in Social Anthropology*. Cambridge: Cambridge University Press.

Rousseau, Jean-Jaques. 1970 [1762]. *The Social Contract and Other Political Writings*, trans. Victor Gourovitch. Cambridge: Cambridge University Press.

Sax, William. 2002. 'A Divine King in the Western Himalayas', in *Dancing the Self: Personhood and Performance in the Pandava Lila of Garhwal*, pp. 157–85. Oxford: Oxford University Press.

Schapera, Isaac. 1938. *A Handbook of Tswana Law and Custom*. Oxford, UK: International African Institute and Oxford University Press.

Spiro, Melford E. 1966. 'Religion: Problems of Definition and Explanation', in Michael Banton (ed.), *Anthropological Approaches to the Study of Religion*, pp. 85–124. London: Tavistock.

Strathern, Marilyn. 1999. *Property, Substance and Effect: Anthropological Essays on Person and Things*. London: Athelone Press.

Turner, Victor. 1953. *Schism and Continuity in an African Society: A Study of Ndembu Village Life*. Manchester: Rhodes Livingstone Institute and Manchester University Press.

———. 1970. *The Forest of Symbols: Aspects of Ndembu Ritual*. Ithaca: Cornell University Press.

van Velson, J. 1967. 'The Extended-case Method and Situational Analysis', in A. L. Epstein (ed.), *The Craft of Social Anthropology*, pp. 29–53. London: Tavistock.

SUGGESTED READINGS

Bennett, Thomas W. 2011. 'Customary Criminal Law in the South African Legal System', in Jean Marie Fenrich, Paulo Galizzi and Tracy Higgins (eds), *The Future of African Customary Law*, pp. 363–87. Cambridge: Cambridge University Press.

Benson, Bruce L. 1998. 'Economic Freedom and the Evolution of Law', *Cato Journal*, 18 (2): 209–32.

———. 2003. 'The Evolution of Law', in Charles Rowley and Friedrich Schneider (eds), *The Encyclopedia of Public Choice*, pp. 561–64. New York: Springer.

Comaroff, John and Simon Roberts. 1981. *Rules and Processes: The Cultural Logic of Dispute in an African Context.* Chicago: University of Chicago Press.

Das, N. K. 1993. *Kinship Politics and Law in Naga Society*. Calcutta: Anthropological Survey of India.

Fenrich, Jean Marie, Paulo Galizzi and Tracy Higgins (eds). 2011. *The Future of African Customary Law.* Cambridge: Cambridge University Press.

Hoebel, Adamson E., and Karl Llewelyn. 1941. *The Cheyenne Way: Conflict and Case Law in Primitive Jurisprudence.* Norman, Oklahoma: University of Oklahoma Press.

Marry, Sally E. 1992. 'Anthropology, Law and Transnational Processes', *Annual Review of Anthropology*, 21: 357–79.

Moore, Sally Falk. 2001. 'Certainties Undone: Fifty Turbulent Years of Legal Anthropology, 1949–1999', *Journal of the Royal Anthropological Institute*, 7 (1): 95–116.

Riles, Annelise. 1994. 'Representing In-between: Law, Anthropology, and the Rhetoric of Inter-disciplinarity', *University of Illinois Law Review*: 597–653.

6

TRIBES AND THE STATE

HIGHLIGHTS

- Political status of tribes
- Colonial and postcolonial tribal policies
- Tribe–state relationships in the present times
- Dispossession and exploitation of tribes and tribal regions

INTRODUCTION

In the anthropological understanding, tribes have always been regarded as the antithesis of the state. Service's (1962) classical definition refers to the tribe as a stage of human society where the society is organised around kinship, and is horizontally and not vertically segmented. Tribes have as their basic social organisation horizontally placed segments, each constituting a kinship grouping such as a clan or other form of descent group. Beyond this kind of society are those that are based on chiefdom, which is not radically different from tribal organisation, as here, one of the segments may gain in power and establish itself as superior. Tribal chiefs do not have coercive powers but rather their powers are based on keeping their subjects happy. Even if the chief does receive tribute, he will have to use it to give lavish feasts or organise elaborate rituals. Often, in tribal societies, persons with ambition have had to compete with each other to establish themselves as chiefs or persons of power like the 'big men' of Melanesia.

The state is a radical departure from those societies that retain some egalitarian values. The state, in its early form, depended upon a strong centre, with an administrative machinery for the collection of taxes and the presence of military and police force to enforce law and order and the will of the power holders. This was designated as a despotic state and has been described by scholars such as Wittfogel (1957). In essence, the state is based upon inequality and coercion.

The nation states that emerged after World War II and the decolonisation of the erstwhile colonies were mostly based upon principles of freedom and democracy. The newly formed Indian republic had a Constitution that guaranteed equality and justice for all its citizens irrespective of caste, class and ethnic affiliation. These states differed from the feudal states in that they were not based upon coercion or a sense of territorial domination but upon a concept of nationhood that emphasised a sense of belongingness and collective consciousness. People belonged to a nation just as the nation belonged to them. Yet, in most states, the nation was imagined not in terms of its masses but by its ruling elite. Thus, the US is imagined in terms of the WASP (White, Anglo-Saxon Protestant) population and not in terms of its indigenous population of Native Americans and a sizeable population of African Americans, or people of various ethnic and cultural identities. Similarly, according to Pandey (1991: 559), what goes by the name of Indian national culture is actually 'Brahmanical, Hindu, consumerist'.

More importantly, the formation of these nations was not based upon consensus, least of all from the people who inadvertently became part of them even while they were on its fringes, sometimes quite literally, like the people on their borders of nations, or metaphorically, when they formed a politically and culturally marginal population like the Native Americans. As nation states defined their identity and consolidated their nationhood, these people on the fringes rarely got the benefit of so-called developmental or nation-building enterprises. Their initial reluctance to be subservient to a higher power as well as their deprivation from the nation's resources is often channeled into political action that may take the form of protest and contestation. At the most radical level, it may take the form of secessionist activities, and at the most passive level, it leads to resignation and apathy.

The state does not have a uniform policy or attitude towards the people on its fringes. A newly forming nation state may initially take harsh measures to bring its population under control and subject them to coercive administrative control. However, the ultimate aim of a democratic state like India is to govern consensually and consolidate its position of legitimacy. Therefore, a democratic state never uses only coercive measures, but often tempers them with positive discriminatory policies of appeasement.

The Indian state can be understood in two phases: the colonial state and the postcolonial state. While pre-colonial India was a fragmented feudal society with many scattered locations of power, loosely consolidated under the Mughal emperors (whose power also varied over generations), the British colonial government attempted to consolidate most of India into a unified colony that they could govern adequately and peacefully. It was during this period that many tribes first tasted the imposition of direct rule on them. The feudal lords quite often engaged with tribes tangentially, leaving them ungoverned but recruiting them for military support if required. The small communities of forest dwellers and relatively isolated tribes were never deemed worthy of much attention. In this context, it is important to take note of Schendel's (2011: 24) comment that '[o]ne aspect often overlooked in general pronouncements about "tribes" in South Asia is the enormous variety of relationships between the "tribes" and their rulers today'. Thus, the tribes of central India, who call themselves 'Adivasi', are part of the majoritarian party politics of peninsular India. The state of Jharkhand came into existence with the efforts of the Bharatiya Janata Party (BJP), a right-wing organisation that is now insisting that the tribes of this region declare themselves as Hindus. In any case, the tribal people of this region consider themselves to be an intrinsic part of the Indian nation, in spite of having a troubled relationship with the state. The predominantly tribal regions of the Northeast have developed an entirely different kind of identity, being situated as they are away from the Indian mainland. They have not yet accepted their total mergence with the Indian state although they are participants in national politics and avail themselves of many facilities from the state.

> **While pre-colonial India was a fragmented feudal society with many scattered locations of power loosely consolidated under Mughal emperors, the British colonial government attempted to consolidate most of India into a unified colony that they could govern adequately and peacefully.**

THE COLONIAL STATE AND TRIBES

The colonial state performed only certain actions with respect to tribes—it attempted to create typologies and classifications, used force to subjugate tribes, and also tried to maintain peace and harmony, at least superficially, while it extracted resources and levies. Since most tribes were scattered over inhospitable terrains and were rarely settled cultivators, the British state either left them alone or tried to convert them into settled and tax-paying citizens. Thus, the three aspects of British rule with respect to tribes may be identified as: (i) classification, (ii) subjugation and (iii) protection or isolation.

The three aspects of British rule with respect to tribes may be identified as classification, subjugation, and protection or isolation.

Since tribes differ in their livelihood, population and social organisation, the policies towards them also differ. The factors that affect policymaking at any point of time in history are mostly dictated by the perceived interests of those in power. Thus, as long as the tribes were seen as occupying remote regions and not interfering with the autonomy of the rulers, they were left alone. Over a period of time when those very inhospitable regions were seen as reservoirs of valued goods such as coal and minerals, these tribes began to be seen as impediments to the process of revenue generation by the state.

The British needed to enter the tribal regions mainly to extract timber and coal; at the same time, they were wary of tribes that seemed hostile or resistant to being ruled. Thus, the large tribes of the Northeast like the Angami Nagas, the Konds of Odisha, and the Mundas and Santals of Chotanagpur were subjected to repressive measures as they were perceived as posing a threat to the sovereignty of the colonial state. There was another side to colonial rule. The British maintained an ambivalent attitude towards the tribes, with whom they were impressed and who stirred their curiosity.

The British administrators, educated as they were at Eton, Oxford and Cambridge, were also academically oriented and driven by what they considered as scientific curiosity. As described by Ngully (2014: 44), the British administration, while it was subjugating the natives, was at the same time satisfying its curiosity about the exotic people, whose culture and practices fascinated it. The raids on Naga villages to stop headhunting also provided an opportunity to British officials to collect headhunting trophies and other ritual objects otherwise inaccessible to outsiders. Thus, officers like Hutton have described how they collected their 'trophies' while they suppressed the hostile villages. Many of the colonial administrators also turned into ethnographers and collectors, like Hutton, whose writings provide insight into the lives of the Sema and Angami Nagas, and whose material-culture collections from the Naga Hills enriched the museums in Britain. Henry Balfour in the preface to Hutton's *The Angami Nagas* writes, 'During his eight years of official contact with the hill tribes, Mr. Hutton made a very fine and valuable ethnographic collection, the greater part of which he has most generously presented to the Pitts River Museum at Oxford: a very important gift to his old university' (Hutton 1969: *xvii*). Thus, the British state, as represented by its highly educated and academically oriented civil servants, showed a combination of administration and scholarship, which became rare in the postcolonial times. This academic interest or curiosity, however, did nothing to reduce the coercion or violence unleashed upon the local people; it only facilitated and justified what Ngully (2014: 44) referred to as 'loot': 'Raids and punishment allowed administrators to rummage through and "loot" artifacts of interest as proof of their exotic adventure and then most importantly by virtue of their authority, justify their collections even through violent means as an accepted norm.'

A unique aspect of British administration was their reliance on the power of words. They not only prepared extensive documents about colonial India but also administered by referring to books and documents. Padel (2011: 26) writes, 'Some of the most powerful techniques that have been developed for dominating tribes are located in language, particularly in written language.' In her writing about the Girasia of Rajasthan, Unnithan-Kumar (1997: 54) writes, 'The early British administrators recognized the Girasia as petty landholders who were marginal to positions of state power. The British conception of the Girasias was based mainly on the works of Baden-Powell (1892) and Todd (1899, 1920) for the upper Bombay presidency and Rajasthan respectively.' Various texts such as the *Imperial Gazeteer* (Meyer et al. 1908), *Annals and Antiquities of Rajasthan* (Todd 1899, 1920) and *The Land Systems of British India* (Baden-Powell 1892) continue to serve as the basis for the classification of tribes even in the present times. Thus, just because the Girasia of Gujarat were given a position of landholders, they are even today considered as Other Backward Classes in Gujarat, as against their classification as a Scheduled Tribe in Rajasthan.

The British used the term 'tribe' as a part of a comparative taxonomy (Schendel 2011: 20) where '[c]ontemporary societies that Europeans considered to be farthest behind in time were designated as "tribes", "primitives", "aborigines" or "savages", and entitled the rulers to deal with them as it pleased'. As discussed in Chapter 1, this externally imposed classification that was begun by the British continued for a long period. Labelling and classification may be seen as one of the key contributions of the British state in India, evidence of which is now archived in the form of numerous gazetteers and Census reports as well as in other forms of literature about the people of India. The classifications the British created were both a reflection of their cognition of Indian society as well as of their prejudices about the people they were ruling. The most insidious of these was the creation of the term 'criminal tribes'.

Labelling and classification is one of the key contributions of the British state in India, evidence of which is archived in numerous gazetteers and Census reports, as well as in other forms of literature about the people of India.

THE 'EX-CRIMINAL' TRIBES

The British, in their zeal for civilising the savages, created certain categories of those that they considered beyond civilising. Thus, the most marginal communities, beyond any possibility of redemption, were classified as a category separate from all others. Radhakrishna (2016: 4) argues that the state had the liberty to create its own categories of 'undesirable' people. Entire communities were labelled as 'criminal', identifying those occupations and ways of life that to the British appeared as not amenable to subjugation and regulation.

Quite predictably, they included nomads, wandering bards, performers who travelled from village to village, mendicants and peddlers, none of whom were outside of the local society. These people were all part of the pre-colonial feudal set-up, as part of which they were patronised or at least tolerated by the local rulers and peasants. To the British administrators, these people appeared as outside the pale of Brahminical Hinduism and also antithetical to the peaceful settled lives of the peasantry or settled cultivators. As pointed out by Fourcade (2003), the use of the term 'tribe' for such people, many of whom would be more aptly recognised as castes locally, was again a result of the colonial administration's prejudiced views about who they considered as caste as who as tribe. The conferring of the term 'tribe' enabled the British to exert more force, as 'tribe' was associated with both primitiveness and wilderness and thus qualified for justifiable brutality brought against them. The fact that entire communities were designated as 'criminal' was a derivative of the racist theories about criminality, where crime was often associated with biological inheritance.

The Criminal Tribes Act (CTA) came into existence in 1871, and 'The very text of the Act lays down a pure criminal jurisprudence which would facilitate the application on an arbitrary law' (ibid.: 146). In hindsight, we recognise that the law was arbitrary and was applied mindlessly only in response to mistaken judgements and racist scientific theories that presumed the existence of 'contaminated blood' and believed that crime could be hereditary. Interestingly, this label was never applied to the tribes who lived away from urban areas and had their own territories (people who we recognise today as Adivasi), but only to those who lived in close association with cities and villages and who actually were dependent on others for their livelihood. Their art and skills, such as singing, dancing and helping in rituals, were believed to be unproductive and a drain on the resources of the village and urban communities.

The Criminal Tribes Act was an arbitrary law that was applied mindlessly in response to mistaken judgements and racist scientific theories that presumed the existence of 'contaminated blood' and believed that crime could be hereditary.

Since the propensity towards criminality was assigned not to individuals but to the community as a whole, one way of dealing with this issue was to put such people into detention and corrective facilities. In 1910, these corrective facilities were taken over by the Salvation Army and missionary organisations, and run in conjunction with the police. Fourcade (2003: 148) has quoted from Pouchepadass (1979) that just before Independence, the Census figures indicated that there were 198 so-called criminal tribes with a population of about 2.3 million people. The act was amended in 1876, when it became applicable to Lower Bengal. The original act of 1871 was only applicable to what was then known as the North-west Frontier Province. A further amendment in 1897 enabled the authorities to separate children between four and eighteen years of age from their alleged criminal parents. A complete upgrading of the law in 1911 stipulated that members of the 'criminal tribes' were not to be governed by the general laws of the country but were to be brought under executive authority. 'Thus they were obliged to register themselves, record their fingerprints, and notify the administration every time they changed residence' (ibid.). In this manner, provincial governments of the colonial administration could prevent people from relocating and travelling and from having practically any freedom, even when they were not in jail and had not been charged with any crime formally.

The fact that the local police had all the records of such communities, including their fingerprints and other details, enabled them to nail any member of such a community whenever any petty crime was committed. It was as if a ready bank of criminals was always present on whom the blame could be fixed.

Although formally the law was repealed after the country became independent and a Constitution that promised equality and justice for all Indian citizens was adopted, the reality is quite contrary. The act was discarded in 1952, and it was ordained that these people would be governed by the general laws of the country. However, the stigma of 'ex-criminal tribes' remained with them as did their records with the police, who behaved exactly as the colonial police, rounding them up every time any criminal act was committed in the vicinity of where members of these communities were present. They still remain vulnerable and sitting targets for accusation.

An extensive ethnography of a criminal tribe has been provided by Hatch (1976 [1928]). This pertains to the Kuravers of south India, whom the author describes as a 'remarkable tribe of hereditary criminals' (Fourcade 2003: 152). This nomadic tribe was found in the erstwhile Madras Presidency, in the Tamil- and Telugu-speaking regions. Locally they were known as diviners and palm readers. By and large, as described by Hatch, the Kuravers had thievery as their dharma, although they may have posed as temple servitors or as having a holy occupation to villagers. They worshipped Subrahmanium, the patron of thieves. They are described in Hatch's account as a strongly knit community, where it was difficult to catch anyone for any crime as they provided strong alibis for each other and could also lie expertly. The Kuravers also worshipped Aiyanar, who is the enemy of thieves. They functioned as guards of the village as they were known to be guards of the temples. Fourcade (2003: 156) gives a long list of occupations that Hatch himself has given for the Kuravers. These include adorning gods with flowers, carrying offerings to a temple god, singing praises of gods in a temple, stitching footwear for offering to gods as well as performing the role of salt sellers, basket weavers, bamboo workers and snake charmers. Thus, we find that the accounts of the so-called criminal tribes are mired in contradictions and are full of statements based more on prejudices than on reliable evidence. Most of Hatch's assertions about the Kuravers being hereditary criminals are based on his own conviction than the real data that he provides, with the two often pulling in opposed directions.

Dumont (2001 [1986]) has studied the Piramalai Kallar, a sub-caste of the Kallars, also known as a criminal tribe. He labels the Kallars as a caste and not a tribe. The Kallars were landowners who fought to retain control over their lands. Their participation in armed conflicts was largely to retain their independence from local rulers. They also combined the dual role of being thieves and guardians of wealth. Efforts were made to educate them and not just provide alternative economic avenues as it was clear that robbery was not undertaken only for money but as an ordained profession of value. The charge of rehabilitation passed from one agency to another, and in 1949, the welfare policy was handed first to the Harijan Welfare Department and then to the Rural Welfare Department. However, in spite of efforts put into schooling and the offer of scholarship to young Kallars, the rehabilitation programmes were not very effective. 'Doubtless the major cause for this was the syllabus that derived from British educational models and not from their own lives' (Fourcade 2003: 164). Thus, like all other projects to improve the lives of tribes, these initiatives were a top-down effort rather than one that derived from the needs of the people who were the beneficiaries. After 1947, when the CTA was repealed, efforts were also made for the rehabilitation of these tribes by the state. The state took help of the report prepared by Labour Commissioner T. E. Moir (ibid.: 163). This report put a question mark on the concept of criminality as it stated that nothing that these people did was against local traditions or culture. In other words, in their own milieu, they were not regarded as criminals, nor did they have any self-perception that they were doing anything amoral or wrong. In other words, they did not feel that they were in need of any 'reform'.

After 1947, when CTA was repealed, the state made efforts to rehabilitate the tribes. A report prepared by Labour Commissioner T. E. Moir stated that nothing that these people did was against local traditions or culture.

In contemporary times, the process of rehabilitation remains fuzzy, and most among the ex-criminal tribes remain poor and doubly marginalised by poverty and illiteracy, on the one hand, and the stigma of being 'ex-criminal', on the other. The category of 'ex-criminal' means to the postcolonial police force exactly what 'criminal' meant to the colonial police. These tribes remain as sitting ducks to be targeted for any offence without any evidence. As Fourcade (2003) points out, they are victims of a history that was created *for them* and in which they had no part.

TRIBAL UPRISINGS AND LEADERSHIP (COLONIAL PERIOD)

The second phase of colonial rule was as academically oriented as the first phase, and it involved the active use of force, often leading to bloody wars and brutal subjugation of those who dared to challenge the might of the Raj. As pointed out by most anthropologists and scholars, there is generally a huge prejudice against tribes because they seem antithetical to what goes by the name of modernity and civilisation. Civic society as well as officials who are part of the very same society view tribes as having a lifestyle that actually needs to be dispensed with. However, this is not at all commensurate with how tribes view themselves. They have resisted being drawn into slavery and have fought to retain their lifeworlds that are of great value to them. In writing about the Konds of Odisha, Padel (2011: 12) writes, 'Konds see themselves simply as one of the main races or divisions of mankind. In their myth, Konds are usually the first human beings to emerge out of earth, and have a special relationship with the Earth Goddess.' Very similar myths of origin and world views exist among most other tribes. Many Naga tribes believe that they came out from a cave or from underground. Most believe that they are the direct creation of their deity and hold a special position in this universe. Colonial forces, on the other hand, were convinced that they were 'civilising' them, and this mindset has been inherited by the postcolonial government of India and of other colonies as well. Tribes have faced and continue to face this external imposition, an imposition that introduced an 'element of discontinuity into their history' (ibid.: 22). They have reacted with passive acceptance, withdrawal or active resistance.

A major factor leading to tribal unrest has been that from the colonial period onwards, due to various reasons such as infiltration of outsiders into their areas and the impact of external rule on their earlier independence and ways of life, tribes have been disproportionately impoverished and marginalised as compared to the general population. Maharatna (2005: 16) states that famines, so common during the British rule, affected the tribal population much more than the general population: 'From 1891–1901, tribes as a whole appear to have experienced a substantial decline in their absolute number vis-a-vis a small increase in the general population. This reflected the greater mortality toll among

Due to various reasons such as infiltration of outsiders into their areas and the impact of external rule on their earlier independent ways of life, tribes have been disproportionately impoverished and marginalised as compared to the general population.

tribals during two consecutive major famines that occurred in 1896–97 and 1899–1900.'

In 1855, there was a massive uprising of the Santals against the intrusion of outsiders into their land, in which nearly 30,000, tribal people were killed. Fürer-Haimendorf (1982: 36) referred to the Santal Rebellion of 1855–56 as the last resort of an oppressed people with no other means of redress.

> Among the causes of the uprising were the grasping and rapacious manner of merchants and moneylenders in their transaction with the Santals. The misery caused by the iniquitous system of allowing personal and hereditary bondage for debt, the unparalleled corruption and extortion of the police in aiding and abetting the moneylenders, and the impossibility of the Santals obtaining redress from the courts.

The fiercely independent tribes did not give up their freedom easily and were conscious of the sufferings to which they were subjected as a result of external political impositions. We have a long chronicle of tribal uprising against colonial rule and often of violent encounters. Chaudhuri (1993) provides a detailed historical and anthropological account of the Santal uprising in Barind in West Bengal under the leadership of Jitu Santal alias Jitu Hembram. This uprising was inspired by the Hindu uprising in the region against the British colonisers and was part of the freedom struggle. Yet the Santals were actually victimised by the Hindus more than by anyone else. As Chaudhuri (1993: 110) points out, the Santals accepted Hinduism as a way of protest and defence against the dominant group. Their goal was to shake off foreign rule to create self-rule for themselves, even as they took Gandhi as one of their ideals. Barind was a Santal conclave, where they were isolated after migrating from their homeland in the Santhal Pargana, and this also explains why they tried to accept Hinduism and merged their movement into the larger freedom struggle taking place locally. As reported by Sarkar (2011: 67), starting from around the year 1800, Santals poured into Malda from the Santhal Pargana, and by the year 1900, almost 20,000 Santals had settled down in this region. And interestingly, they were prized by the local landlords in the Barind tract, for their skill in rice farming, thus dispelling the myth that tribes are not cultivators.

The movement of the Santals into Barind was stimulated by land alienation, unscrupulous moneylenders and the seasonal vagaries in the region with only monocropping. Since land-alienation was a common problem for other impoverished peasants, the Santals were joined by them as well. The earlier paternalistic ties between landlord and peasant had declined by the second half of the nineteenth century by the influx of capitalism and British rule. The Gandhian influence had kept violence out of this movement, and women were accorded a high status. In fact, the leader Jitu had installed Kali as his personal deity. Like Birsa Munda, Jitu was also accepted as a religious leader, of the Satyam Shibam Hindu sect floated by him. His main protest was in the form of a no-tax movement, which he justified by saying that the Santals had cleared primary forests to make their settlements and should therefore not be required to pay tax to anyone. Jitu ultimately declared himself to be a 'king' of the Santals and attempted to ascend a throne in the Adina mosque in the vicinity that had earlier been identified by him to have been an abode of Lord Rama, the Hindu deity. As described by Chaudhuri (1993), there is a lot of mystery and myth surrounding the circumstance of his death on 13 December 1932 by police firing inside the mosque.

Thus, the story of Jitu Hembram also ended like that of most other tribal leaders and uprisings, but it is interesting in its divergence from the other movements that were solidly situated within the tribal milieu and followed tribal symbolism. Here, the use of Hindu symbols and ideology in a situation of gross Hindu domination shows how the oppressed were using the same structures to overcome their oppression as they believed was being used by their oppressors. Jitu had strongly insisted on ritual avoidance of pig and fowl, and aspired for the conversion of Santals to a clean Shudra status within the Hindu caste system. He was also opposed to Muslims. According to Sarkar (2011: 68), it is possible that tribes like the Santals developed a self-contempt by being defrauded by *diku*s (outsiders), mainly Hindu landlords and moneylenders, and as an aspect of their negative self-image, they sought out the ways of the very diku who they perceived as their prime enemies. Jitu's example also shows that tribal uprisings were not simply tribal in nature but had close interrelationships with local political ideologies and cultures. Thus, Sarkar (2011: 66) says that 'Jitu's legend, moreover, strongly underlines a complex political relationship with the local elite: of sharing, of contesting, as well as of recreating, or trying to recreate, each other's political activism.' Again, as Sarkar points out, the Santals became part of the social landscape because even in contemporary times, the name of Jitu Santal is remembered in Malda as the name of a legendary hero of this region and not merely as a Santal leader (ibid.). In Chhattisgarh, a megalith has been raised to commemorate the tribal leaders who had sacrificed their lives for the sake of freedom, and the first name is that of Tilka Manjhi, who killed the British resident, Augustus Cleveland, with a bow and arrow in 1784. His contribution is being recognised now by renaming Bhagalpur University as Tilka Manjhi University.

In Chhattisgarh, a megalith commemorates the tribal leaders who sacrificed their lives for the sake of freedom, and the first name is that of Tilka Manjhi, who killed the British resident, Augustus Cleveland, with a bow and arrow in 1784.

A relatively unknown chapter of tribal uprising has been recorded by Meena (2016) about the tribals of Rajasthan. The story of Govind Guru is similar to other stories of tribal uprisings, where, as already pointed out, famines, oppression by rulers and repression of the marginal people played key roles. During the period of 1898–1900, there was widespread famine in the areas of Dungarpur, Udaipur, Banswara and Pratapgarh as also the adjoining areas. The local Rajput rulers played their game according to the dictates of the British officials, and they enjoyed great camaraderie among themselves. The tribals were being exploited by all power holders who extracted *begar* (unpaid slave labour) from them and did not provide any succour to them even in times of failure of monsoon and famine. The landlords and moneylenders took every opportunity to exploit the tribals and take advantage of their innocence. The hungry tribals had very little recourse but to take to crime, primarily looting food and other essentials. The rulers were not interested in mitigating the tribals' suffering, but only in suppressing what they regarded as 'crimes' so that the tribals were subjected to extreme oppression and cruelty and their numbers dropped in this region due to migration and deaths.

Tribal preachers like Govind Guru, Sengaji, Kuriya Bhagat and Joriya Bhagat, who were inspired sages, tried to boost the sagging morale of the tribal people and at the same time made them aware of their rights. They told the tribal people to refuse begar and also demand their rights. As a consequence of standing up for the tribals, Govind Guru was arrested and imprisoned in 1898, at the time when the tribes were suffering from all sides. Joriya Bhagat was also hanged by the British for his protests against atrocities committed on his people. After his arrest, Govind Guru attained a hallowed status and was able to unite the tribes of the regions of Rajputana as well as neighbouring Gujarat. Most of these gurus encouraged the tribal people to give up drinking alcohol and take up the ways of the Hindu saints. By the first decade of the twentieth century, Govind Guru had set up his location at Mangadh Hills from where the last battle with the British was fought, when thousands of tribals gathered to protest against their rulers. The British sent their armies and mowed down the tribals, armed with only bows and arrows, with their guns. Here, the feudal lords and the British Raj colluded to crush the Adivasis and their holy men in a concerted show of power.

Some of the tribal leaders who stood up against the colonial state attained iconic status, one of the most well-known being Birsa Munda. Birsa Munda was a tribal leader of Chotanagpur, now in Chhattisgarh, a leader today venerated by the local tribals as divinity. The British had, in their land acquisition policies, handed over large tracts of land to revenue collectors known as zamindars. These were the local power holders who the British appointed to collect taxes on their behalf. The tribes has no idea of private ownership and even when the British took over large areas of forests, claiming that they were 'wasteland' (since they were not under cultivation and no one staked a claim to them), they did not know how to claim what was theirs for time immemorial. Thus, the people who had considered themselves as belonging to the forest and to the land of their ancestors

Some of the tribal leaders who stood up against the colonial state attained iconic status. One of the most well-known, Birsa Munda, was a tribal leader of Chotanagpur, venerated by the local tribals as divinity.

were suddenly bereft of the land and its resources and also coerced to pay taxes to an unknown entity. This led to widespread resentment and many tribal people stood up against what they considered as unwarranted intrusion by outsiders into what was legitimately their domain.

Birsa's movement has been studied by many anthropologists (Fuchs 1966; Roy 1912; Sachchidananda 1964; Singh 1983). The eminent social writer Mahashweta Devi has written a remarkable book on Birsa, *Aranyer Adhikar* (1977). The region where Birsa lived was under the traditional *khuntkatti* system of land tenure. Inadvertently, the British let in the zamindars and the moneylenders (diku) into this land, unleashing untold miserly for the simple tribes and posing a threat to their livelihood. Community lands were alienated and individual tribal persons were forced into bonded labour as they could not pay taxes or pay back the moneylenders. The Birsa movement was the culmination of several uprisings and resistance movements from 1789 to 1832. Between these years, the Mundas engaged in several armed uprisings as more and more land was usurped from them. The Raja of Chotanagpur gave away many villages to Sikhs and Muslim landowners, depriving the Menki and Munda of their cultural traditions by the imposition of these alien ways of life. This precipitated in collective political action by the joint efforts of the Munda, Ho and Oraon, the major tribes of this region.

The Birsa movement was the culmination of several uprisings and resistance movements from 1789 to 1832. Between these years, the Mundas engaged in several armed uprisings as more and more land was usurped from them.

The Christian influence on the tribes also led to their empowerment as they had a new script and were educated by the missionaries. The Christian converts led a movement known as the Sardari Agitation in 1858. Singh (1983: 33) has divided this movement into three phases: agrarian phase (1858–81), revivalistic phase (1881–90) and political phase (1890–95). The persistent goal in all these phases was the restoration of cultivation rights to the tribals. In 1867, 14,000 Christian tribal persons filed a petition against a local officer and the Raja of Chotanagpur, and over a period extending from 1869 to 1882, 482 villages were registered in the name of the local tribes. However, the Sardars, as Christian-convert leaders were known, were not satisfied with piecemeal reform and wanted a complete restoration of what they believed to be their 'past glory' as well as all their ancestral land. In 1881, the Munda tribe pressed for total claim over the entire Chotanagpur area, and under a leader who called himself 'John the Baptist', the tribe set up a so-called kingdom at Dolsa. The leader, who had borrowed his name from a major Christian saint, had many followers calling themselves 'Children of Mael'. Christianisation had given a lot of self-confidence to the tribal people—since Christianity preached equality and justice, the tribal followers mistakenly believed that they would get what they were entitled to from the British rulers. However, in reality, the Sardars, in spite of being Christians, were persecuted and scattered.

Even the leadership of a Christian missionary, C. Lievens, who led the tribal people in organised land restoration movements by mass agitations, did not succeed. The government asked Lievens to leave the region and the movement was cut short. The Munda and other tribes thus lost faith in the missionaries and the British government, and were left searching for someone who would provide succour to them from the diku. Thus, when Birsa, the son of a poor peasant with a smattering of education from a German mission, entered the scene, the local tribal people were desperate for a leader. Birsa had entered the mission in 1886 and stayed there till 1890, and he was taught that if he could become a good Christian, he would get back all that was lost to him—the land as well as the glorious past. However, with obvious disillusionment, Birsa reverted to his original tribal religion as the promises made by the Christian missions failed to materialise.

A dramatic turn of events took place when Birsa attained divine status. It is believed that he was enlightened in a dream, where he dreamt that Singbonga (the great god of the Mundas) had entrusted him with the task of delivering his people from the authorities (the British state), the zamindars and the old religion. Like all prophets, Birsa too turned towards a reformation of tradition. Similar to other millenarian movements, he ordered his people to kill all white pigs and white fowls as they were believed unclean. (It is possible that this was a symbolic rejection of the White rulers.) Birsa made prophesies—reflecting the apocalypse as predicted in biblical Book of Revelation—that fire and brimstones would come from the heavens and all would die except those near him. This doomsday prediction was believed by many Mundas, who let their cattle loose, wore new clothes like on a festival and flocked to Birsa. However, nothing happened and the cattle in the meantime destroyed all the crops causing famine. But the followers kept their faith and did not lose hope. They followed Birsa, believing him to be a god.

Birsa continued his agitation against exploitation, and the state officials were worried that they would not get any revenue if people kept neglecting their cultivation. There were warrants issued for Birsa's arrest, and people turned violent. It became a war, with the tribals on one side and the Hindu and Muslim zamindar and traders on the side of the rulers and the state officials. The zamindars made exaggerated reports to the higher authorities and the police about Birsa's attempts to kill many people and cause chaos. In 1895, he was arrested and served a sentence of two years in prison for rioting and causing unrest. His following became even stronger after his persecution, and his status as a prophet was confirmed. Large numbers of people flocked to the jail to pay homage to Birsa.

Continued famine and widespread distress caused even more people to turn to him as a way of overcoming the harsh realities of their daily existence. Birsaism, with its revivalistic character, promised deliverance and a hope of better days to come. Birsa preached the arrival of Sat Yuga, and the movement picked up with many young people joining in and the experienced preachers continuing with their preaching of what Birsa wished to convey to his people. Birsa's death in jail turned him into a legend, and today the Mundas and other tribes of Chotanagpur worship him as *bhagwan* (god). He has become a key symbol of their aspirations for freedom from the diku and for attaining self-respect.

Other tribes too fought for their freedom and integrity and, most of all, to preserve their cosmology and ways of life. Thus, even when they appear to be passive, tribes have their own, mostly spiritual, ways of dealing with problems, and they are always ready to put up a fight even if it is a last resort. Even though the Mundas did not win their war, they were able to create a demi-god, in the form of Birsa Munda, to be an inspiration to them forever.

THE COLONIAL STATE AND TRIBES: POLICIES OF SEGREGATION

Apart from violent usurpation and classification—the two central aspects of the colonial state in its dealings with tribes—was a third aspect, which was antithetical to both these aspects. This was the policy of segregation and separation, which was practised in some parts of India, like the Northeast. Although the British kept their hold on the far-off regions, coming down on practices like headhunting among the Nagas, they were not interested in spending too much energy on those areas where they did not have much trading and commercial interests (Ao 1972: 479). However, the Naga Hills and parts of the Northeast opened up during World War II, when the Japanese came right up to Kohima and Imphal, where war cemeteries still stand as mute spectators to the ravages of the war. The tribes of this area remained loyal to the British, fending off the incoming Japanese bravely. Ao (1972: 480) quotes from an article published in *The Times* of 29 December 1944, which described how the Naga people kept the road open for Field Marshall Alexander's army to retreat in the rain, when the roads had become dangerous. The local villagers fought in both the Assam Rifles and the Assam Regiment, and acted as allies and spies for the British army. The Japanese failed in their efforts to win over the Nagas to their side. This encounter with the outside world brought about significant changes in the Naga perspective. The British helped the Nagas form their first political council to deal with the outside world. The first political institution to be established in this region, by the name of the Naga Hills District Council, was established with help from the then Deputy Commissioner of Naga Hills, C. R. Pasweey. Later on, in February 1946, a congregation of tribes changed the name of this body to Naga National Council (NNC). This organisation gradually developed into the major political face of the unified Naga people in the postcolonial period. It appears that Pasweey himself patronised Zapu Phizo, who was the first leader of the futuristic Naga nation, and is still regarded with as much veneration as Birsa Munda is in central India.

The north-east frontier of India along with Nagaland was protected by the Inner Line Regulation of the British, which restricted the entry of outside people into these areas, a policy that prevails even today. Indian citizens too need special permission to enter these regions, which are secured by a border protection that does not allow easy entry. Outsiders are not allowed to possess land and property in these areas. Even in other parts of India like in the East Godavari District, the colonial government promulgated some laws to prevent undue and excessive land alienation of tribes. The Agency Tracts Interest and Land Transfer Act, 1917, was passed by the British administration to bring some relief to the tribes of this area. The act, if properly implemented, should have put an end to most of the land alienation taking place in this area. But given the simplicity of the tribes and the cunning of the outsiders, as well as corruption at the level of police and law-enforcing agencies, most tribal land has changed hands and little remains with the original tribal owners.

The north-east frontier of India along with Nagaland are secured by a border protection that does not allow easy entry. Outsiders are not allowed to possess land and property in these areas.

The act of 1917 remained in force till the Andhra Pradesh Scheduled Areas Land Transfer Regulation was passed in 1959. There were other acts to follow and the Government of India Act, 1919, paved the way for the Government of India (Excluded and Partially Excluded Areas) Order, 1936, which ordained that the laws meant for more developed regions should not be applicable to the 'backward' areas occupied by tribes who could be adversely affected if such legislations were extended to them. This law had divided these areas into 'excluded' and 'partially excluded areas'. The former were placed under the discretionary and direct rule of the governor, while the latter were within the field of ministerial responsibility with special powers to the governor for the administration of these areas. As is clear, these were protective measure where the state was making a direct intervention, superseding the general laws of the land in order to give special protection to those sections of the society considered more vulnerable than others. Such laws and acts were meant to give some kind of protection to marginal people, as the state is morally seen as responsible for the overall welfare of its people. The legitimacy of the state depends upon such acceptance by the people, yet as we have seen over the years, some people always remain more important to the state than others.

POSTCOLONIAL STATE

The postcolonial Indian state is widely recognised as following in the footsteps of its predecessor, the British Empire. The army, the police and the administration have remained almost intact even after the withdrawal of the imperial government. The creation of the Indian Constitution, with its emphasis on equality, justice and freedom, also made provisions for the so-called backward and marginal sections of Indian society. To this end, tribes were listed in the Constitution under the name of Scheduled Tribes. By the Census of India, 2011, there are about 461 officially recognised tribes in India, and they constitute about 8.2 per cent of the population of India. The Government of India category of 'primitive tribal group' (PTG) has now been replaced by the term 'particularly vulnerable tribal group' (PVTG). This category includes tribal groups characterised by (i) pre-agricultural level of technology, (ii) stagnant or declining population, (iii) extremely low literacy and (iv) subsistence level of economy. The use of the word 'primitive' in the earlier classificatory terminology drew criticism from academics and activists who considered 'primitive' as derogatory and against the dignity of the people so labelled. The change in terminology is meant to highlight the fact that the miserable conditions of these tribes, many of which are forest dwellers, is not because they lack in terms of capability or human potential but because their ways of life, which have their own merits, are under threat from others. This is also to emphasise a rapidly gaining philosophy and outlook, mostly derived from environmental concerns, that the subsistence modes of livelihood pursued by these people and their deep knowledge about the

One of the ways in which the Constitution provided for the tribal populations was by listing them as Scheduled Tribes. By Census 2011, there are about 461 officially recognised tribes in India, constituting 8.2 per cent of the population.

environment may be more sustainable than the modern, industrial ways of life.

A slew of programmes, including reservation in jobs and educational institutions, were promised for tribes under the official designation of Scheduled Tribes, as no finite characteristics were ever identified for defining a tribe. In spite of much academic debate, the word 'tribe' is used only with reference to the Government Schedule. At the same time, the state was defined in terms of its personnel, most of whom belonged to the upper echelons of Indian society in terms of caste, religion and occupations. The nation was thus defined in terms of a 'mainstream' that certainly did not include tribes. Most policy planners and power holders still associated tribes with the image of 'primitive', 'savage' and 'superstitious', and, most importantly, with being in need of 'development'. The first prime minister of India, Jawaharlal Nehru, in the company of some philanthropist, anthropologically inclined persons like Elwin, did have an ideologically liberal view of tribes. Nehru's Tribal Panchsheel, as outlined in Elwin's *A Philosophy for NEFA* (1959), envisioned a future for tribes that would be largely free from external interference and would be focused on orthogenetic development. While such a vision led to the seclusion of some parts of the country by an Inner Line, most tribes were not beneficiaries of such policies. Each successive Five Year Plan had rising allocations for the so-called development of tribes. But these were only lip service. The major problem lay in that all policymakers were making plans that emanated from the top, without taking into account the people for whom they were meant. There was always the condescending attitude that tribes were not mature enough to think for themselves, a legacy that the postcolonial state inherited from the colonial rulers.

The eminent anthropologist Vidyarthi (1984: 112) has given the example of such a miscalculation for the hill tribes of Bihar, the Hill Paharias, who practised shifting cultivation. The monolithic version of development followed by policymakers as well as social workers envisaged a process of 'rehabilitation' for these hill tribes that involved bringing them down from their original habitats and settling them on the plains as settled cultivators. In his anthropological study among these people, Vidayarthi administered some 50 schedules to them with an array of questions to be answered. In their responses, the Hill Paharias said that they would prefer death to coming down from the hills that have been occupied by their forefathers for centuries. Moreover, they were absolutely averse to leaving their practice of shifting cultivation. The aversion of officials to shifting cultivation is often framed within an ecological rhetoric as they claim that such a mode of cultivation is harmful for the environment. But ecological studies point to something quite contrary, arguing that given that this mode of cultivation has stood the test of time for centuries without exhibiting any harmful effect on the environments where it has been practised is itself proof that it is not harmful to the environment. In fact, in places where this practice was stopped, it was found that forest regrowth was adversely affected as the saplings of many trees such as the sal trees of central India failed to come up when the forest undergrowth was not removed by burning and which ended up suffocating the saplings.

Shifting cultivation often leads to the growth of a lush and diverse forest as many different kinds of plants, creepers and tubers are planted. A long period of fallow also helps in the regeneration of the original vegetation, which is often made more vigorous by the firing that rejuvenates the soil. Shifting cultivation is, however, antithetical to administration by the state as it is not compatible with individual ownership, cash cropping and the creation of large amounts of surplus for the market. The rhetoric of the state against shifting cultivation is thus more to do with the needs of a capitalist state than the environment. In his book *Pastoral Politics: Shepherds, Bureaucrats, and Conservation in the Western Himalaya*, Saberwal (1999) has similarly shown that the drive of state agencies against pastoral ways of life has everything to do with politics and very little to do with environmental concerns. The efforts to take people out of the forest or make them give up a subsistence form of economy are towards fulfilling the state's goals of getting everyone to participate

The state views shifting cultivation as incompatible with individual ownership, cash cropping and the creation of surplus. The efforts to make people give up subsistence economy are intended to get everyone to participate in the cash economy.

in the cash economy and to pay taxes. In addition, sedentary people are easier to administer and control.

Fürer-Haimendorf (1982) has written about his studies on the plight of tribes in the Warangal region of Hyderabad that fell under the jurisdiction of the Nizam of Hyderabad's government in the colonial times. His writings, consolidated under the title *Tribal Hyderabad*, were submitted to the Revenue Department, and Grigson, the local British resident, dealt with them favourably. In 1943, schools were opened for Gond children and Gond teachers were trained, a special officer was appointed and land *patta*s were given to many tribal people in this region. The Tribal Areas Regulation Act benefitted the tribes of this region considerably and they gained confidence by having their own land in their own names and also having functioning panchayats of their own to regulate their affairs. Such panchayats continued to function even up to the 1980s, although the Tribal Areas Regulation Act was repealed in 1963. Hyderabad State had been partitioned earlier in 1956, and the merging of the Telangana and Andhra districts took place, giving rise to the long drawn-out demand for a separate state of Telangana, which was realised only in 2016. The earlier act was replaced by the Andhra Pradesh Scheduled Areas Land Transfer Regulation, 1959. While this act continued to protect the land of the tribes, it did not have any provision for tribal panchayats and no role for the social service officers who had done good work during the Nizam's era.

Well-intended policies and legislations have not brought about any significant transformations in the condition of tribes in India. There are severe infrastructural shortcomings in tribal regions, and tribals are becoming minorities even in states that were created specifically for them.

In the postcolonial period, there have been specific budget allocations for tribes in the successive Five Year Plans. The postcolonial government set up the Sub-committee on Excluded and Partially Excluded Areas, which coined the terms 'Schedule V' and 'Schedule VI' for these areas, during the period of 5–7 September 1949. A Tribal Advisory Committee was also set up to advise the state regarding the governance of these areas. Yet there has been many a slip between the legislations, policies and plans, and their execution. Well-intended plans, policies and legislations have not brought about any significant transformations in the condition of the tribes of India, who continue to be marginalised and among the most poor, illiterate and exploited sections of Indian society. There are severe infrastructural shortcomings in tribal regions. The electoral politics of numbers is playing against the tribals, who are becoming minorities even in the states that were created specifically for them. Thus, in contemporary times, tribes are a minority in states like Jharkhand and Chhattisgarh. Nathan and Xaxa (2012: 4) write, 'At the heart of these infrastructural deprivations is political marginalization, or political exclusion. Even in an electoral sense, the adivasis do not count for much, with 8 percent of the total population, most often distributed as minorities amongst other communities.'

LAND AND LEGISLATIONS WITH RESPECT TO TRIBES

The attempts of the colonial state and the British administration to provide some protection to tribes from the usurpation of their lands and also to prevent excessive exploitation at the hands of outsiders has already been discussed. The Constitution of free and democratic India was committed to providing a just and equal society to its citizens. The Indian Constitution not only guarantees a life free of exploitation and violence but also has special provisions for those sections it deems most susceptible to such acts, especially by outsiders. Politically, at least in India, all tribes are part of the Indian nation, yet the Constitution of the country gives them some privileges to practise their age-old customs and civil laws. The criminal justice system is the same for all Indian citizens, although at the local level, people may try to deal in their own way with those acts that may not constitute serious crimes. The creation of the category of 'Scheduled Tribes', that is, those tribes that are protected by the Scheduled Areas acts, was done towards such a goal. The sub-committee for the protection of tribal rights denied permission for tribal land to be sold or otherwise alienated from tribal hands, and also forbade industries to be set up in Scheduled Areas for fear that such an entry would not be conducive to the welfare of the tribal people.

However, with the country rapidly transitioning to a capitalist form of economy and liberalisation, there is increasing pressure to make inroads into the land and habitats of the tribes, as most of the tribal dominant areas are the ones that have huge reserves of the much-coveted resources such as coal, bauxite, iron, uranium and other minerals, and thick forests and rich natural biodiversity. Radhakrishna (2016: 370–408) provides a detailed account of the plight of tribals. She gives the relevant figures and data pertaining to the extraordinary quantity of mineral wealth found in the three states of Odisha, Jharkhand and Chhattisgarh, which ironically house a large population of tribals in these very sites of mineral wealth, and also have a high number of 'backward districts' (Jharkhand, 19 districts out of 22; Odisha, 27 out of 30; and Chhattisgarh, 15 out of 16). 'Literally hundreds and thousands of adivasis have been displaced losing their land, livelihood, culture, and identity because of these measures to develop the region, without deriving any benefit out of the projects or industries' (ibid.: 374). The Land Acquisition Act, 1894 (amended 1984), did not guarantee the right of refusal to landholders as all land acquisition was in 'national interest' (though often in the interests of private companies). The Working Group on Land Relations formed under D. Bandyopadhyay in 2006 had recommended giving extensive powers to the gram sabha under the Panchayats (Extension to Scheduled Areas) Act (PESA), 1996. The working group formulated extensive rules in favour of Adivasis and strongly recommended that all rehabilitation be completed before the commencement of the project concerned. But land is still acquired under the outdated Land Acquisition Act.

As described by Radhakrishna (and many other scholars), the Maoist 'label' is now often being used by the state to suppress any legitimate demands made by tribes. At the moment, Maoist operations have spread so wide that they are now perceived as the greatest 'internal security' threat (Radhakrishna 2016: 381), and the states of Chhattisgarh, Jharkhand, Andhra Pradesh (also now Telangana), Odisha and Bihar account for 91 per cent of the known Maoist violence in the country. The clearing of the Saranda forest that is particularly rich in minerals to corporations has initiated state-run operations like Operation Green Hunt, which specifically targets the removal of tribals and the opening up of the area for outside investments. Heavily armed police and army in these regions are slaughtering unarmed and small populations of tribal men and women. Even worse was Salwa Judum, the state's policy to arm tribals against tribals. From the period of 2005 to 2011, the combined forces of armed gunmen provided by contractors, traders and miners (approved by the state) were used along with those of the local tribals, who were instigated against their own brethren to clear land for the corporates. Six hundred and forty villages were burnt down and eliminated, and 3,50,000 tribals displaced, their women raped, children killed, and youth either killed or maimed for life. 'Villages sitting on tons of iron are effectively de-peopled and available for the highest bidders' (ibid.: 385). Following this, companies like Tata and Essar have entered these regions for mining.

During 2005–11, Salwa Judum, the state's attempt to arm tribals against tribals, left 640 villages incinerated, 3,50,000 tribals displaced, women raped, children killed, and youth either killed or maimed. Following this, companies like Tata and Essar entered these regions for mining.

Where mining is already in place, any protest is dealt with a heavy hand, such as in Odisha where the police personnel often outnumber the protestors (ibid.: 388). The aim is to create an atmosphere of fear by an exaggerated show of strength. In addition to increasing local police presence, the Central Reserve Police Force (CRPF) and the India Reserve Battalion are also being used to intimidate tribals. 'The police and paramilitary only target those opposing the project, while allowing company goondas to openly attack protestors with impunity' (ibid.: 389). In addition, false charges are always framed against activists and people opposing the corporates. They are put in long police detention and not granted bail as a means of keeping them 'away' from action. In short, the democratic government of a free India is actually even worse than the colonial state as the stakes are now in billions of dollars, and the states are largely under control of the corporates. At the same time, protests have not stopped, and Adivasis are willing to face bullets to save their land, livelihoods and ways of life as they realise that they are nothing without these.

Successful Adivasi campaigns have also happened, and the national and international human rights, environmental and other liberal non-governmental organisations have been in continuous support.

The question that has been raised again and again is in terms of prioritising development in so-called national interest and the contradiction this poses as it threatens the ways of life, livelihood and cultures of millions of people who occupy these territories. There is also the question of environment as it is being realised that forests and biodiversity are also precious resources that humankind needs to preserve for its own survival. In terms of laws of the land and the role of the state to ensure the welfare of all its citizens, a great deal of dilemma exists. Ratnabali (2015: 130) writes:

> In the context of the principle embodied in Article 46, a question arises as to whether acquisition/destruction of a Scheduled Tribe's land/space/site including those having cultural/religious significance on account of development project is a violation of this principle or not on the basis that it is form of social injustice? If the community displaced by such a project does not get the benefit from it, rather its living condition deteriorated post-displacement, will it not result into their exploitation for the benefit of others? In these circumstances can we say that the State had failed on both the counts?

From the legal point of view, our Constitution had realised that a nation cannot progress without giving priority to the poor and underprivileged. Towards this end, the Directive Principles of State Policy (DPSP) were borrowed from the Irish constitution. These principles are directly related to social justice and economic democracy, yet these have never been implemented in their true spirit. For example, the Forest Rights Act, 2006, recognises the importance of biodiversity and the rights of flora and fauna, but does not recognise the rights of the forest-dwelling people even though they have been part of the life of forests since time immemorial. It is only in more recent times that the Convention on Biodiversity, short form for Convention on Biological Diversity, formulated by the United Nations in 1992, has recognised the value of indigenous knowledge in conserving the environment, especially forests. The forest-dwelling tribes have been removed from the forests and never rehabilitated properly, though it is actually impossible to rehabilitate them given that their lives are totally tied to the forest.

The Scheduled Areas did not come under the Panchayat Act of 1992, as they were seen as having their own customary bodies of self-governance. Later under PESA, a modified form of the Panchayat Act was extended to these areas as well. Ratnabali (2015: 139) has listed some of the relevant points of this act:

1. State legislation on panchayats should be in consonance with the customary law, social and religious practices, and traditional management practices of community resources.
2. The independence and competency of every gram sabha to safeguard and preserve the traditions and customs of the people, their cultural identity, community resources and the customary mode of dispute resolution should be maintained.
3. The gram sabhas have the power to approve the plans, programmes and projects for social and economic development before such plans, programmes and projects are taken up for implementation by the panchayat at the village level.
4. The gram sabha shall be responsible for the identification or selection of persons as beneficiaries under poverty alleviation and other programmes.
5. The gram sabhas or the panchayats at the appropriate level should be consulted before acquiring land for development projects in the Scheduled Areas, and before resettling or rehabilitating persons affected by such projects in the Scheduled Areas. The actual planning and implementation of projects in the Scheduled Areas shall be coordinated at the state level.
6. The recommendations of the gram sabhas or the panchayats at the appropriate level shall be made mandatory prior to granting licenses or mining leases for minor minerals in the Scheduled Areas.

On the face of it, it would seem that such legislations should work wonders for tribes and the preservation of their land and resources. But at the level of implementation, this is not at all the case. There are many breaches of the PESA Act, as unscrupulous government officials in collusion with corrupt political figures and multinational companies interested in exploiting resources in Scheduled Areas find many ways to get around such stringent provisions for safeguard. Often, illiterate tribals are made to sign on documents so that consent for a project may be obtained without the actual knowledge or real consent of the people. Sometimes, a few tribal leaders are bought off by bribes and made to sign on behalf of their people. Sometimes, consent is not even taken and the project is given a go-ahead, and by the time the tribes realise, it may be too late. At times, police and army coercion is used to take the consent by force.

Ratnabali (2015: 235) has researched the Tangkhul Nagas of Chodang village in Manipur, displaced or affected by the Thoubal Multipurpose Project, which involves the building of Mapithel Dam. When the initial survey for the dam was being conducted about 25–30 years back, the villagers had no inkling of what a dam was. When they asked their state legislative assembly representative about it, he in turn asked them whether they had asked for a dam to be built in their area. When they innocently answered in the negative, they were told that they were lucky that they were getting the dam, without asking for it. They were also told that when the dam would be built, they would be able to catch huge fish without making any efforts and would become prosperous. It was only after 20 years that they realised what the dam actually meant by way of their displacement and the destruction of their environment. And this is happening in a Sixth Schedule area for which the laws are extremely strong. The people are now protesting, and predictably, the government is retaliating by using its military might. There is a legal battle underway. As described by Ratnabali, there were strong protests against the dam and the government had to deal with it by fortifying the construction area of the dam with military personnel. The villagers in turn formed organisations and sent representation to the National Commission for Scheduled Castes and Scheduled Tribes highlighting the violation of their rights by the state. They have also fielded a case in court against the government for not complying with the National Rehabilitation Policy and for not coming up with a comprehensive state policy on development-induced displacement and rehabilitation.

According to a young activist from Manipur, who spoke at a meeting in Chhattisgarh in the month of March 2017, the National Hydroelectric Power Corporation had made promises of providing jobs to all affected youth and also providing subsidised electricity to the people of Manipur to compensate for the submergence of villages because of Mapithel Dam. The Loktak Hydroelectric Project in Manipur has submerged 82,000 acres of fertile paddy fields, and similar empty promises had been made. None of the promises have been fulfilled.

This is a story that has been repeated again and again, with tribes losing their rights in spite of legislations and protective policies in place. Thus, in spite of many acts, especially those directed towards the protection of tribal land and resources, 'tribal lands have continued to pass from tribes to non-tribes' (Xaxa 2008: 48). As described by Xaxa, during the first three Five Year Plans, more than 50,000 Scheduled Tribe and 10,000 Scheduled Caste families were uprooted from the Jharkhand area alone to make way for the construction of public works like roads and dams and other projects, mainly directed towards benefitting the city people and elite. The private sector displaced even larger numbers, and most of this has been done with no adequate rehabilitation and relocation. The story of development of the Indian nation has seen the displacement of millions of tribals from their lands and also immense degradation of the environment. The displaced people have been deprived of their habitat, livelihoods, nutrition, religious shrines and, most importantly, their dignity and personhood. The irony is that even as excellent legislations and provisions exist on paper, they are never implemented properly.

The story of development of the Indian nation is the story of displacement of millions of tribals from their lands and immense degradation of the environment. Even though excellent legislations exist on paper, they are never implemented properly.

The National Thermal Power Corporation (NTPC) was the first to formulate an effective rehabilitation policy in 1993. As is well known, coal-mining is extremely deleterious for the environment and leads to deforestation, destruction of flora and fauna of both land and water, and rising temperatures, which results in loss of livelihoods of local people. In such a scenario, most local people lose their subsistence activities and are reduced to becoming mining labour. The NTPC was forced to formulate a rehabilitation and resettlement (R&R) policy under pressure from the World Bank, which refused to provide any grants to projects that did not have any such policy. However, there has hardly been any visible effect of such a policy as the officials have a very prejudiced view of the tribes that are affected. As pointed out by Ratnabali (2015: 188), 'It was a clearly development oriented policy, instead of being people-centric. The policy is also silent on the principle of "striving for minimum displacement".' Technocrats and bureaucrats have an attitude of apathy towards tribal people, who are regarded as not quite human.

Even in the name of preservation of the environment, that is, by the creation of national parks on the lines of those in Western countries, the state has deprived tribes of their age-old lifestyles that were often within these protected areas. Karlsson (2000), in his study of the Rabhas, who live in the forests of the Duars region in north Bengal, has described how, over years of deprivation, the Rabhas now regard the *sarkar* (state) as their prime enemy. This is not surprising, considering that the Duars forests and most others in the country have been denuded not by the activities of the forest-dwelling tribes but by the colonial government and later by the postcolonial state.

The British had completely denuded the tendu reserve forest and heavily deforested the Buxa reserve forest to supply railway sleepers for the building of the Bengal–Duar railway line. At present these areas are being preserved and attempts are being made to regenerate them as conserved Tiger Protection Areas in the Alipurduar region of West Bengal in the Eastern Bhabhar area of the Himalayan foothills, but the tribes are no longer welcome in these forests. During the colonial period, large tracts of forest were given to the European tea growers to make tea estates, which now make this region famous for its supply of Darjeeling tea to the world. But the tribal people, who have protected both flora and fauna in these forests, are being forcibly evicted even as realisation is dawning that perhaps they are the best custodians of forest wealth. For example, in referring to Project Tiger, the tiger conservation programme launched by Government of India in 1973, Sheshadri (1995: 237), an expert on tiger conservation, wrote that the 'fundamental mistake of Project Tiger was its neglect to recruit the local communities in conservation and running of the reserves'. The eviction of tribes from forests has resulted in a people versus state attitude so that the very tribal people who had protected the forests for so long now identify it with the state and even contribute to its destruction.

The successive policies of the Indian state, especially after its pursuit of economic liberalisation in 1992, have been to put greater emphasis on the interests of corporations, big business and economic growth as against overall welfare and social justice. The redefining of the nature of 'public purpose' for which the state can acquire land has been left to the state. The new policies have a clear priority to favour corporates over local people as well as the environment. In the words of Ram Dayal Munda, who was the president of the Indian Confederation of Indigenous and Tribal Peoples, about 20 per cent of all tribal people from across India have been displaced and evicted from their traditional lands by large-scale development projects like dams and mines—'they now live on the roads as "internal refugees"' (quoted in Karlsson 2000: 16). Shortsighted and immediate gains are taking precedence over long-term benefits of inclusive growth.

THE MILITARY AND POLICE

At a meeting of indigenous youth held in Ranchi, Chhattisgarh, in March 2017, the participants were unanimous in identifying the police and the military as one of the prime enemies of tribal people. Speaking at the seminar, Rameshwar Oraon, a retired senior police officer and chairperson of the National Commission for Scheduled Tribes, said that the greatest violator of human rights was the state. The basic oppressive character of the state never changes, whether it is a feudal, socialist or democratic state. Power is more likely to be misused than used for any useful purpose. Many innocent tribal people are being killed by being labelled as militants. Even if it is proved that they were innocent and compensations are given, the lives lost can never be got back. Oraon also said at the seminar that his long stint as a police officer had made clear that most policemen were neither sympathetic nor sensitive to the issues of the tribes. For the police, tribes are not even human.

The Armed Forces (Special Powers) Act (AFSPA), as it is applied to states like Manipur and Nagaland, has escalated violence and underground activities. With the elderly women's nude protest after the rape and killing of the young woman Manorama in July 2004, the then prime minister Manmohan Singh had apologised and handed over Sangla Fort, which was then housing the Assam Rifles (whose personnel were guilty of this heinous crime), to the people of Manipur. It is now a museum and has many sacred sites of the local Meities. The AFSPA is a more draconian version of the earlier Armed Forces Special Powers Ordinance, 1942, used by the British during World War II to suppress the Indian freedom struggle, and its modified 1958 version is being used by the Indian state to suppress its own people. As Subramanian (2016: 357) describes for the state of Manipur,

> [w]ith the prolonged imposition of the Act, the cycle of violence has spread geographically and in intensity. Enforced disappearances, arbitrary executions, torture, rape, housebreak, loot, arbitrary detentions etcetera have become every day features of life in Manipur. And yet, few perpetrators of these gross violations of human rights were ever persecuted. Thus, the Armed Forces enjoy complete impunity and immunity under the Act.

The immunity offered to the armed forces has also encouraged the state police to misuse its powers, and the police and the paramilitary continue to kill people and indulge in other acts of intimidation and violence to oppress locals. The state government remains hand-in-glove with the oppressors, and the people killed are often no other than protestors of various projects of the government like dams and mining. 'Indeed the number of killings of "suspects" by the police are even considered achievements and the perpetrators are rewarded with cash incentives, medals and gallantry awards by the state government which ultimately serves as stepping stones to promotion' (ibid.: 359).

The Independent People's Tribunal (IPT), set up in New Delhi and organised by the Human Rights Law Network (HRLN), met in Imphal in 2009 (Subramanian 2016: 364). The IPT found severe violations of human rights including torture, rape and murder, and it suggested the immediate repeal of AFSPA. But this has not happened under the plea of internal security. Pregnant women, young boys and other innocent, unarmed people have been killed under no provocation but to increase the 'numbers' for the police personnel to show that they have been actively engaged in fighting 'terrorism'. There are ambivalent opinions about the role of the army and police, but the heavy-handed approach of the state has not yielded any fruitful results. Many people believe that since many of the tribes are situated in border areas, there is a need for vigilance over them to protect the national borders. During my fieldwork on the Indo-Tibet border, I found that an amicable relationship is possible, but it depends on the attitude of the army regiment posted in that region. A lot depends on how much the army personnel identify with the local people. For the northeast region, the interaction with the army has been hostile and full of misunderstandings, which has been further exacerbated by AFSPA.

SUMMARY

Virginius Xaxa has made a significant remark with respect to the policies of empowerment of marginal sections of Indian society by saying that while sections like the Scheduled Castes, who have been oppressed for centuries, are in need of empowerment (as they have never had power), it is a different situation for tribes. These are people who have had power and independence and then have had this power and independence taken away from them by a state that now takes on a paternalistic attitude by trying to 'empower' them. The state, especially the postcolonial state, has always regarded tribal people as 'backward' and in need of development, and it has constructed a rhetoric of passing down 'benefits' to tribes, as from a superior to an inferior level.

The many constitutional provisions for tribes (Sharma 2001) do not account for the circumstances under which they became impoverished and came to be in need of such benefits. In fact, as Xaxa (2008: 39) has also pointed out, 'Tribes, who have always enjoyed freedom and equality in their own societies did not benefit much from citizenship rights.' In fact, they have mostly resisted being incorporated into the larger Indian nation state, even after it became a democratic nation, because for them, this incorporation into a larger state meant disempowerment rather than any kind of empowerment. Thus, in independent India, tribes have been continuously losing their economic, political, cultural as well as social rights.

Tribes have mostly resisted being incorporated into the larger Indian nation state, even after it became a democratic nation, because for them, this incorporation into a larger state would have meant disempowerment rather than any kind of empowerment.

The peasants among tribes who have been semi-integrated into mainstream society, like the Gonds, Santhals, Mundas and Konds of central India, have the least access to power, having always been dominated by the local rulers. Later they came directly under colonial rule and then under the Indian state. The Hindu moneylenders, forest contractors and, later in the day, the globalising economy have all negatively impacted tribes.

The forces of democracy have not been too kind to tribes as well. The feudal system had extended protection to some tribes, who either had their own feudal chiefs, like the Gonds of Bastar and the Naga tribes of the Northeast, or enjoyed royal patronage like the Bhils of Rajasthan. In Rajasthan, the Bhils had been loyal allies to the local kings and chieftains, and were regarded as equivalent to the Rajputs in valour and skill. After the demise of the feudal system, all the power shifted out of the hands of the tribal rulers, as few of them had as much resources and education as the bigger royal houses of India. In Rajasthan, the Bhils, who had given up on agriculture to pursue a martial way of life, suddenly found themselves to be redundant in the present system. They have now been reduced to being daily-wage labourers and eke out a marginal existence. The institution of Panchayati Raj, with its mandatory reservation for Scheduled Tribes and Scheduled Castes, has not brought much relief to tribes, especially in regions where they live in close proximity to dominant Hindu castes. Here, persons of the dominant caste groups, like the Palliwals in the village Dabok in Rajasthan, merely put up a candidate from the tribal community as a proxy for their own power. It is only in tribal-dominated areas like the Northeast where tribes have real power.

For smaller and more homogenous communities like the Jad Bhotiyas (Channa 2017), the incorporation into Indian democracy and the compulsory imposition of an electoral system has done more harm than good. From 1992, the 73rd Amendment in the Indian Constitution made significant changes in the tribes' participation in Indian democracy, with the formation of the statutory gram panchayat. The majority of Jads view the process of internal elections as an intrusion into their community life. As one young man narrated to me when I was doing fieldwork in this area (Channa 2017: 35), 'The *sarkar* (government) has pitted brother against brother and sister against sister. We had a harmonious community life before but now factions have been created within us.' This shows how mindless the introduction of macro-democratic policies can be and how they can have a deleterious effect under certain conditions. The Jads had very little by way of internal stratification. They never had any concept of headman or village council. Most affairs were settled by mutual negotiations, but now internal rifts are appearing in the community, and when rifts appear, there are ways in which internal differences can be highlighted. In earlier times, these differences (like having a different lineage god) were not taken into account or were played down in the interests of the larger community, but now these are being played up. Thus, 'Jads exhibit the uneasy and problematic relationship that may exist between "democratic values" and democracy as an institutional set up, with its hierarchies and administrative mechanisms' (Channa 2017: 47). 'Thus to them democracy appears as hierarchy rather than equality, a curtailment rather than freedom of choice' (ibid.).

Some tribal activists have voiced concerns over the manner in which indigenous institutions are being eroded and replaced. However, sometimes these arguments are loaded and different stakeholders may have different opinions, for example, as mentioned earlier, the Naga women would rather comply with the Indian Constitution that gives more advantages to women than go by their own customary laws.

The lumping together of Scheduled Tribes and Scheduled Castes, as in need of beneficiary policies, does not do justice to either of them. From a status of political autonomy, cultural independence, high social status and a life of dignity in their own habitats, tribal people have been largely reduced to a subservient status within a state that, while being benign and just in principle, is represented by personnel who are anything but just and who are deeply entrenched in the hierarchical values of a caste- and class-based society. In the construction of the nation and the interpretation of nationalism, there is a significant bias towards a mainstream identity that certainly does not include the diversity of tribal identities across India. The very denial of the diversity among tribes, the non-recognition of their languages and the richness of their indigenous knowledge, indicates the inherent prejudice against all that tribes stand for. Roy Burman (1994: 69), in his critical analysis of the paternalistic policies of the state, suggests the replacement of paternalistic protection by an 'authentic partnership approach'. There is a need to understand tribes as a part of civil society, as people who have made and are still capable of making significant contributions to the nation, not as converts to a 'modern' way of life, but as themselves, with their own centuries of stored wisdom and sustainable lifestyles that have served to preserve some of the only remaining ecologically sustained regions of this country.

REFERENCES

Ao, Alemchiba. 1972. 'Problems of Readjustment to a New Situation (With Special Reference to the Naga Tribe)', in K. Suresh Singh (ed.), *The Tribal Situation in India*, pp. 477–85. Simla: Institute of Advanced Studies.

Baden-Powell, B. H. 1892. *The Land-systems of British India*. Oxford: Clarendon Press.

Channa, Subhadra Mitra. 1992. 'The Classical Ethnographies', in Subhadra Mitra Channa (ed.), *Nagaland: A Contemporary Ethnography*, pp. 11–40. New Delhi: Cosmo Publications.

———. 2017. 'Seeking Identities on the Margins of Democracy: Jad Bhotiyas of Uttarkashi', in Vibha Arora and N. Jayaram (eds), *Democratisation in the Himalayas: Interests, Conflicts, and Negotiations*, pp. 27–53. New Delhi: Routledge.

Chaudhuri, A. B. 1993. *State Formation among Tribals: A Quest for Santal Identity*. New Delhi: Gyan Publishing House.

Devalle, Susan B. C. 1992. *Discourses of Ethnicity, Culture and Protest in Jharkhand.* New Delhi: Sage Pub.

Dumont, Louis. 2001 [1986]. *A South Indian Subcaste: Social Organisation and Religion of the Piramalai Kallars.* London: Oxford University Press.

Fourcade, Marie. 2003. 'The So-called "Criminal Tribes" of British India: Colonial Violence and Traditional Violence', in Gilles Tarabout, D. Vidal and E. Meyer (eds), *Violence and Non-violence: Some Hindu Perspectives*, pp. 143–75. New Delhi: Manohar.

Fuchs, Stephen. 1966. *Rebellious Prophets: Study of Messianic Movements in Indian Religion.* Bombay: Asia Publishing House.

Fürer-Haimendorf, Christoph von. 1982 *Tribes of India: The Struggle for Survival.* Berkeley: University of California Press.

Hatch, W. J. 1976 [1928]. *The Land Pirates of India: An Account of the Kuravers, a Remarkable Tribe of Hereditary Criminals, their Extraordinary Skill as Thieves, Cattle-lifters, Highway Men and their Manners and Customs.* Delhi: Concept Publishing Company.

Hardiman, David. 1987. *The Coming of the Devi: Adivasi Assertion in Western India.* Delhi: Oxford University Press.

Hutton, J. H. 1969 [1921]. *The Angami Nagas.* London: MacMillan.

Karlsson, B. G. 2000. *Contested Belonging: An Indigenous People's Struggle for Forest and Identity in Sub-Himalayan Bengal.* Richmond Surry: Curzon Press.

Maharatna, Arup. 2005. *Demographic Perspectives on Indian Tribes.* New Delhi: Oxford University Press.

Meena, Hari Ram. 2016. *When Arrows Were Heated Up: A Story of Tribal Struggle against British Colonialism.* New Delhi: Niyogi Books.

Meyer, W. Stevenson, R. Burn, J. Sutherland Cotton, W. Wilson Hunter and Great Britan India Office. 1908–31. *The Imperial Gazeteer of India.* Oxford: The Clarendon Press.

Nathan, Dev and Virginius Xaxa (eds). 2012. *Social Exclusion and Adverse Inclusion: Development and Deprivation of Adivasis in India.* New Delhi: Oxford University Press.

Ngully, Meripeni. 2014. 'Stories in a Curiosity Box: John Henry Hutton Administrator-Collector in the Naga Hills', in Michael Heneise (ed.), *Passing Things On: Ancestors and Genealogies in Northeast India*, pp. 33–52. Dimapur: Heritage Publishing House.

Padel, Felix. 2011. *Sacrificing People: Invasions of a Tribal Landscape.* New Delhi: Orient BlackSwan.

Pandey, Gyanendra. 1991. 'In Defense of the Fragment: Writing About Hindu-Muslim Riots in India Today', *Economic and Political Weekly*, 26 (11/12): 559–72.

Pouchepadass, J. 1979. 'Delinquance de Function et Normalization Colonial: Les "Tribus Criminelles dans l'Indebritannique', in *Les Marginaux et les Exclus dans l'Histoire*, pp. 122–54. Paris: Plon.

Radhakrishna, Meena (ed.). 2016. 'Introduction', in *First Citizens: Studies on Adivasis, Tribals, and Indigenous Peoples in India*, pp. 1–30. New Delhi: Oxford University Press.

——— (ed.). 2016. 'Epilogue: Violence of "Development" and Adivasi Resistance—An Overview', in *First Citizens: Studies on Adivasis, Tribals, and Indigenous Peoples in India*, pp. 370–408. New Delhi: Oxford University Press.

Raguviah, V. 1962. *The Yanadis*. New Delhi: Adim Jati Sevak Sangh.

Ratnabali, Kongbrailatpam. 2015. *Law and Developmental Policies: Impact on Tribals' Cultural and Religious Space*. New Delhi: Abhijeet Publications.

Roy Burman, B. K. 1994. *Indigenous and Tribal Peoples: Gathering Mist and New Horizons*. New Delhi: Mittal Publications.

Roy, S. C. 1912. *The Mundas and Their Country*. Calcutta: Kuntaline Press.

Saberwal, Vasant. 1999. *Pastoral Politics: Shepherds, Bureaucrats, and Conservation in the Western Himalaya*. New Delhi: Oxford University Press.

Sachchidananda. 1964. *Culture Change in Tribal India*. Calcutta: Bookland.

Sahlins, Marshall and Elman R. Service (eds). 1973 [1960]. *Evolution and Culture*. Michigan: University of Michigan Press.

Sarkar, Tanika. 2011. '"Rebellion as Modern Self-fashioning": A Santal Movement in Colonial Bengal', in Daniel J. Rycroft and Sangeeta Dasgupta (eds), *The Politics of Belonging in India: Becoming Adivasi*, pp. 65–81. London and New York: Routledge.

Schendel, William van. 2011. 'The Dangers of Belonging: Tribes, Indigenous Peoples and Homelands in South Asia', in Daniel J. Rycroft and Sangeeta Dasgupta (eds), *The Politics of Belonging in India: Becoming Adivasis*, pp. 19–43. London and New York: Routledge.

Service, Elman Rogers. 1962. *Primitive Social Organization: An Evolutionary Perspective*. New York: Random House.

Sharma, B. D. 2001. *Tribal Affairs in India: The Crucial Transition*. New Delhi: Sahyog Pustak Kuteer.

Sheshadri, B. 1995. *Call of the Wild: Survival in the Sun*. New Delhi: Sterling Pub.

Singh, K. S. 1972. *Tribal Situation in India*. Simla: Institute of Advanced Studies.

———. 1983. *Birsa Munda and His Movement 1874–1901*. Calcutta: Oxford University Press.

Subramanian, K. S. 2016. 'Bleeding Manipur: Repeal the Armed Forces (Special Powers) Act 1958', in K. B. Saxena and G. Hargopal (eds), *Marginalization, Development and Resistance: Essays in Tribute to S. R. Sankaran, Vol. 2: Dalits and Adivasis*, pp. 353–72. New Delhi: Aakar Books.

Sundar, Nandini. 2007. *Subalterns and Sovereigns: An Anthropological History of Bastar 1854–2006*. Delhi: Oxford University Press.

Todd, James. 1899, 1920. *Annals and Antiquities of Rajasthan* (Vols 1 and 2). London: Joseph Burridge Books.

Unnithan-Kumar, Maya. 1997. *Identity, Gender and Poverty: New Perspectives on Caste and Tribe in Rajasthan*. Oxford: Berghahn.

Vidyarthi, L. P. (ed.). 1984. 'Anthropology and Tribal Policy: A Case Study among the Maler Pahariya', in *Applied Anthropology in India*. Allahabad: Kitab Mahal.

Wittfogel, Karl. 1957. *Oriental Despotism: A Comparative Study of Total Power*. US: Yale University Press.

Xaxa, Virginius. 2008. *State, Society, and Tribes: Issues in Post-colonial India*. Delhi: Pearson Longman.

———. 2016. 'Formation of Adivasi/Indigenous People's Identity in India', in Meena Radhakrishna (ed.), *First Citizens: Studies on Adivasis, Tribals, and Indigenous Peoples in India*, pp. 33–52. New Delhi: Oxford University Press.

7

THE PRESENT AND THE FUTURE

Globalisation, Identity and the Road Ahead

HIGHLIGHTS

- Tribal identities, tribal futures, contestation of identities
- Environmental issues and development
- Tribes and the nation

INTRODUCTION

In the twenty-first century, tribal people are certainly on a path that has taken them on a long journey away from their ancient roots. In this sense, they are no different than anyone else. All people evolve, transform and change. Everyone has hopes and aspirations for a future, and all have changed from what they were to something that they have become, but this is a never-ending process as people continue to change with the passage of time. Today tribes look different, even though they do dress up at times to put up a show, like we all do. So there are times when 'tradition' is celebrated, but this reinvention of tradition is always oriented towards the future. When we look back to the past, it is only to validate some future agenda. Tribal people today represent a spectrum, from hunter-gatherers in forests and shifting cultivators, pastoralists and settled cultivators to physicians, engineers, teachers, politicians, ministers and even global citizens. But no matter where they are, they are not untouched by time. Even if they live in the forest, they are aware of forest guards, of so-called Maoists, of police and miners. This is not to say that in the past they were unaware of outsiders, as forest people were always engaged in trade and social interactions with settled cultivators. But today, the nature of interactions has changed, and this process of change is continuous and never-ending.

Interestingly, the path to transformation is never linear—people change, only to look back and reinvent their identities, to create new traditions, like the Horn Bill Festival held in the Northeast or the newly emerging Sarna festivals in Chhattisgarh, which combine the old and the new in a synchrony that is consonant with their present lifeworlds. The Horn Bill Festival, for example, brings together a number of tribes that were hostile to each other in earlier times but today are interested in forging a common political identity. In cities around India, like Delhi and Mumbai, there are associations of tribals, especially of young people, who are trying to keep their culture alive. For example, Sarna dances are held in Delhi, where local people from the central Indian tribes, mostly the young, dress in their traditional attire and dance. At times, elders are called upon to teach and train the youth. Thus, one of the most emphasised characteristics of being a tribe—that they are isolated or localised—is no longer applicable in this global world. People born in Manipur or Chhattisgarh may now be anywhere, in Chennai, Mumbai or San Francisco, but they remain tribal as long as they identify with their roots and ethnicity.

If we try to understand tribal people as they are in the twenty-first century and as they prepare to move forward, there are several major dimensions of their lives that we need to consider, such as the following:

1. Literacy and education
2. Identity and political aspirations
3. Internal stratification
4. Ecology and issues of 'development'

None of these dimensions is independent of the others as one aspect influences the other and often forms a pre-condition for the others. This classification is merely for theoretical simplification and to facilitate the understanding of some very complex processes.

LITERACY AND EDUCATION

Almost all tribal people have only in recent times moved from an oral tradition towards literacy, and some like the Tangkhuls have had their written languages created for them by European missionaries. Scripts have also been borrowed from neighbouring literate and dominant cultures, like the Bengali script used by some tribes of northeast and central India. Literacy has also followed on the heels of Christianisation, with missionaries carrying the burden of 'civilising' tribes along with showing them the way to 'salvation'. This religious and cultural transformation has played a dual role. On the one hand, missionaries drilled in the idea among tribes that they were savages and backward before they became Christians and that their modernity and education were solely gifts of the missionaries. Young people of the Northeast parrot such sentiments even today. On the other hand, the adoption of literacy has contributed to the emergence of common identities that was not possible earlier. As Shimreiwung (2014: 157) puts it, 'it also laid the foundation for creating a common language for a tribe characterized by having as many dialects as the number of villages'. The missionary William Pettigrew created the written language for the Tangkhuls in the nineteenth century. He arrived at Ukhrul in 1896 and created a common written language using the Roman script. Although the purpose of the missionaries was purely to civilise the local people, the effect of having a common language, reading from the same books and singing the same songs enabled the coming together of a people under a common nomenclature that went a long way in forging a common political identity, supported by the creation and adoption of common cultural elements.

Although the purpose of the missionaries was purely to civilise the local people, the effect of having a common language went a long way in forging a common political identity.

Emerging identities like Naga and Kuki have been possible only by the availability of a common language so that the internal divisions between numerous dialects could be overcome and people could come together on larger platforms to assert their political identities. The merging of tribes into the larger political entity of the Indian state gave to many of them the realisation that tiny fragmentations will not serve the purpose of giving them their rights, especially as numbers tend to matter in a parliamentary democracy. Thus, for diverse tribal communities to come together, it was imperative to be able to communicate in a common language if they were to assert their common issues. Nagaland, under greater influence of European missionaries, adopted English as the common language, and Arunachal, surprisingly the state most isolated physically, adopted Hindi, the national language.

Many tribal folklore, ways of life and even medicinal systems were converted into written documents by the advent of writing and literacy among tribes. Just like Pettigrew, who wrote the first Tangkhul language dictionary, Paul Olaf Bodding created the first Santal language dictionary and also painstakingly documented the Santal system of healing and medicine as also their cosmology and folklore. Some students of Pettigrew like Y. K. Shimray took to writing in the Tangkhul language and created a substantial body of literature. The Tangkhul literary society was founded in 1938, and it published a magazine of which Shimray was the editor. It is to be noted that the larger and more dominant tribes like the Santals, the Tangkhuls, the Angamis and Sumi Nagas were the ones who took initial advantage of the spread of literacy and education. The Santali script, called Ol Chiki, was created by a tribal scholar, Pandit Raghunath Murmu. He first conceptualised the script in the 1920s and gave it a final shape in the 1940s (Mohapatra 2001: 75). The Santals are among the largest tribes who had early access to literacy—being in close contact with outsiders led not only to their exploitation but also their emancipation. In their efforts to fight external exploiters, they were also able to educate themselves. Today, Santali literature exists, as do newspapers and magazines published in Ol Chiki.

Smaller tribes were smothered within the larger local identities. Literacy and education have also begun to create hierarchies within the relatively homogenous tribal groups. For the past few decades, in spite of the tenuous political links with the Indian mainland, many tribal students have begun to enter institutions of higher learning like colleges and universities across India. There is, as a result, a generation

Literacy and education have begun to create hierarchies within the relatively homogenous tribal groups. Those already in positions of proximity to the mainstream and those who have not suffered much deprivation have taken away the share of those more disadvantaged.

of tribal persons, serving as officers, teachers and workers in various offices and agencies all across India. This has also been possible because of the reservation policies with respect to Scheduled Tribes. However, even now, the number of students from these communities in institutions of higher learning is limited. There is a feeling even among tribal people that only some individuals or few privileged communities among tribes have taken maximum advantage of these provisions. As mentioned in Chapter 1, only nine out of the 500 recognised Scheduled Tribes are dominant. It is apprehended that those already in positions of proximity to the mainstream and those who have not suffered much deprivation have taken away the share of those more disadvantaged.

In tribal-dominated regions like the Northeast, only those belonging to dominant tribes like the Tangkhuls are disproportionately represented as compared to smaller tribes in the same region. Similarly, the Apatanis of Arunachal Pradesh, Khasis of Meghalaya, the Santals and the Mundas of central India, the Bhotiyas of Uttarakhand are among those one is likely to find in Delhi and Mumbai. The least literate and least advantaged are the Yanadis, the Tharus, the Garos, the Konds, the Van Gujjars, the Bondos of Odisha and similar tribes, whose modes of livelihood located them in inaccessible areas and who were also less influenced by outside forces such as the missionaries and the impact of education and literacy. Many of these tribes voluntarily shunned literacy and education as they had a world view and cosmology that were not compatible with urban and literate ways of life. Many prefer their traditional modes of life to mainstream ways. For example, the Konds of Odisha have successfully resisted the destruction of their livelihood and environment by a multinational corporation Vedanta. The choice was clear for them. Others are not so lucky, and tribes that were once the proud owners of forests and hills, like the Birhors and Bison Horn Marias, are destitute occupants of urban slums, plying cycle rickshaws or working as daily labourers.

Thus, literacy and education—the means to participation in the mainstream economy and society—were either not available to the bulk of tribal people or were voluntarily avoided by them as they preferred their own ways of life. There was also the creation of a tribal elite in this process, which effectively blocked the way for many others. As has been observed, advantages of education and modernisation tend to be inherited over generations, and some families rise over others and tend to secure their positions permanently. As observed by Maharatna (2005: 54), demographic statistics indicate that tribals have the least literacy rate as compared to other marginal groups like Scheduled Castes and Other Backward Classes. Further, 'the gap between tribal and non-tribal literacy rates widened during the 1970s and 1980s especially for females' (ibid.). This is not because the educated tribals stopped giving education to their children, but because the expansion of education was more among the other groups while tribes lagged behind. Maharatna (2005) raises the question as to why the literacy rates of tribal women are lower in spite of the general observation that women among tribes enjoy a higher status than among non-tribes. From the statistics provided by work figures from the Census and the National Sample Survey, it becomes clear that women among tribes work much more productively than their non-tribal counterparts and play important roles in the tribal economy. Jayachandran (2001: 14–15) gives the example of Jhabua district that is predominantly tribal and where female work participation is nearly 80 per cent, but female school attendance is only 15.2 per cent in the age group of 5–14 years (an age group in which the maximum number of girl children go to school even if they drop out later).

Tribes may show some improvement in their parameters of poverty and education, but in terms of relative deprivation or in comparison to the non-tribal population of India, they are falling behind and not catching up with others.

As pointed out by Xaxa (2012: 29), tribes may show some improvement in their parameters of poverty and education, but in terms of relative deprivation or in comparison to the non-tribal population of India, there is clear indication that they are falling behind and not catching up with others. According to Mathur (2008), cited in Xaxa (2012: 23–35),

> in 1993–94 for example the proportion of the tribal population falling below the poverty line was 51.14 per cent as compared with 35.97 per cent for the country as a whole. By 2004–2005, the share of the tribal

> population living below the poverty line had declined to 46.5 per cent, as compared to only 27.6 per cent for the population as a whole.

Thus, it is apparent, as also endorsed by most other tribal studies, that tribes are not the beneficiaries of any programme directed towards the improvement of life in general.

The category of Scheduled Tribes is a blanket term applicable to all tribes irrespective of their location and status. There exists only one subcategory, that of the Particularly Vulnerable Tribes, which, in any case, are hardly in a position to be literate or educated. Tribal people are themselves aware that the benefits meant for them are cornered by a few. In Chapter 1, we saw how only a few tribes were more dominant than others, even though the total numbers of tribes are quite high. Some tribes may be de-scheduled or, as was related to me by young tribals in West Bengal, some officials refuse to recognise educated tribal men as belonging to a 'tribe', and dissociate them from the identity of their own fathers.

In my interaction with Bhils in Udaipur, there was a sense that the government could not be depended on for doing anything for the marginal. Shah (2011: 220) writes based on her study of the Munda tribes that the word the Mundas most frequently associated with the state was *shosan* or exploitation. Most tribal people who are not the creamy layer benefitting from government-run programmes find themselves at the wrong end of 'development', including opportunities for education. One major reason for the apathy of the state towards tribal education could be the historical fact that the tribals who were the first to rise against the state were the ones who had received education from the missionaries. 'The first movement for a separate state of Jharkhand was the result of social and educational work of Christian missionaries from late eighteenth century in the area—they created a different class of adivasis' (Shah 2011: 222). There was a similar situation in the Northeast and such other tribal regions that came under influence of educational social workers.

Most tribal people who are not the creamy layer benefitting from government-run programmes find themselves at the wrong end of 'development', including opportunities for education.

There is also a counter-movement where Hindutva-driven organisations are trying to indoctrinate tribal children into believing that they are Hindus. However, there is also an emerging self-consciousness that is propelling tribal people to be self-reliant and to depend on their own abilities. The youth are looking for avenues of self-development, including going back to some of their own ways of life. They are also trying as much as possible to get educated, but it is not always a possibility given that educational facilities for poor tribal students are not the best. There is considerable prejudice on the part of teachers who look upon tribal children as inherently lacking in the capacity to learn. Many small children find it difficult to learn in alien languages that they do not speak at home. At the same time, tribes also wish to be educated in more universal languages that will connect them to the outside world.

Most tribes still retain their original languages and dialects even as they are able to converse with each other and with outsiders in more universal languages like English and Hindi. The smaller tribes are the ones most likely to be multilingual as they have to communicate with other dominant groups who also put the onus of communication on the smaller group. For example, the Kota of Nilgiris studied by Wolf (2005) numbered only about a 1,000 individuals at the time they were studied, their population having steadily declined over the years. They reportedly speak their own dialect, the language of the Badagas, their dominant neighbours, and Tamil, as it is the language of the state. Many also speak Hindi and English if they are educated and are going to school.

The dominant tribes in particular regions are better able to propagate their own tribal languages, like the Santals. Some tribal areas, like Shillong in Meghalaya, have a flourishing education system with excellent schools being run by missionaries and a university of repute (North-eastern Hill University or NEHU). Many students from neighbouring areas like Nagaland, Assam and Manipur go to Shillong to get a good education. Once tribes learn a connecting language, there is a way open for forging larger alliances beyond the confining boundaries that had earlier separated even villages from one another. For example, when they are away from their home states, students from the Northeast bond together as 'northeasterners', irrespective of the inherent fissions that may have historically existed between them. A common language such as English enables them to connect. At times, several different identities are swallowed within one dominant identity for political gains. For example, referring to Meghalaya, Ramirez (2014: 46) writes, 'For the Karbis and Tiwas landlocked by the boundary inside the heavily Khasi dominated State of Meghalaya, Khasi ST status might possibly be very attractive.'

The present generation of educated youth is learning to connect with each other across regional and cultural divides under global identities such as 'indigenous'. The Internet and the many social networks enable forging of relationships across a wide geographical region that may extend across the world. Global recognitions of identities such as those of the indigenous peoples enable the coming together of different tribes on a common platform on common agenda. The very process of globalisation that is driven by a global capitalism creates common situations and hence also common enemies, which enables the marginal to talk to each other across huge social and cultural divides. Global capitalism makes conditions such as mining, deforestation, displacement, internal colonisation and environmental racism a common vocabulary understood by the exploited and marginalised globally (Moody 2007). The positive side of economic liberalisation is that it makes cash available to people who earlier only had barter or the subsistence economy to rely upon. This access to a cash economy makes travel, national and international political participation, and spending on items of symbolic capital like religious shrines possible. Thus, economic transformations are adjunct with many other kinds of possibilities and changes. They also enable the emergence of voices that were earlier muted as they did not have any access to any platform. But economic and political empowerment is manifested in multiple ways.

The present generation of educated youth is learning to connect with each other across regional and cultural divides under global identities such as 'indigenous'. This has enabled the coming together of different tribes on a common platform.

IDENTITY AND EMERGING CONSCIOUSNESS

The tussle with the central government over the use of the designation 'indigenous' as against tribal is one of the many issues that the young and the educated are finding as a common thread to forge common identities. There is still an ongoing discourse on the use of terms such as 'tribe', 'Adivasi', 'Scheduled Tribes' and 'indigenous', and the so-called tribal people are still not sure about which term they should use and which one is the most empowering for them. There is an ongoing discourse in academia on the use of these terms (Radhakrishna 2016; Rycroft and Dasgupta 2011). Since the term 'tribe' is now universally recognised as a colonial product (Devalle 1992), a section of scholarship is oriented towards the emerging efforts at 'decolonisation of knowledge' in a way that 'exponents of decoloniality aim to recognize, negotiate and move beyond the political and intellectual limits of a colonial/post-colonial patterning' (Rycroft and Dasgupta 2011: 6). This means that there are efforts to redeem some of the labels and concepts like 'tribe' that had an inherently insidious political agenda aimed towards serving the colonial regime's economic interests.

There is an ongoing discourse on the use of terms such as 'tribe', 'Adivasi', 'Scheduled Tribes' and 'indigenous', and the tribal people are still not sure about which term they should use and which one is the most empowering for them.

Another very important issue is the way 'development' is being interpreted and how a monolithic version of this development is being thrust upon tribal people. 'Indigenous' is no longer associated only with being 'original' to a place. It is increasingly being associated with the processes of dispossession and the lack of a political voice. The indigenous are those who are on the fringes of the centre of power. People identifying as 'indigenous', such as the Indigenous Youth Network of India, are bringing together various tribes from the different regions that speak different languages and worship different deities. Under the blanket category of common oppression, they can identify their common enemies and unite. As already discussed in Chapters 1 and 6, such designations are often used variably and for different goals, for instance, 'Scheduled Tribe' is used to negotiate with the Indian state, while 'indigenous' is used for international networking, and 'Adivasi' for internal self-assertions. Most tribes, no matter how small, realise that they have multiple levels of identity and, therefore, multiple platforms for negotiation. Today, no tribe is in a position that it is not acutely aware of the presence of others in its life and not aware of how these external forces affect it. Most tribes are also keenly involved in processes of negotiations, protests and assertions. Thus, even though the state of Jharkhand came into existence by the efforts of the BJP, a right-wing political party ideologically committed to Hindutva, the tribes of Jharkhand today are opposing the efforts to classify them as Hindus. As Shah (2011: 223) argues, the Jharkhand tribes wish to unite under their own common language, Nagpuri, an Adivasi cultural heritage based on *jal, jangal, jamin* (water, forest and land), and their original Adivasi religion, Sarna. They wish to revive their original political organisation based on the Parha system, which is linked to the sacred and constructed as different from the 'amoral' politics of the state (ibid.).

The designation 'Scheduled Tribe' is used to negotiate with the Indian state, while 'indigenous' is used for international networking, and 'Adivasi' for internal self-assertions.

At the meeting of the Indigenous Youth Network held in Chhattisgarh in March 2017, the common enemies identified were, first, the media, second, the state and, third, the police and army, who are seen as representatives of the state. The media was firmly blamed for blacking out all news on indigenous people, especially those involving police torture, military action and deprivation. It is for this reason that several dominant tribes with flourishing languages like Santali have started publishing their own newspapers. In the Northeast too there are papers and magazines in Tangkhul and Nagamese (a synthetic language that evolved with the forging of a common Naga identity). The media is seen as the foremost enemy because it is seen as having the power to counter the monopoly of the state machinery for repression, a power that it fails to exercise. The pen could, if it so wished, highlight the plight of the marginalised, but it rarely does so, except to write about insurgencies and about the ultra-left working in tribal belts. There is a common sentiment among the tribal youth and educated persons that the popular media is 'sold' to the rich and the powerful.

According to Surya Singh Besra, a prominent Santali leader and littérateur, who has translated *Gitanjali* by Rabindranath Tagore and *Madhushala* by Harivansh Rai Bachchan into the Santali language, there is need to recognise the tribal as an ethnic and cultural identity on the part of the civil society in India. The identity of Jharkhand and Chhattisgarh should not be only by residence but by ethnicity. The non-tribal, more educated, and politically and socially dominant persons form the dominant groups in tribal states such as Jharkhand and Chhattisgarh, which have a sizeable population of non-tribal people. There is now an increasing assertion by tribes of their ethnic and cultural heritage. For example, the Mundas and Oraons of Chhattisgarh are now reaffirming their ancient Sarna religion and the Supreme God Sing Bonga. They are under pressure from Hindutva dominant political groups to declare themselves as Hindus (Xaxa 2008: 46), something that is being rejected by the tribes of this region. In Manipur, there is a revivalism of the original religion of Sona Mahi, by the Vaishnavite Meities, long recognised as Hindus. 'A cult like *Doinipolo*, *Seng Khasi*, or the celebration of *Gangngai* by Rongmei Nagas, stands as a resistance to such processes of Hinduisation or Christianisation. The participation of Christian Hmars and Lusheis in traditional festivals like *Butu Khuong Lawm*, *Chaopou Kut*, *Mim Kut* or *Chapchar Kut* brings back a renewed sense of tribal identity' (Biswas and Suklabaidya 2008: 102).

In the villages near Udaipur, the local Bhils are reclaiming their traditional deities and celebrating their annual festivals in their villages. The celebration of these annual festivals ensures that all the people who leave the village as daily wage labourers in cities come back at least once or twice a year, and people reconnect with each other and reaffirm their family ties. I was told by several men (while doing fieldwork in this region in the summer of 2016) about how earlier they never came back even to meet their families once they were taken away by the contractors to work as labourers in the big cities. These simple folk from the village lost their bearings in the cities and practically forgot their kith and kin. But today, as they told me, the deity ensures that they come back for its worship: 'It is the power of the devta that brings us back so that we do not get lost in the wilderness of the city.' There is a considerable resurgence of religiosity among tribes and marginal people. Much of it has to do with the tensions created in their lives by urbanisation, displacement and migration. The destruction of local environments and livelihoods is forcing many of them to become migrant labourers, and for these independent and simple people, the shift from a free to a stressful life means a great change. The collective worship of local deities gives them a sense of belonging and helps re-establish kinship and village ties, which serve as a buffer for the stress created by urban slum life. Also, the access to some cash income gives them the means to spend money for festivals and, at times, refurbish the local temple or re-establish some place of worship. The sense of pride to be able to do this is also a great boost to their self-esteem and identity.

Such ethnic assertions, which appear to be drawing upon the past, are actually oriented towards the future. Tribes are now looking towards a future where they hope that they will be recognised by their own identity and will be able to hold a place in Indian society where they are not submerged within other identities. Even those that have become Christians, like the tribes of the Northeast, are now trying to move away from too much Westernisation towards creating an identity based on their culture. This includes the retention of their traditional material-culture items like shawls and jewellery, songs and oral traditions. Some elements of beliefs still continue from ancient times like the belief in 'guardian spirits' (Khongreiwo 2014: 74) that is retained by Christian Nagas. Thus, belief in the benevolence of certain mountain spirits and field spirits is still prevalent among all Nagas, irrespective of their conversion to Christianity.

Tribes are now looking towards a future where they hope that they will be recognised by their own identity and will be able to hold a place in Indian society where they are not submerged within other identities.

Literacy helps in creating a literature that is focused on the tribes' present-day conditions and future aspirations. Shimreiwung (2014: 162) writes, 'We also find the construction of Tangkhul's identity and image in written literature being highly influenced by political aspirations, a form that was in variations from folk narratives and oral history.' The reinvention and revitalisation of tribal material culture is one big step towards the contemporary identity formation of tribes. According to Odyuo (2014: 53), 'Although production of Naga art has lost its ritualistic significance, it has been taken up again with vigour. And that constitutes a continuity, renaissance or reinvention of traditional creativity.' Traditionally, material culture has been mostly for utilitarian or ritual value, although this did not mean that the objects created did not have high aesthetic standards. The same designs and techniques are today used for making objects of mixed utility and artistic value. Tribal art is being marketed as craft and for purely decorative and aesthetic purposes. Although craft forms and techniques were never individually owned and all such knowledge belonged to the community, today, with the art entering the market, individual artists are also getting recognition. The Gond artist, Jangarh Sing Shyam, for example, has attained international fame and is now given almost iconic status. Innovative artists from among tribes are being recognised at home and abroad, and many are travelling and exhibiting their art as art, with both commercial and artistic value. Even within the community, some individuals are getting artistic recognition and being showcased as icons of the community. 'For example, among contemporary basket makers known for their distinctive style is Selie at Khonoma village an expert weaver of a fine ritual basket called khopi, which is used by the Angami Nagas only on festivals such as the Terunyi, Sekrenyi and Thekranyi' (Odyuo 2014: 59).

Tribal art is also being used in more global art forms like the fashion industry. Tribal colours, motifs and designs are being used on ties, T-shirts, bags and jackets, items of clothing not traditionally worn but now being used as symbols of a modernising tribal identity. Both men and women often wear such motifs and designs on their formal Indian and Western dresses to assert that even being modern, they have not given up on their identity. Traditional fabrics, designs and motifs are being used in the global fashion and textile industry. As described by Odyuo (2014: 61), 'Emerging young Naga fashion designers such as Zos Zhasa, Atsu Sekhose and Imcha Imchen among others, in inventing their own styles that reflect their version of modernism with traditional touch suggest the melding of Naga identity with changing taste and styles in global fashion.' At the same time, since there is no copyright as such on the use of the label tribe or tribal, a lot of things are also being marketed by opportunist entrepreneurs, exploiting the 'tribal' label. Ethnic chic, a term that has now attained marketable status, is often used to pass off mass-produced goods that lack the authenticity of individually crafted items. However, even this commodification has helped project tribes as having value and artistic merit, something that has given them some standing in civil society. Tribes have begun to take pride in their art and craft and to showcase their authentic culture.

In universities around India, tribal students form their unions, network with each other, have food festivals and connect with non-tribal students. Even those regions that are still involved with secessionist movements, like Manipur and Nagaland, are getting a foothold in the mainstream, and interactions with local people can at times be on more or less equal terms as colleagues and friends. Tribal artists and craftspersons go to cities to participate in festivals and exhibitions. There are internationally known tribal artists and writers, like the Naga writers, Easterine Kire and Temsula Ao. There are also many performing artists, singers and dancers whose work is now getting acclaim both nationally and internationally. Globalisation is also connecting tribal people to similarly situated people all across the world. They are able to present their problems at international forums and send representatives to the UN and the ILO. Participating in universal education systems, learning national and international languages, making contacts on cyberspace and being connected to the rest of the world has helped tribal people realise their identity, and they are now confident to face the world as themselves.

CONTESTING IDENTITIES

Among the grievances of tribes is that they have had names and identities imposed on them. There are many communities, like the Bhotiyas, that do not recognise themselves in their official name. As recorded by Channa (2013), this pastoral community of shepherds in a village on the upper Himalayan ranges recognises themselves as Rongpa, a name by which outsiders never refer to them. The common local name for them is Jad, and the official records mention them only as Bhotiya. But the latter is a generic name and includes many more such small communities, each with their own distinct identities, but which were perhaps too small to be recognised officially.

When the identity of a nation was created by incorporating a large number of units, some were not important enough to be recognised individually. Many of them did not, and perhaps still do not, exist in official documents. Often, they exist as something they do not recognise as their self-identity. Thus, their 'inner selves' are de-recognised, and many have to struggle with imposed 'outer selves', which are identities to which they do not feel that they belong. Yet, they often have to take on these imposed selves because of practicality, power hierarchies and political negotiability (Channa 2013: 13). It is possible that in their own reflections, the Angami and the Sumi think that they are Angami and Sumi and not just Naga; many may be identifying in terms of their clans and lineages. Yet they will respond to the identity of 'Naga' and also do it somewhat willingly.

When the identity of a nation was created, some identities were not important enough to be recognised individually. Thus, as 'inner selves' are de-recognised, many struggle with imposed 'outer selves', to which they do not feel that they belong.

When the resources at the disposal of people grow and their vulnerability decreases, the larger identities may be discarded, at least in some situations, in favour of more parochial ones. Thus, individual groups now put under blanket categories, Naga being one of them, are finding it difficult to remain united as more power is coming their way. There is a distinct disjunction when they are opposed to the Indian nation (as in case of the AFSPA) and when they are fighting assembly elections as part of the Indian democracy. When it comes to power-sharing, a renegotiation of identities emerges. This negotiation is often done with a futuristic agenda like forming alternative interest groups when the earlier interest groups begin to lose their meaning. Earlier many similar groups had found it expedient to gather under a large, encompassing umbrella of identity, but in changed circumstances these identities may fall apart or at least reassert themselves.

A case in point is the Zeliangrong, a confederation of tribes, where each constituent unit has been trying to recreate its identity to fit in with a new sense of belonging. The data on the Zeliangrong was compiled by my student Mary Panmei, herself a Zeliangrong. Zeliangrong is an acronym composed of three tribes, 'Ze' from the Zeme, 'Liang' from the Liangmei and 'Rong' from the Rongmei. The term 'Zeliangrong' was coined in a conference of the Zeme, Liangmei, Rongmei and Puimei of Manipur and the Naga Hills of Assam, on 15 February 1947 at Imphal. Since the colonial period, there has been confusion over their identities in the common nomenclature of the Zeliangrong. This was due to the imposition of exogenous names by the Meitei rulers of Manipur that were recognised by the British and Indian governments. In the nineteenth century, British ethnographers used nomenclatures like Zeme, Aroong, Kutcha Naga or Mejhamah and Kachcha Naga Empeo to refer to the Zemes of North Cachar and Naga Hills (Butler 1875; Grange 1840; Soppit 1885). In Manipur, McCulloch (1859) and Brown (1874) used nomenclatures like Songboo and Pooeeron to refer to the Kabui (Rongmei) and the Puimei. They used Quireng (Lyeng) and Kabui to refer to the Liangmei, the Rongmei and the Puimei. T. C. Hodson, in his book *The Naga Tribes of Manipur* (1911), clarified the confusion, and the name 'Kabui', a Meitei word, was officially used to designate the Songboo (Rongmei) and the Pooeeron (Puimei). Hutton in his monumental monograph *The Angami Nagas* (1921) explicitly described the ethnic and racial composition of the 'Kacha Naga' as comprising three groups, namely, Zeme, Liangmei and Maruongmei.

The ethnonym 'Kabui' is a Meitei word used in the ancient chronicles of Manipur, before the British usage of the term. According to the chronicles, the term 'Kabui' is used to mean the Rongmei and the Puimei. The differentiation between the Rongmei and the Puimei was indicated in the *Cheitharol Kumbaba*, the royal chronicle of Manipur. During the reign of King Bhagyachandra (1763–98), the name Kabui Anouba (New Kabui) was used to mean the Puimei. The claim that Puimei was older than Kabui and that the British adopted 'Kabui' from Puimei is completely wrong. The term 'Kabui', which is not a Rongmei word, was given by the Meitei to mean the Rongmei and the Puimei. Although it has several historical references, Kabui is a misnomer.

Some enquiries show that 'Kacha Naga' is an Angami word derived from 'Ketsa' or 'Ketsu' meaning deep forests or forest dwellers. Originally, it was adopted to mean the Zeme of Naga Hills. This name was also used for the Liangmei who live in the Naga Hills and Manipur. Hutton and U. G. Bower employed the term 'Kacha Naga' to mean the Zeme, Liangmei and Rongmei. This description is believed to be wrong and not acceptable to the Zeliangrongs. However, in Manipur, 'Kacha Naga' means the Zeme and Liangmei only as per the Scheduled Tribe List [All Zeliangrong Students' Union (AZSU)].

At the end of the British rule in 1947, two nomenclatures, 'Kacha Naga' and 'Kabui', remained, referring to Zeme, Liangmei, Rongmei and Puimei. To replace the foreign-imposed names, the ethnonym 'Zeliangrong' came into existence. After the formation of the state of Nagaland, 'Kacha Naga' was replaced by Zeliang (Zeme and Liangmei), whereas Rongmei was barred. Zeliang is given Scheduled Tribe status under 'Any Naga Tribe' in Nagaland, devoid of Rongmei. In Manipur, 'Kacha Naga' (Zeme and Liangmei) and Kabui (Rongmei and Puimei) were declared as Scheduled Tribes in 1956 without the consent of the respective people. In Assam, under the provision of 'Any Naga Tribe', only the Zeme is recognised as Scheduled Tribe, debarring the Liangmei and the Rongmei. Hence, the collective identity of the Zeliangrong, which has been imposed and recognised in different nomenclatures, is wrong and unacceptable to the Zeliangrong people. There are interesting observations that can be made on the basis of the preceding discussion. First, it seems that the first chroniclers of the Naga tribes, the British administrators, picked up nomenclature not from the 'wild' tribes of Manipur and Nagaland, but from far more 'civilised' sources, namely, the royal chronicles of the kings of Manipur and perhaps people from the plains of Assam, which explains why the names used by them were many and differed greatly from the original indigenous ones. The British had certainly not asked any of the natives as to what they were called or what they wished to be called. Thus, Kabui is said to be a misnomer by the present-day bearers of that name, implying that it did not originate from them.

These misrepresented nomenclatures obviously were the products of interactions between one set of power holders with another set, and the people concerned were never consulted. This is, however, not at all an isolated incidence of such imposed nomenclatures or even identities. In the post-Independence context, identities have also assumed greater significance, as getting labelled as a separate 'tribe' in the Indian Schedule means that one is entitled to certain benefits. But one must not attribute the search for identities to only a pragmatic goal but also link it to the sense of an 'inner self', a validation of what one believes one's self to be.

The continued struggle of some tribes to get recognition on their own terms now involves the educated sections of these tribes. Also within a democracy, the universal franchise has given some political weight to the collective voice of a people. In Manipur, since the recognition of Kacha Naga and Kabui as Scheduled Tribes in 1956, there have been persistent demands for the alteration of these two nomenclatures. In 1960, the Zeliangrong Naga Union (ZNU) demanded that Government of India recognise the Zeliangrong. In January 1966, freedom fighter Rani Gaidinliu raised her demand for a Zeliangrong district and for the recognition of Zeliangrong as a separate Scheduled Tribe in Assam, Manipur and Nagaland (Kamei 2004). A great conflict took place in Nagaland in 1976, when the Rongmei were excluded in the list of the indigenous tribes of Nagaland. Rongmei as a separate tribe or Rongmei as a part of 'Zeliang' was not considered. In Manipur, the issue was about changing the nomenclatures Kacha Naga and Kabui into the collective name of Zeliangrong.

In 1975, the Zeliangrong Student Union of Manipur (ZSUM) submitted a memorandum to Government of India for the collective status of the Zeliangrong as a tribe. Again in 1983, there was a movement by the Zeliangrong People Convention (ZPC) under the leadership of Gaidinliu for the recognition of the Zeliangrong as a Scheduled Tribe and to provide a separate homeland. The AZSU and other Zeliangrong organisations of Assam, Manipur and Nagaland organised several *dharnas* (demonstrations) and submitted memorandums (1992, 1994, 1996, 2005) to the prime minister of India and other higher officials on their demands for the common identity of the Zeliangrong.

On the recommendation of the Hill Areas Committee, the government of Manipur decided to recommend the following proposal in respect of the recognition of the Zeliangrong as a Scheduled Tribe. Any Zeliangrong tribe includes Zeme and Liangmei in lieu of Kacha Naga, and Rongmei and Inpui in lieu of Kabui. Also, there is a demand for a separate recognition of Zeme, Liangmei, Rongmei and Puimei (Inpui) by some vested interest groups. Nevertheless, most of the Zeliangrongs as a whole are against the divisive policy of the collective identity of the Zeliangrong people.

From the preceding analysis, one finds that slowly the rights to decision-making are passing from the hands of the external elite to those of the indigenous elite, composed mostly of the formally educated, so that we find that students are playing a key role as much as the local politicians. When such new identities are being asserted, they are obviously being done as a political strategy and to serve the future political agenda of some people. When we look at the traits that are being evoked to stake a 'common' identity, it becomes obvious that, as Bayart (2005) puts it, culture is a 'construct'. The Zeliangrong are the descendants of the same ancestors. The common identity of the Zeliangrongs as an ethno-cultural entity is based on (i) common origin and history, (ii) ethnic and linguistic affinity, (iii) common social structure based on kinship and lineage, (iv) cultural homogeneity, and (v) a common political system. Racially and linguistically, the Zeliangrong belong to the Naga-Bodo sub-family of the Tibeto-Burman linguistic group (Grierson 1903). All the five characteristics mentioned are both sufficiently generalised and also non-challengeable, yet they suffice to create a sense of commonality, if one wishes to believe in it.

> **Slowly the rights to decision-making are passing from the hands of the external elite to those of the indigenous elite, composed mostly of the formally educated, so that students are playing a key role as much as local politicians.**

The case of the Zeliangrong is one among many such instances of identity contestation and renegotiation. Eyingbeni et al. (2012: 13) discuss a similar situation for the Chakesang—an acronym that does not describe any spatial or linguistic affiliation: 'The term Chakesang,

(CHA+KHE+SANG) which is a recognized tribe in Nagaland, is an acronym for three groups of people, or basically linguistic groups, namely, "Cha" for Chokri, "Khe" for Kheza, and "Sang" for Sangtam.' However, today Sangtam refers to an altogether different tribe in the Tuensang district in Nagaland. Strangely enough, the Tuensang district was never a land for the Chakesang people. Sangtam was then inappropriately used to refer to a linguistic community called Pochuri who are today a full-fledged tribe in Phek district. Besides, the Chakesang tribe is also constituted by yet another linguistic group known as 'Zhamai' or 'Zavame'.

Similar instances of imposed names are found from all across the world. According to Triloki Nath Pandey, Professor Emeritus, Department of Anthropology, Santa Cruz University (2017, personal communication), the Zuni of North America, recognised by the name 'Zuni' by all academics and administrators, do not call themselves as such. For them, their name is Shibi (meaning, the people). Thus, names and labels are decidedly not derivatives of ground-level realities or represent the self-identities of people. They reflect the convenience as well as administrative requirements of those in power. The fact that these labels are not going unchallenged is illustrative of shifts in power, like the acquisition of a voice by those who were silent earlier. The tribal elite, the educated and the powerful can speak in their own voice. This, of course, does not mean that all the powerless have found a voice but that the power equations and balances are shifting.

INTERNAL STRATIFICATION AND CONFLICTS

Tribes have always been largely egalitarian, as the subsistence activities they engaged in did not produce the kind of surplus that leads to real stratification. Among them, practically everyone was engaged in food-producing and other activities needed for daily sustenance. Even at present, my colleagues and students at the university, tell me how they participate in shifting cultivation, rice growing, roof making and other domestic activities when they go to their villages. But at the same time, participation in the national democracy, fighting elections, holding ministerial posts, even becoming industrialists, and getting economic and political power in the national and global arenas, has created a thin strata of tribal people who are now part of the elite mainstream. Some of them may retain their roots, but some work with agencies like the state, the corporates and other interest groups with disregard to their own environment. Another problem may be the creation of factions competing over resources, and this may lead to conflict between different tribal communities and groups. Divisions are also found between tribes following religions different from their original ones, like the friction between Christians and non-Christians in Jharkhand.

There are also internal regional differences that are sometimes hidden behind a common political identity. For example, as pointed out by Biswas and Suklabaidya (2008: 282), the Nagas in Manipur and those in Nagaland have different histories, and they are integrated within different regional identities. Even within Nagaland, there is less of common history between the eastern and the western Nagas. Even in terms of political entities, there are irreconcilable differences between the two factions of the Naga separatist group National Socialist Council of Nagaland (NSCN)—NSCN (K) and the NSCN (I-M)—but they are only united with respect to a common 'other'. Das (2017: 56) writes that while the Indian Schedule recognises only 17 Naga tribes, in reality there are as many as 36 Naga sub-tribes. There is considerable internal politics between the majority and the minor tribes. After 1997, Nagaland was divided between the forward and backward areas, the latter consisting of those regions that were practically ungoverned during the colonial period and where the benefits of education were not available. Das (2017: 60) describes how the Nagas of the more prosperous and urbanised regions of Kohima, Dimapur and Mokochung regard the eastern Nagas, like the Mon and Tuensang groups, 'as "others", who were often described as being the "wildest" and most "aboriginal" of all Naga tribes. The informants cited how these eastern tribes continued to observe "authentic" Naga rituals, followed shamanistic practices like animal sacrifice, and were unwilling to change, and therefore were relatively backward.' Thus, it is interesting to note that even tribes consider those among themselves who still follow tribal practices to be 'backward'.

Similarly, there are many factions and divisions within the Mizos, the Arunachalis and others, and often, these divisions renegotiate their positions and alliances. Thus, sub-national identities such as Naga and Mizo, and even of Adivasi and tribe, are much more oppositional identities than those with an internal unity. The tribal world is no longer homogenous and non-stratified, and as history often tells us, it probably never was. In contemporary times, the tribal world is heterogeneous and internally stratified, composed of competing units that may contest with each other over power and resources. Among the tribes of the Northeast, there is a tilt towards Westernisation instead of an Indian identity. They feel that Westernisation makes them reject the domination of the Indian mainland, and also allows them greater freedom and possible association with a more global culture. Thus, as identities develop, they develop not as monoliths but as multiple selves. A tribal person working in Delhi, for example, may have an identity as a citizen of India and a member of a professional group; they would have colleagues and friends among non-tribals. But at the same time, there is also the tribal self, the gendered self and the person belonging to a specific clan or a village. An individual responds to different situations, foregrounding the self that is most appropriate for that occasion. Selves are not necessarily contradictory even if they appear to be so. In situations of modernity and globalisation, tribes are responding in a variety of ways. The more educated and more urbanised they are, the processes of self-reflexivity are more profound. It is the educated elite that is in a more contradictory situation as it is pulled by the forces of modernity, on the one hand, and is much more self-aware about its identity, on the other.

An individual responds to different situations, foregrounding the self that is most appropriate for that occasion. Selves are not necessarily contradictory even if they appear to be so.

The claims to an identity such as 'tribe', 'indigenous' or 'Adivasi' are also quite often informed by the goals to which such an identity is manipulated than to some altruistic ideology. For example, the continued use of the term 'tribe' in South Asia, is driven by the necessity, even if reluctantly, for the people designated as such and activists to negotiate with the state to 'claim group rights' (Schendel 2011: 24). Thus, stakeholders are limited by the official use of this term, and by the fact that most rights and claims are legally and constitutionally framed using the term 'tribe' or Scheduled Tribe in India. The term 'Adivasi', in popular usage by central Indian tribes, is completely foreign to the tribes of the Northeast, who prefer 'indigenous' to 'Adivasi', as the latter conjures up for them an identity, namely, of belonging to peninsular India, that they reject. Moreover, 'Adivasi' is used by the tribes of central India as an oppositional term to caste Hindu, with whom they live in close proximity. In contrast, the tribes of the Northeast practically reject any association with caste Hindus, and being located in tribal-majority states, these tribes do not have the problems of living in close proximity to non-tribals. The state of Mizoram, for example, has 95 per cent tribal population, while other states in the region have more than 80 per cent. The roots of the term 'Adivasi' are from Sanskrit or Hindi, languages that are regarded by the Northeast tribals as foreign.

Schendel (2011) is particularly sceptical of the term 'indigenous' as it can create hostility and divisiveness, even as many groups claim this identity in pursuit of their political ambitions. As Schendel (2011: 29) points out, '"Indigenous" is anything but a registered trademark. It can be claimed by dominant groups to eliminate aliens.' This can happen quite often between groups, both of which have a claim to being 'indigenous' in terms of belonging to an 'oppressed' category. The concept of 'homeland', which took root in South Asia with the partition of the Indian subcontinent, is being played out continuously over the years, leading to the fracturing of regions into smaller and smaller segments, as one can see in the proliferation of states in India, and the consequent increasing divisiveness with the creation of imagined 'others'. Such divisiveness is also a consequence of globalisation, which is a simultaneous process of global economic flows and consequent creation of fractured identities competing with each other in this global arena of a capitalist market. Globalisation is creating xenophobic tendencies along with the technological and economic connectivity that it makes possible. In India, indigenous people are getting further divided as they are getting alienated from the non-indigenous, for example, there is a renewed demand for creating Inner Line regulations for domestic tourists in Manipur, leading to consequent strife between communities, both of which claim indigenous identities. Clashes between 'tribal' people—for instance, between Bodos and Santals in Assam, or the attempts of the Arunachal Pradesh government to oust the Chakmas and Hajongs by saying they do not belong to this region—indicate how divisiveness has a way to multiply itself, once set in motion.

The 'horizontal fraternity' that a term such as indigenous may foster can also under stress and the spectre of diminishing resources give way to 'imagined communities of differences' (Schendel 2011: 30). However, such claims are often belied and almost always contested, as such neat categories of bounded people and territory rarely exist, given the ethnographic reality of migration and movements of people. Even the Gonds, assumed to be belonging since time immemorial to a region called Gondwana, have been shown to have migrated from Maharashtra, during the rule of the Maratha ruler Raghoji Bhonsle around the the 1740s (Prasad 2004). Most tribal ethnographies and accounts unfettered by the earlier colonial assumptions of equilibrium and lack of history indicate similar movements and fuzzy boundaries.

There are two major connotations of the way 'indigenous' has been imagined and used in recent discourses about marginalised people across the world. One is with reference to a 'claim to a particular part of the earth's surface on the basis of history' (Schendel 2011: 25), which in simple terms implies a territorial association of primordial belongingness. The second, as Schendel puts it, is in terms of 'being oppressed by later arrivals in the territory, or being exploited by post-colonial states that treat indigenous territories as internal colonies' (ibid.). In India, scholars like Roy Burman, Xaxa and Padel have taken indigenous in the second sense of the term as, given the ethnographic situation of India, the first claim is difficult to sustain. In this sense, the postcolonial construction of 'indigenous peoples' as 'dispossessed' of land, biodiversity and mineral resources, and their knowledge about these (ibid.: 31) has also brought attention to the environmental aspect of the discourse, namely, the ecological

There are two major connotations of the way 'indigenous' has been imagined in recent discourse about marginalised people: one, implying a territorial association of belongingness, and two, in terms of being oppressed or exploited.

degradation and loss of biodiversity, the consequent climatic changes and what is today perceived as the failure of 'capitalist modernity'.

ECOLOGY AND ISSUES OF 'DEVELOPMENT'

The issue most troubling to tribes is the loss of their resources and land to outsiders. The educated elite are in a more privileged position to both understand the nuances of this process as well as resist it. The smaller and weaker sections of tribes everywhere are the worst sufferers. For example, the Tharus of Uttar Pradesh have become minorities in their own land, where they were the majority. Even though populations are rising everywhere, it is only tribes that are losing their populations. The status of nutrition and health among them is dwindling at an alarming rate. The level of malnutrition among tribal children below the age of five is alarming and is much higher than the national average.

At the same time, there is a global discourse on the environment that is available to the tribal intellectuals and activists. The global focus on climate change and environmental issues, which are being caused by the very processes and discourses of development leading to displacement and distress to tribal people across the world, is reaching tribes as well. The young generations of educated tribal people are critiquing the activities of mining and construction of dams, overt urbanisation and deforestation in terms of not only their own welfare, but also the global environmental discourse. They are putting themselves forward as custodians of the global wealth. Tribes are being seen and are also seeing themselves as conservators of the natural forests and the biodiversity considered precious for the future of the world.

Tribes are being seen and are also seeing themselves as conservators of natural forests and biodiversity, which are considered precious for the future of the world.

Environmental concerns and the focus on concepts such as indigenous knowledge and local knowledge are giving a new lease of life to tribal lifeworlds. Tribes are now realising that they are no longer to be regarded as primitive and backward but that their centuries-old livelihoods and knowledge have relevance for both the present and the future. They are the representatives of what is now being seen as an 'alternate modernity' (Schendel 2011: 28). Many tribal people of the Northeast are now finding ways to show that their jhum cultivation is scientifically and environmentally sustainable. Concepts of sustainable development are being reframed within the rhetoric of tribal world views like the 'jal, jangal, jamin' slogan of the tribes of central India. Tribal people are able to frame their demands not only in terms of political and social identity, but also in terms of a discourse of logic and rationality that is far from the earlier perception of tribes as backward, primitive and in need of development. As put by Karlsson (2000: 141):

Tribal people are framing their demands not only in terms of political and social identity, but also in terms of a discourse of rationality that is far from the earlier perception of tribes as primitive and in need of development.

> It is obvious that tribal people's struggles for land and forest more and more will be carried out in the domain of "eco-politics". A central feature of such politics is to establish "sustainability". The present conflict in northwestern India between nomadic Gujjars, or Van Gujjars, and the State/Rajaji National Park is a prime example of this.

The creation of reserved forests and the exclusion of the traditional forest dwellers has been a very unwise decision, as instead of protecting biodiversity and creating a safe environment for endangered animals such as tigers and elephants, it has actually led to both degeneration of forests and the depletion of animals. Savyasaachi (2007: 474) writes with respect to the Simlipal Tiger Reserve in Odisha:

> The core area where wildlife is to be protected is open to reckless exploitation. In collaboration with forest officials, poachers kill animals for tusks, hide and other exotic foods. Also their methods harm the forest. For instance, trees are sprayed with insecticides to kill elephants, and tigers are killed when they are young as their coats are in good condition.

In the sub-Himalayan villages near Simla, I have seen brown patches on the mountainside, which villagers told me were the government-protected forests. These brown patches were flanked by the lush green cover of the individual-owned forests. The village people use these individual forests for extraction of timber, minor forest produce and even hunting. It is the traditional knowledge and wisdom of the local people that enables them to maintain these forests in a sustainable way. People from the outside extract resources with no concern for the future, as these resources do not belong to them. As one old man from a Himalayan village told me,

> I had got a person from outside to trim some of my trees as I was too sick to do it myself. But those people came and uprooted the trees from the roots, instead of trimming them from the top. They were interested in extracting the maximum amount of timber. They were not interested to save the lives of the trees.

Thus, outsiders, whether they are forest guards, government officials or poachers, have no real interest in the forest. They all regard it as an exploitable resource and not as something that is sacred. In my work on the Jad Bhotiyas of Uttarakhand (Channa 2013), I have reported that local villagers consider each Deodar tree in the forest as a deity and the forest as a temple. Such sentiments cannot be expected from outsiders. It is only recently that Government of India, having been advised by experts, has revised its forest policy to include the forest dwellers as partners for the sustainability of forests. But there is only a half-hearted implementation of the same (Dungdung 2015).

There is a developing discourse on the relevance of knowledge other than the one that has propagated as authentic knowledge, science and rationality. Facing the prospect of global environmental disasters, the world is no longer sure about the efficacy of Western science and a global consumerist culture. The words and sayings of indigenous people are beginning to carry some weight as their ways of life have proven to be far more sustainable than the technology-driven rationality of Western science. The increasing momentum of environmental movements and the rise of environmental consciousness across the globe are also bringing about some change in attitudes towards the indigenous peoples (Sharma 2009). It is now increasingly evident that the land and resources held by indigenous people across the world are acting as buffers against unmitigated climate change. It is these people who have retained original forests, hills and mountains and not crushed them for profit. 'Resilience and change is embedded in indigenous knowledge and know-how, diversified resources and livelihoods, social institutions and networks, and cultural values and attitudes. Therefore, policy responses to climate change should support and augment indigenous resilience' (Shimrah 2014: 254). Even leading organisations like the Intergovernmental Panel on Climate Change do not take into account indigenous knowledge, as they do not consider it as scientific evidence. But many scholars and institutions are investigating alternative sources of knowledge and also alternative roads to development, and it is certain that the present indigenous or tribal people are going to play a key role in the future of the world. The time is certainly ripe to consider them as worthy of respect and as the bearers of sustainable knowledge. It is also time to take a different path to development, which is oriented towards happiness and contentment.

Scholars in the postmodern world are disillusioned by the way the world is hurtling towards self-destruction and anomie. Carmack (2015: 350), citing the work of the anthropologist Keesing (1981), pleads that instead of trying to find revolutionary political solutions that have a record of failing, we should try to learn from the lives of the simple tribal people who have a better record of survival and of maintaining 'balance and harmony in the ecosystem of which we are a part' (Keesing 1981: 503). Keesing, who makes a similar point, argues that this does not imply that we go back to the notions of the 'noble savage' or romanticise the life of tribes, which also has many shortcomings and sufferings, but rather look for some practical solutions to enable us to live better and get relief from some of the negative aspects of modern social life (ibid.). Keesing suggests that people today should try to carry out more economic activities within the setting of the family and community, maintain family support for child care and 'mutual social concern in everyday life' (ibid.), and carry on the social relations of mutuality and care developed in childhood to adult life like caring for one's aged parents and older relatives. Keesing also suggests that society should strive for continuity over generations rather than create a new set of values for each generation, thus retaining the importance of the elderly in society. Moreover, it is always better to look for political and legal solutions in more intimate face-to-face situations rather than go for abstract and impersonal settings.

> Keesing recognized that to create a new, more personal egalitarian way of life in the context of the complex, modern world would be seen as utopian, but he pointed out that tribal peoples have proven over the millennium that they were extremely flexible in adapting their cultures to changing external conditions. This suggests that more egalitarian cultures might be uniquely adaptable, perhaps even in the post-modern era. (Carmack 2015: 350–51)

SUMMARY

In summing up, let us examine the key question that was raised in Chapter 1, namely, what are tribes? The label 'tribe' is only an arbitrary and politically informed one—the term used could even be indigenous, aborigine or First Nation or something else. While considering the Indian nation, anthropologists tend to go by the official category of Scheduled Tribes, although as we have seen, such labels are also often historically conditioned and politically manipulated. In India, tribes can be identified largely, though not totally, by the following criteria:

1. Self-identification as a distinct community is a crucial criteria, although as in case of the Zeliangrong, this identity can also change over time. But at any given point of time, it is best to go by the way a community identifies itself.
2. Tribes mostly have a subsistence-based, pre-capitalist economy. All forms of what Wolf (1966) refers to as paleotechnic modes of adaptation are found among tribes, namely, hunting-gathering (foraging), pastoralism, shifting cultivation and subsistence agriculture. This does not mean that tribes do not participate in cash and market economies, but that they do so only to a

limited extent. Again, a large number of tribes now live in cities and have urban, Westernised or modern lifestyles. They remain tribes because of their ancestry and historical association.

3. Tribes have a nature-centric cosmology that emphasises harmony and balance between the human and the non-human worlds. Ways of life based on sharing and cooperation rather than competition and hierarchy make the tribal or indigenous way of life an example for sustainable living. Again, these aspects now have limited applicability, and urban tribal people may no longer sustain these values.
4. Tribes have regional or ecological identities but not the kind of rigid boundaries as was presupposed earlier, for example, the pastoral communities in the high Himalayan pastures and villages distinguish themselves from the cultivators in their neighbourhood but may marry or otherwise relocate in the villages of other pastorals in the same ecological zone. The important thing in terms of identity is the sharing of a world view and the ability to communicate with each other.
5. Tribes may have distinctive cultures but can also be part of larger cultural zones, where they share some cultural traits with others but have some distinctive markers of their own identity, for example, the Naga tribes share many aspects of their culture, habitat and ways of life but are yet distinguished from each other by distinct traits of dress, dialect or specific rituals.
6. Tribes have their customary laws and principles of justice that form a part of the larger body of jurisprudence based on community values and social relations rather than abstract principles of individualism and objective rules. By constitutional provisions, tribes still have the right to use their civil codes but are managed by the criminal law of the country. Many subdivisions of tribes, especially women members, are now contesting the continued use of customary laws that they feel are patriarchal in nature.
7. Politically, most contemporary tribes are part of the larger nation state, but at one time in the pre-colonial past, they had their distinct political identities and bodies.

As students of anthropology, we should not take anything for granted but work as per the data that we collect on the ground. Substantive data and empirical knowledge is the best way to understand who tribes are. Students need to develop their own understanding of each situation as it is encountered on the ground. Tribe has to be understood as an analytical category built from empirical situations, and as such, there is always the possibility of reformulation, relocation and revisiting what we already know.

REFERENCES

Bayart, Jean-Francoise. 2005. *The Illusion of Cultural Identity*. Chicago: University of Chicago Press.

Biswas, Prasenjit and Chandan Suklabaidya. 2008. *Ethnic Life-worlds in North-East India: An Analysis*. New Delhi: Sage Publications.

Brown, R. 1874. *A Statistical Account of Manipur*. Calcutta: Government Printing Press.

Butler, John. 1875. 'Rough Notes on the Angami', *Journal of Asiatic Society of Bengal*, 44: 307–46.

Carmack, Robert M. 2015. *Anthropology and Global History: From Tribes to the Modern World-system*. Boulder, New York and London: Rowman and Littlefield.

Channa, Subhadra Mitra. 2013. *The Inner and Outer Selves: Cosmology, Gender and Ecology on the Himalayan Borders*. New Delhi: Oxford University Press.

Das, Debojyoti. 2017. 'The Politics of Census: Fear of Numbers and Competing Claims for Representation in Naga Society', in Vibha Arora and N. Jayaram (eds), *Democratisation in the Himalayas: Interests, Conflicts, and Negotiations*, pp. 54–79. New Delhi: Routledge.

Devalle, Susan B. C. 1992. *Discourses of Ethnicity, Culture and Protest in Jharkhand*. New Delhi: Sage Publications.

Dungdung, Gladson. 2015. *Mission Saranda: A War for Natural Resources in India*. Jharkhand: Deshraj Prakashan.

Eyingbeni, Hümtsoe-Nienü, Paul Pimomo and Venusa Tunyi. 2012. *Nagas: Essays Responsible For Change*. Dimapur: Heritage Publishing House.

Grange, E. R. 1840. 'Expedition into the Naga Hills on the Assam Frontier', *Journal of the Asiatic Society of Bengal*, 9 (2): 947–66.

Grierson, George Abraham. 1903. *Linguistic Survey of India, Vol. 3—Tibeto-Burman Family, Part 2: Specimens of the Bodo, Naga and Kachin Groups*. Calcutta: Government Printing Office.

Hodson, T. C. 1911. *The Naga Tribes of Manipur*. New Delhi: Low Price Publications.

Hutton, J. H. 1921. *The Angami Nagas*. London: MacMillan.

Jayachandran, U. 2001. 'Understanding School Attendance and Children's Work Participation in India', *Journal of Educational Planning and Administration*, 15 (1): 1–24.

Kamei, Gangmumei. 2004. *The History of the Zeliangrong Nagas: From Makhel to Rani Gaidinliu*. Delhi: Spectrum Publications.

Karlsson, B. G. 2000. *Contested Belonging: An Indigenous People's Struggle for Forest and Identity in Sub-Himalayan Bengal*. Richmond Surry: Curzon Press.

Keesing, Roger. 1981. *Cultural Anthropology: A Contemporary Perspective*. New York: Holt, Rinehart and Winston.

Khongreiwu, Rammathot. 2014. 'Landscapes, Memories and Pre-Christian Tangkhul Naga Eschatology', in R. Vashum (ed.), *Encountering Modernity: Situating the Tangkhul Nagas in Perspective*, pp. 62–89. New Delhi and Chicago: Chicken Neck.

Maharatna, Arup. 2005. *Demographic Perspectives on India's Tribes*. New Delhi: Oxford University Press.

Mathur, Ashok. 2008. 'An Overview of the Jharkhand Economy and Perspectives on Human Development', background paper read at the national seminar on 'Growth and Development in Jharkhand: Perspectives and Policies', Ranchi, 4–5 July.

McCulloch, William. 1859. *An Account of the Valley of Manipur and the Surrounding Hill Tribes*. Calcutta: Bengal Printing Press.

Mohapatra, Shyam Sundar. 2001. 'Formation of Ol Chiki Script and the Process of its Transmission', in Nita Mathur (ed.), *Santhal Worldview*, pp. 74–89. New Delhi: Indira Gandhi National Centre for the Arts and Concept Publishing Company.

Moody, Roger. 2007. *Rocks and Hard Places: The Globalization of Mining*. London: Zed Books.

Odyuo, Iris. 2014. 'The Impact of Globalization on Naga Art', in Michael Heneise (ed.), *Passing Things On: Ancestors and Genealogies in Northeast India*, pp. 53–71. Dimapur: Heritage Publishing House.

Prasad, Archana. 2004. 'Reinterpreting Tribal Livelihood Systems: Underdevelopment and the Local Political Economy in Central India, 1800–1940', in B. B. Chaudhury and Arun Bandopadhyaya (eds), *Tribes, Forest and Social Formation in Indian History*, pp. 109–20. New Delhi: Manohar.

Radhakrishna, Meena (ed.). 2016. *First Citizens: Studies on Adivasis, Tribals, and Indigenous Peoples in India*. New Delhi: Oxford University Press.

Ramirez, Philippe. 2014. *People of the Margins: Across Ethnic Boundaries in North-East India*. Guwahati: Spectrum Publishing House.

Rycroft, Daniel J. and Sangeeta Dasgupta (eds). 2011. *The Politics of Belonging in India: Becoming Adivasis*. London and New York: Routledge.

Savyasaachi. 2007. 'The Tiger and the Honeybee', in Mahesh Rangarajan (ed.), *Environmental Issues in India: A Reader*, pp. 471–82. Delhi: Pearson Longman.

Sharma, Subhash. 2009. *Why People Protest: An Ecological Analysis of Ecological Movements*. New Delhi: Publications Divisions, Ministry of Information and Broadcasting, Government of India.

Shah, Alpa. 2011. '"Who Cares for a New State": The Imaginary Institution of Jharkhand', in Daniel J. Rycroft and Sangeeta Dasgupta (eds), *The Politics of Belonging in India: Becoming Adivasis*, pp. 217–30. London and New York: Routledge.

Schendel, William van. 2011. 'The Dangers of Belonging: Tribes, Indigenous Peoples and Homelands in South Asia', in Daniel J. Rycroft and Sangeeta Dasgupta (eds), *The Politics of Belonging in India: Becoming Adivasis*, pp. 19–43. London and New York: Routledge.

Shimrah, T. 2014. 'Global Environmental Change: Perceptions, Challenges and Adaptation Strategies in Tangkhul Indigenous Communities', in R. Vashum (ed.), *Encountering Modernity: Situating the Tangkhul Nagas in Perspective*, pp. 245–67. New Delhi and Chicago: Chicken Neck.

Shimreiwung, A. S. 2014. 'Print Culture and the Rise of Identity Consciousness in Oral Society: Trajectories in Conception of Community Identity in Tangkhul Literature', in R. Vashum (ed.), *Encountering Modernity: Situating the Tangkhul Nagas in Perspective*, pp. 154–70. New Delhi and Chicago: Chicken Neck.

Soppit, C. A. 1885. *A Short Account of the Kachcha Naga (Empeo) Tribe in the North-Cachar Hills with an Outline Grammar, Vocabulary and Illustrative Sentences*. Shillong: Assam Secretarial Press.

Wolf, Eric. 1966. *Peasants*. Englewood Cliffs, New Jersey: Prentice Hall.

Wolf, Richard K. 2005. *The Black Cow's Footprints: Time, Space and Music in the Lives of the Kotas of South India*. New Delhi: Permanent Black.

Xaxa, Virginius. 2008. *State, Society, and Tribes: Issues in Post-colonial India*. Delhi: Pearson Longman.

———. 2012. 'Tribes and Development: Retrospect and Prospect', in Dev Nathan and Virginius Xaxa (eds), *Social Exclusion and Adverse Inclusion: Development and Deprivation of Adivasis in India*, pp. 23–35. New Delhi: Oxford University Press.

SUGGESTED READINGS

Agnihotri, S. 2000. *Sex Ratio Patterns in the Indian Population: A Fresh Explanation*. New Delhi: Sage Publications.

Béteille, André. 1998. 'The Idea of Indigenous People', *Current Anthropology*, 3 (2): 187–93.

Bodding, P. O. 1986. *Studies in Santal Medicine and Connected Folklore*. Calcutta: The Asiatic Society.

Chaudhuri, A. B. 1993. *State Formation among Tribals: A Quest for Santal Identity*. New Delhi: Gyan Publishing House.

Chaudhuri, B. B., and Arun Bandopadhyay (eds). 2004. *Tribe, Forest and Social Formation in Indian History*. New Delhi: Indian History Congress and Manohar.

Elwin, Verrier. 1944. *The Aboriginals*. Bombay: Oxford University Press.

Fourcade, Marie. 2003. 'The So-Called "Criminal Tribes" of British India: Colonial Violence and Traditional Violence', in Gilles Tarabout, D. Vidal and E. Meyer (eds), *Violence and Non-violence: Some Hindu Perspectives*, pp. 143–75. New Delhi: Manohar.

Friedman, J. 1994. *Cultural Identity and Global Process*. London: Sage Publications.

Guha, Sumit. 1999. *Environment and Ethnicity, 1200–1901*. Cambridge: Cambridge University Press.

Hardiman, David. 1987. *The Coming of the Devi: Adivasi Assertion in Western India*. New Delhi: Oxford University Press.

Hobart, Mark. 1993. *The Growth of Ignorance: An Anthropological Critique of Development*. London: Routledge.

Karlsson, B. G., and T. B. Subba (eds). 2006. *Indigeneity in India*. London: Kegan Paul.

Kaviraj, Sudipta. 1993. 'The Imaginary Institution of India', in Partha Chatterjee and Gyanendra Pandey (eds), *Subaltern Studies, Vol. 7*, pp. 1–39. Delhi: Oxford University Press.

Kelkar, Govind and Dev Nathan. 1991. *Gender and Tribe: Women, Land and Forests in Jharkhand*. New Delhi: Kali for Women.

Mathur, Nita (ed.). 2001. *Santhal Worldview*. New Delhi: Indira Gandhi National Centre for the Arts and Concept Publishing Company.

Miri, Mrinal (ed.). 1993. *Continuity and Change in Tribal Society*. Simla: Indian Institute of Advanced Studies.

Nathan, Dev (ed.). 1997. *From Tribe to Caste*. Simla: Indian Institute of Advanced Studies.

Roy Burman, B. K. 1994. *Indigenous and Tribal Peoples: Gathering Mist and New Horizons*. New Delhi: Mittal Publications.

Saxena K. B., and G. Hargopal (eds). 2016. *Marginalization, Development and Resistence: Essays in Tribute to S. R. Sankaran, Vol. 2, Dalits and Adivasis*. New Delhi: Council for Social Development and Aakar Books.

Shah, Alpa. 2010. *In the Shadows of the State: Indigenous Politics, Environmentalism, and Insurgency in Jharkhand*. Durham: Duke University Press.

Sheshadri, B. 1995. *Call of the Wild: Survival in the Sun*. New Delhi: Sterling Publishers.

Skaria, Ajay. 1999. *Hybrid Histories: Forest, Frontiers and Wilderness in Western India*. New Delhi: Oxford University Press.

Troisi, J. 1978. *Tribal Religion: Religious Beliefs and Practices among the Santhals*. New Delhi: Manohar.

Vidyarthi, L. P. 1963. *The Maler: A Study in Nature-Man Spirit Complex of a Hill Tribe*. Calcutta: Bookland.

INDEX